EX LIBRIS

A VERY
PRESENT HELP

A VERY PRESENT HELP

God's Power
In Our Lives

Compiled by the editors of Guideposts

"God is our refuge and our strength,
a very present help in trouble…"

PSALM 46:1

CARMEL • NEW YORK 10512

Table of Contents

In Day-to-Day Faith

You're about to meet the people who have told their stories in Guideposts magazine. You're going to recognize some of them because their names have been in the news. Some of them, you'll be meeting for the first time. But no matter who they are, the problems they write about—and triumph over—are the problems that confront us all from day-to-day. The who's and what's and where's of these stories are as vivid and varied as life itself.

Who: an astronaut's mother...a World War I flying ace...a middle-aged mechanic...the first black player in major league baseball...an ice-cream maker...the exiled publisher of Havana's oldest newspaper...a lustrous Hollywood star...a Pennsylvania farmer and his wife...a backwoods trapper...the wife of a ship's captain...a bomb squad officer.

Where: a high-security prison in Northern California...the only drug store in a tiny South Dakota town...the waiting room of Washington's Union Station...the rustic hills of Appalachia...a tough inner-city ghetto...the kitchen of a comfortable suburban home... the U.S. Embassy in Teheran...the corridors of a convalescent home...the deck of a disabled ship.

What: a kidnapping by ruthless South American terrorists...an impossibly difficult boss...a bout with cancer...a three-year-old lost in the woods...a hurt too big to forgive... a crisis of faith...an estrangement between father and daughter...an erupting volcano... a career gone sour...a battle of wills...a troubled marriage.

And what is it that links these Guideposts people together? It's that they've all felt God's power in their lives.

A very present help.

*Captain Eddie Rickenbacker (far left, in civilian clothes)
during World War II*

MARCH 1945

I Believe in Prayer... *by Captain Eddie Rickenbacker, former president of Eastern Airlines*

There are a lot of things concerning the human mind and soul that we don't know much about. We get glimpses of them when in times of danger or suffering we cross a little way over the line of ordinary thought.

As I roared down the last stretch in an automobile race years ago, I felt that I could control that machine with my mind and that, if it finally collapsed, I could run it with my mind.

If I had said such a thing then, the boys would have called me crazy. Even now I can't explain it. But I believe that if you *think* disaster you will get it. Brood about death, and you hasten your demise. Think with confidence and faith, and life becomes more secure, more fraught with action, richer in achievement.

Perhaps such things as the control of mind over matter and the transmission of thought waves are tied up together, part of something so big we haven't grasped it yet. It's part of us and part of the Something that is looking after us. It's one of the things that makes me believe in personal protection and in life after death. I have difficulty putting it into words.

A strange thing happened to me some years ago. I was flying to Chicago. It was a Sunday afternoon in the middle of December, and the weather was miserable. There was a lot of ice. We suddenly lost the radio beam. For a long time we cruised back and forth trying to pick it up. Fog was all around us. We were lost, off the beam, and flying blind. Our two-way radio

went out, and we had lost all communication with the world. For seven hours we flew— where, we didn't know.

Darkness was coming on. Then, suddenly, we saw a break in the murk. The pilot brought the ship down to within one hundred feet, and we saw lights go flashing by on a four-lane highway. We followed it for some distance.

Then we saw a red glow away off to the right, headed for it, and saw a river gleaming. We flew up that river, and out of the six-thirty dusk of winter I saw the Toledo-Edison sign flashing. Skimming the roofs, we circled and landed at the airport. We had just enough gas left for 11 minutes of flight.

We had flown blind, without a beam, but we were on a beam, just the same. I like to think it was the "Big Radio" that kept us going—the Thing that keeps all of us flying safely through the fog and night, toward some mysterious and important goal. The "Big Radio" is a two-way job. You've got to keep tuned with It, and you have to talk back. I believe in prayer.

One day in France, during World War I, with only one magneto on my Newport biplane functioning, I was attacked by three German Albatross planes. I came out of a dive so fast that the terrific pressure collapsed my right-hand upper wing. No matter what I tried, I couldn't come out of that whirl of death. I often wish I could think as fast under

first issue of Guideposts, March 1945

normal conditions as I did during that drop. While I fought the controls and tried to get the engine going, I prayed:

"Oh, God," I said, "help me get out of this."

As a last desperate act, I threw my weight to the left-hand side over the cockpit and jammed the controls, then jammed the engine wide open. The thing suddenly sputtered and vibrated violently, and the plane sailed away, on her one good wing, for France. I held it like that all the way home.

This escape and others I have had were not the result of any super-ability or super-knowledge on my part. I wouldn't be alive if I had to depend on that. I realized then, as I headed for France on one wing, that there had to be Something else. I had seen others die— brighter and more able than I. I knew there was a Power. I believe in calling upon It for help.

On a rainy night in February 1941, I had the worst accident of my life. As I look back on the agonizing days in the hospital that followed, I realize there was a reason behind it all. It was a test and a preparation for what was to follow.

In the four months I lay in that hospital I did more thinking about life and death than I had ever done before. Twenty-one months later I was adrift in an open lifeboat with seven other starving men, most of them so young that they needed the strength and understanding of a man who had been down in the valley of the shadow, who had suffered and made sense out of his suffering. To those men I was able to bring the distilled essence of the religious philosophy I had developed while in the hospital.

Once, while there, I almost died from a throat hemorrhage.

"Here," I said, "is death."

Then it dawned upon me in a flash that the easiest thing in the world is to die; the hardest is to live. Dying was a sensuous pleasure; living was a grim task. In that moment I chose to live. I knew from experience that abandonment to death was a sin. I wasn't quitting. I had work to do, others to serve.

Many things came to me. I realized I wasn't *afraid* to die, because I had lived so much, in good ways and bad, that I no longer felt the youthful pang of not having lived at all. And when I finally came around, I saw life and death and the meaning of the Golden Rule more clearly than I had ever known.

I had taken that clarity with me to the rubber raft in the South Pacific after our plane crashed. Throughout those 24 days of blistering sun and nights of ghastly chill I never lost faith, and I felt that we were adrift for a purpose. I saw life had no meaning except in terms of *helping* others.

I think man instinctively does not interest himself in others. He does it only by an act of will, when he sees that "I am my brother's keeper" and "Do unto others" are the essence of all truth.

My experiences and the suffering through which I passed have taught me that faith in God is the answer to life.

Rosalind Russell (1912–1976), noted for her portrayals of witty, sophisticated career women in scores of motion pictures, also won wide acclaim on the Broadway stage. But perhaps her greatest triumph was her gallant fight against arthritis and cancer. After her death, this poem was found tucked in her prayer book.

> *"Trust Him when dark doubts assail thee,*
> *Trust Him when your faith is small,*
> *Trust Him when simply to trust Him*
> *Is the hardest thing of all."*

OCTOBER 1954

A Medal for Freddie *by Rosalind Russell, actress*

Lanky, graying, Hans Christian Adamson was visiting us in Hollywood when we noticed the first strange turn in our old battle. We were at dinner, back in 1942. It was a long table, I sat at the head of it; Hans Adamson was at my right; and my husband Freddie Brisson, sat at my left. We were all chatting, when suddenly Hans reached into his pocket and fished among his coins.

Now, Hans and my husband were close friends in spite of the 20 years difference in their ages. They were both officers in the Air Force. Hans Adamson was one of the best-read men I have ever known, which is why Freddie and I took so seriously his views on religion.

Hans was also an agnostic.

Not anti-religious; he was interested in religion, but there were things he could not accept with his rational mind. Back at his home, on the East Coast, he used to attend church occasionally with his wife Helen. But we had the feeling it was more out of respect for her, than for her beliefs. Hans often said he envied people who could believe without understanding. "But that's as far as I can go," he would tell us during our long talks. "I try to understand your churches and your little medals and things. But I cannot. So I cannot believe."

That's why it struck us as so peculiar when Hans fished among his change that night and brought out a medal.

"Freddie," Hans said, and it seemed that his voice rose higher than usual, "Freddie, I stopped at the PX and got you one of those flying medals. St. Joseph of Copertino. I think he flew or something. You're going to do a lot of flying, and I want you to have this."

With that, the second strange turn occurred. My hand shot out. I grabbed Hans' sleeve. I spoke very impulsively.

"No. Keep that yourself."

"Why?" Hans asked. "I don't want any medals. I got it for Freddie. He's a Catholic and he believes in these things."

I realized I had spoken sharply, and I tried to soften it down. "What I mean is, you keep it for now, Hans. You just keep it for now."

We all kind of looked at each other, and I tried to change the subject. The dinner party was ruined. But in my mind, I sensed a premonition that actually I had done the right thing...that Hans was trying to tell us something with that medal.

Three months later, Hans phoned my husband that he was going on a secret mission across the Pacific and that he would be coming out to California for a visit.

We all spent the day together in Beverly Hills. Hans kept saying that he felt nervous. He had never talked that way before. There is not a bit of cowardice in Hans Adamson yet he kept saying the trip had a fatality about it.

Rosalind Russell and husband
Frederick Brisson, 1951

Frankly, we thought nothing about it at the time. But then, at six the next morning, the phone rang.

It was Hans.

"Will you do something for me? Will you call Helen and say good-bye again?"

I was puzzled why Hans didn't call his wife himself. At first I thought he was afraid of alarming her by calling so early. But I answered: "Of course I will."

Then, once more, Hans said something about the trip. And I at last saw that he had really called to seek help. Right out of the blue, I sat bolt upright in bed.

"Hans, do you have that medal that you tried to give Freddie some time ago?"

Hans was silent for a moment, as if he didn't want to answer.

"Yes," he finally admitted, "I've got it in my pocket with my change."

"Well. Now mind you, I don't think anything is going to happen. But if it does, if something should go wrong, you take that medal out and put it in your hand and hold on to it."

There was a prolonged silence. I thought I had offended Hans. When he did answer, it was with the single word:

"Yes…"

After he hung up, I couldn't get back to sleep.

"What's the matter?" Freddie asked.

I told him I felt something was going to happen. I wished I had explained more to Hans about the Catholic use of medals, how we don't claim special powers to the medal itself, how the medal helps us focus our prayers, reminds us of our need for prayer. But I had missed my chance.

We were about to get up when Freddie mentioned: "Oh, by the way, Roz. Hans has a rather famous companion for his trip across the Pacific."

"Yes?"

"Captain Eddie Rickenbacker…"

It was perhaps the most famous airplane crash in history. Captain Eddie Rickenbacker, Hans, and six others, on a secret mission, went down in the Pacific.

You know the story. Twenty-four days were to pass before their rubber rafts were finally spotted. Twenty-four days of torture for us too …waiting…

From Wednesday, October 21, 1942, through Saturday, we were more or less hopeful. We learned what had happened. The plane had missed its island destination in the night, probably through faulty instruments.

By the fourth day, most of my own personal hope had dwindled. By the end of the first week, I had given up all hope. The chances of surviving the crash for more than a few moments seemed slim to me. A week spent on a flimsy rubber life raft under a hot tropical sun, with no protection, would surely kill any survivors.

But my husband thought Hans was still alive. Freddie had that simple kind of trust I have seen so often, especially in men.

In 1946, Rosalind Russell portrayed the Australian nurse, Sister Kenny (1886–1952), in a film of the same name. Years before the Salk vaccine, Sister Kenny pioneered a treatment for polio that brought hope to the afflicted—but was scorned by many in the medical establishment (Guideposts 1960). Yet, whenever her integrity was challenged, she remembered her mother's advice: "Anyone who angers you, conquers you."

"You must understand," I said, "that Hans is not a young man."

But even as I was saying this, Freddie whispered with great depth to his voice:

"He's alive. I know he is alive. He's getting strength from somewhere…"

I thought of the medal, and for a fraction of a moment almost believed.

Time began to be counted in weeks. The second week passed, and the third began. The search party was cut down in size. We knew that only a few routine patrol planes were continuing the endless task of searching for the tiny rubber rafts on the ocean. Eighteen days passed. Nineteen and twenty.

And then, suddenly, it was all over.

On the 24th day, the rafts were spotted. The headlines shouted, but we felt strangely quiet. As if we were being drained of the last of some sort of strength.

On the 25th day, the rescues were made. We learned that Hans was still alive, although from the very first reports he was on the critical list. The men were kept in overseas hospitals for five weeks before they could be moved.

Then, just before Christmas, I got a call at the studio. It was from my husband, at the Air Base. The hospital plane was coming into San Francisco. Hans had sent a message that he wanted me to be there, that he had something that he wanted to tell me.

We saw Captain Rickenbacker first. He stepped off the plane, perhaps the thinnest man I have ever seen. His shirt stuck out inches, literally, from his neck. His 80-year-old mother was there to greet him. He walked toward her and she toward him for a few paces. Then they stopped. You could feel the pulses of emotion between them. I had to turn away, because it was something I could not watch.

I was told to get on the plane. Freddie and I climbed a ladder and were inside. I had never seen anything like it: so warlike and barren and canvasy. Hans was in bed. He looked worse than Rickenbacker.

I was so upset seeing him and remembering the old Hans that I tried to keep the conversation on trivial things: welcome home, how good it was to see him alive. I had to say that, rather than how well he looked, because of course he looked anything but well.

Freddie looked at Hans and said: "I don't remember hearing about your hand."

The hand was bandaged.

"It's hurt a bit," Hans answered.

And with that he slowly removed the bandage.

There, cupped in his hand, was the medal.

From holding it in the same position for weeks, his hand muscles had frozen so that he could not straighten his fingers. The medal had worked its way into his flesh. Hans looked up at me.

"I didn't even let them take it away in the hospital."

The plane was silent while with his other hand Hans pried the medal loose. Then, softly, he spoke again.

"It's all right, Roz. I understand at last.… May I give Freddie the medal now?"

Rosalind Russell and Sister Elizabeth Kenny

MAY 1957

The Saga of "Big Molly" *by Van Varner, editor*

Big Molly was a legend in her own time. She lived in a small manufacturing city of the Midwest—a town where everyone knew her or knew, at least, her reputation. As a reporter sent there in search of her story, I was not long in finding people who remembered her well.

"She was a real gutterbum," a policeman told me. And he had reason to know.

"She had the foulest tongue I ever heard—female or male," recalled a man who had worked in the same industrial plant with her. "It made some of the guys in the shop turn white hearing a woman talk that way."

The housewives I interviewed had a standard reply: "No decent person would go near her."

"Big Molly?" a prominent judge said, repeating the name to gain time for a judicious answer. "That woman was a synthesis of sin." Then he talked about drinking and roughhousing, illegitimate children, indecent public exposure, a wrathful temper. He mentioned Molly's prostitute mother and her husband, whom she had sent to jail.

As people spoke, a picture of her took shape in my mind. Big, not unhandsome, strong. She was boisterous and bossy, playful, yet sudden-tempered. Her walk, short and snappy, seemed to derive its propulsion from the half-mad-at-the-world expression set firmly on her face. As for her voice, you could have heard it "from here to the corporation limit."

Altogether, Big Molly was a lusty, profane, powerhouse of a woman.

For five years she had been an overhead crane operator in the local machine plant. Perched high up in the crane's cab, she'd shuttle across the top of the shop looking for machinery to hoist, pipes and scrap to move around. To most people this was man's work, but to Big Molly it was literally child's play. She had fun doing it.

She had fun, too, sitting in the shop office, telling the men dirty stories or leaning out of the cab hollering, whooping and watching guys fleeing beneath her. Even men whose reputations were anything but lily-white would beat it out of her way lest they be socially tainted.

Molly was fighting angry the night she was fired, the night she not only let a ton of metal crash into a turning machine, but let it run on until the top was ripped off and the rest reduced to smithereens.

That was five years ago. After that, Molly seemed to disappear. Most people lost track of her, but she continued to live in the same town. She was living there when I found her.

Our meeting took place in a kitchen, a bright kitchen, bustling with women making sandwiches and stuffing eggs. Outside, dozens of children were shouting at play, impatient to be off on a picnic. One of those

*One word. To celebrate an important anniversary, the founder
of the Salvation Army, General William Booth, wanted to send a
cable to each of the Army's worldwide branches. He wanted to find
a single word that would define everything the Salvation Army
stood for. "What word would you have chosen?" Gerald Bath
wrote in Guideposts (1957). In the end, General Booth's message read:* Others.

kids was Molly's. His name was Dickie and he
was eleven years old.

It didn't seem possible that the woman
making that pot of coffee was Molly. She was a
large person, all right, and about 40 years old.
But where was the loudness, the hardness, the
animal vigor?

"You want to write a story about me?" Molly
said, a trifle bewildered. "Why? Because I was
so bad once?" Her voice was soft, her manner
humble, helpful. She spoke with a twang, col-
loquially, with gnarled syntax—the speech of a
woman who had had little or no education.

Her words came haltingly, it was not an easy
story. A lifetime of poverty; brothers and sisters, many of whom died early and unneces-
sarily; a father who deserted and a mother who
was sick most of the time. With little schooling,
no church ties, and no family restrictions,
Molly had matured early into a free-living girl
who slugged at life and yelled loud for attention. And attention, to Molly, was the same as
affection.

Dickie was the son of her short and unhappy
marriage to Arthur Bemis, a laborer who
sometimes worked, sometimes didn't. After
their divorce, Arthur was supposed to send
money to help with Dickie's upkeep, but there
were long periods when he didn't, and Dickie
would be taken away by the welfare people.
Eventually, Molly had Arthur thrown into the
workhouse for nonsupport. Later, after she
was fired from her job, times were worse than
ever before. Molly fought to keep Dickie with
her but it was hard to do that, especially when
there wasn't any money left for food. Then, in

the worst period of all, Molly became ill, very
ill. But just before she went into the hospital, a
postcard arrived from her ex-husband.

"Dear Dickie— How are you?" That's all
it said.

Molly got in touch with Arthur and asked
him to come take care of Dickie during her
hospitalization. Surprisingly he did, and the
father and his six-year-old became friends.

One day the two of them were walking down
an alley when Dickie spotted a playground
behind a big house on one of the main streets.
He wanted to rush off and play on the swings,
but Arthur told him to ask permission first.
There was a lady in the yard.

"Of course you can swing here. Anytime,"
said the lady. That was Dickie's introduction to
the Salvation Army.

He went back again and soon was a part of
the Army's regular play program. And when
Molly came out of the hospital, a lady from the
Salvation Army went out to see her and care
for her. As she got better, Molly came into
some of the meetings the Captain invited her
to—some of the Army's Home League meetings in which subjects such as child-care were
taught.

Molly became genuinely interested. She
began to react to this new kind of attention.
Simultaneously, Arthur got a job in town—he
was showing no signs of leaving either Dickie
—or her.

In time, Molly and Arthur and Dickie, the
three of them, began coming into some of the
Army's other meetings where they sang hymns
and talked about religion.

In the early 1970s, Walter Hoving—then chairman of Tiffany—was trying to raise money for a home for troubled girls. Deliverance came when he created a pin for a church friend that said TRY GOD. It proved popular and he decided to sell TRY GOD pins through Tiffany, with profits going to the girls home. People bought thousands. As Walter said in Guideposts (1984), "The pin that rescued the home, spells out the guidance that saves the lost girls. Or anyone who strays into a wilderness. Try God."

One night the Captain said to Molly, "Are you saved—do you feel the need for Jesus?"

Molly felt strange, peculiarly exhilarated, more alive than she had ever believed possible. Then, during the service, just when she was expecting something but didn't know what, Dickie went up to the altar and knelt there. It was not long before Molly was there kneeling with him, and then Arthur.

Since then, Molly and Arthur have re-married. Arthur has a steady job as a maintenance man and Molly has discovered undreamed of talents as a homemaker.

Only recently Molly went back to work nights, this time as a cook in a diner. It wasn't, however, because she had to, but because she is working to save five hundred dollars—her pledge to the Salvation Army's fund for building a new headquarters in town.

What happened to Molly? Why is it that the only time she goes into bars now is to sell *War Cry,* the Army magazine? Why is it that people on the street say, "I don't believe it" when someone points Molly out as being *the* Big Molly? Why this startling change of personality?

Molly told me the answer in one sentence.

"I found the Christ that was in myself."

DECEMBER 1965

Beautiful Prayers *by Dr. Samuel Shoemaker*

An alcoholic who was fighting to stay away from drink made a daily visit to church. "Jesus, this is Jim," he'd say, as he fixed his eyes on the cross.

A woman in utter despair, unfamiliar with God or prayer, knelt, clasped her hands and cried, "Somebody...something!"

A simple French peasant, seen going into the cathedral day after day, was asked what happened to him when he went there. "Oh," he replied, "I just look up at Him and He looks down at me."

These may seem almost childish prayers in their simplicity and sparsity of words. But any of us who has learned even a little of prayer knows that we are "not heard for our much speaking." There is great power in utterly simple words said from the heart with faith.

Marian Anderson with her mother

MARCH 1954

Grace Before Greatness *by Marian Anderson, singer*

Failure and frustration are in the unwritten pages of everyone's record. I have had my share of them. But if my mother's gentle hands were not there to guide me, perhaps my life in music would have ended long ago.

The faith my mother taught me is my foundation. It is the only ground on which I stand. With it I have a freedom in life I could not have in any other way. Whatever is in my voice, my faith has put it there.

We were poor folks. But there was a wealth in our poverty, a wealth of music, and love and faith. My two sisters, Alice and Ethel, and I were all in the church choir—the junior, not the senior one. There is still a vivid memory of our mother and father, their faces shining with pride, watching us from the front pews. And when I was six, I was once fortunate enough to be selected to step out in front of the choir and sing "The Lord Is My Shepherd."

It was a Baptist Church we attended in Philadelphia. But my mother taught us early that the form of one's faith is less important than what's in one's heart.

"When you come to Him," she said, "He never asks what you are."

My father died when I was twelve, and my mother's burden became heavier. Before she became a housewife, and the mother of three daughters, she was a schoolteacher. Now she became a father to us as well as a mother and earned our whole livelihood by taking in washing. It was terribly difficult for her, I know, but

she would not even hear of any of us children leaving school for work.

During these years, I began to have my first opportunity to earn a little money by singing. They were almost entirely Sunday evening concerts for the church, or for the YWCA and the YMCA.

Many people were kind to me: teachers who took no fees, those who urged me forward when I was discouraged. Gradually I began to sing with glee clubs and churches in other cities. After one minor effort in Harlem, a group of well-meaning people hastily sponsored a Town Hall concert for me in New York.

It seemed at once incredible and wonderful. But I wasn't ready: indeed, I was far from it either in experience or maturity. On the exciting night of my first real concert I was told Town Hall was sold out. While waiting in dazed delight to go on, my sponsor said there would be a slight delay. I waited five, ten, fifteen minutes. Then peeked through the curtain.

The house was half empty! I died inside. But when the curtain went up, I sang my heart out. And when the concert was over, I knew I had failed. The critics next day agreed with me, but what they said was not so important. I was shattered because within me I felt I had let down all those people who had had faith in me.

"I'd better forget all about singing, and do something else," I told my mother.

"Why don't you think about it a little, and pray a lot, first?" she cautioned.

A year after Marian Anderson told her story in Guideposts, she made her debut with New York's renowned Metropolitan Opera in The Masked Ball. *She was the first black to sign on as a regular member of the company. Overcoming color barriers was something that Miss Anderson did often during her career, always with the grace she embodied before and after her greatness was acknowledged by music critics around the world.*

She had taught me to make my own decisions when I could, and pray for the right ones when I could not. But I did not heed her now. I refused a few offers to sing at other concerts. I avoided my music teacher. For a whole year I brooded in silence. My mother suffered because I was not expressing myself in the only way I knew happiness. But she knew I had to find my own way back alone. From time to time she just prodded me, gently:

"Have you prayed, Marian? Have you prayed?"

No, I hadn't. Nothing would help. I embraced my grief. It was sufficient. But in those tearful hours there slowly came the thought that there is a time when even the most self-sufficient cannot find enough strength to stand alone. Then, one prays with a fervor one never had before. From my torment I prayed with the sure knowledge there was Someone to Whom I could pour out the greatest need of my heart and soul. It did not matter if He answered. It was enough to pray.

Slowly, I came out of my despair. My mind began to clear. No one was to blame for my failure. Self-pity left me. In a burst of exuberance I told my mother:

"I want to study again. I want to be the best, and be loved by everyone, and be perfect in everything."

"That's a wonderful goal," she chided. "But our dear Lord walked this earth as the most perfect of all beings, yet not everybody loved Him."

Subdued, I decided to return to my music to seek humbleness before perfection.

One day, I came home from my teacher unaware that I was humming. It was the first music I had uttered at home in a whole year. My mother heard it, and she rushed to meet me, and put her arms around me and kissed me. It was her way of saying:

"Your prayers have been answered, and mine have too."

For a brief moment we stood there silently. Then my mother defined the sweet spell of our gratitude:

"Prayer begins where human capacity ends," she said.

The golden echo of that moment has always been with me through the years of struggle that followed. Today I am blessed with an active career, and the worldly goods that come with it. If sometimes I do not hear the echo and listen only to the applause, my mother reminds me quickly of what should come first:

"Grace must always come before greatness," she says.

Dr. Peale, 1959

JANUARY 1959
Light Your New Year With Hope   *by Norman Vincent Peale, editor-in-chief*

I once saw hope save a woman's life.

Emilie Batisse was 79 years old when she was struck by a hit-and-run driver, and nobody expected her to live. She insisted on staying in her musty, old clapboard house, and it was there that the nurse let me in about a week after the accident.

Mrs. Batisse lay wrapped in plaster from hips to heels, but her voice was firm. "Sit right down to a cup of tea, Norman Peale," she said. "You're cold."

The little room was cluttered with the mementos of a lifetime: a paisley shawl, a child's drawing of a horse (lavender), shelves of much-loved, much-thumbed books. Mrs. Batisse, I thought, was living in the past. Then, to my surprise, I noticed a row of about ten brand-new poetry books that looked as if they had never been opened. I asked Mrs. Batisse if she cared for poetry, and her answer was one of the greatest testimonies to hope that I have ever heard.

"I love poetry," she said, "but I haven't read those yet." As she looked at them her whole face lighted up. "I'm saving them for my old age."

She did, too. She lived to read those books many times. When she finally died at 91, she was planning a trip to Europe.

What *is* hope? Hope is wishing for a thing to come true; faith is believing that it will come true. Hope is wanting something so eagerly that—in spite of all the evidence that you're not going to get it—you go right on wanting it.

And the remarkable thing about it is that this very act of hoping produces a kind of strength of its own.

Every doctor is familiar with this strength-giving function of hope—so much so that Cornell University's medical school once conducted an investigation into the effects of hope on the body. After completing the research, Dr. Harold G. Wolff wrote an article for *Saturday Review* in which he reported as a medical fact that when a man has hope, he is "capable of enduring incredible burdens and taking cruel punishment."

One of Doctor Wolff's studies involved the 25,000 American soldiers imprisoned by the Japanese during World War II. These men were subjected to long months of inhuman treatment, forced labor, insult, poor food, filth. Under those conditions, many died, and almost all were sick. But there were a few who, with identical treatment, showed only slight damage from those nightmare months in prison.

Now here is the important thing. Interviews with those men revealed no physical superiority, but simply a far-above-average ability to hope! In prison they drew word pictures of the girls they would marry; they designed their future homes; in the middle of the jungle they organized seminars in business management.

Doctor Wolff believes it was hope that kept those boys well—indeed in some cases, kept them alive.

As Guideposts prepared to celebrate its 40th anniversary, we editors were struck by the recurrence of the number 40 in the Bible. Noah spent 40 days on the ark (Genesis 7:4). Moses and the Israelites, while searching for the Promised Land, wandered 40 years in the desert (Numbers 14:33). And Jesus fasted for 40 days in the wilderness (Mark 1:13). All of these accounts seem to represent a spiritual journey. Can you think of others?

Learn to hope! It's easy to say, but how do we do it?

In the first place, I think we have to know what it is that we hope for.

If that sounds obvious, ask yourself right now what you want most out of life. For prisoners of war, the answer was easy: They wanted freedom. But for most of us, as long as we're in reasonably good health and know where next month's rent is coming from, desire has lost its sharp edge, and hope doesn't work its magic in our lives.

So the first step is to find out what your one strongest desire is. Be honest with yourself and don't be afraid to say "a larger house," or "a prettier face and figure." Then challenge yourself. Pretend that you're 80 years old and looking back over a life in which your heart's desire has been granted. Are you satisfied? Perhaps so; but if not, keep challenging yourself until you come up with your answer.

For the hope that you settle on must be your own, not one that you vaguely feel you should have, but one that in reality you do have. This is an area where people often fail in trying to learn the art of hoping. They think they ought to wish for, say, a better world or greater understanding. This is certainly admirable, but to be effective your hope must be fervent enough to govern everything you do. I frankly suspect that most of us would make a greater contribution to others by genuinely hoping for our emotional-physical health than by nobly pining for a better world.

And second, after you've defined your own hope, I think it's important to give it a sym-bol—something concrete that you can center your thoughts around.

Do you remember the story of Jeremiah and the field of Anathoth? What a marvelous symbol of hope that was! Jerusalem was under seige; almost everyone agreed that the kingdom was doomed—everyone, that is, except the long-bearded old prophet, Jeremiah.

Just as the armies of Babylon reached the gates, Jeremiah taught his people a great lesson in hope. Calling together a large number of witnesses, and with a great show of attention to all the legalities, Jeremiah purchased a plot of land outside the city. For, said Jeremiah, we will be taken away, but we will come back. And during all the long years of captivity, the memory of the field that Jeremiah had purchased in faraway Judah was a symbol of the restoration to come.

In modern times, too, a symbol can give staying-power to hope.

I read once, in the *Chicago Tribune*, the amazing story of Leo Algimas. Among the thousands herded into concentration camps by the Nazis was Leo's family. Like the others, they endured incredible hardships, but because they had a symbol for their hope they never slipped into the despair that engulfed so many.

What do you suppose this symbol was that gave them such courage? It was a tiny piece of paper torn from a box of chocolates made in Chicago. This particular candy company prints a little American flag on the bottom of all its boxes, and that was the scrap of paper

How do we find God? For a long time, Fulton Oursler (1893–1952), the author of The Greatest Story Ever Told, *made a restless search. Then, one day, in the midst of despair, he wandered into a New York church: "The best I could manage was to admit to myself that I wished I could believe.... And that was enough!" In Guideposts (1950), Oursler outlined the paradox of accepting God. "Faith is a gift," he wrote, "but you can ask for it!" He did.*

that the Algimas family passed from hand to hand in their barbed-wire enclosure. They looked at it, held it and whispered, with eyes shining, about the army of liberation that was coming.

A symbol is not the same thing as positive proof. The Algimas family did not know that the Allies would win the war. In fact, the war news given to the prisoners was edited strongly in favor of the Germans. Hope seems to have little to do with proof. Emilie Batisse had no evidence that she would get well; it was difficult to see how the Hebrews would ever see Jerusalem again, yet they went on hoping. They were like the White Queen in *Alice in Wonderland.*

"One *can't* believe impossible things," said Alice to the Queen.

"I daresay you haven't had much practice," replied the Queen. "When I was your age, I always did it for half an hour a day. Why, some-times I believed as many as six impossible things before breakfast."

And symbols help us to fix our minds on the "impossible." The greatest symbol that the world had ever known was also the hardest to believe. A tiny baby sleeping in the manger of a stable was supposed to signal the kingdom of God on earth.

For the hope of the world, what a wonderful symbol! Hope has nothing to do with the odds and logic of the situation. Few would have believed the baby of this humble Jewish couple would change the destiny of mankind. But we know today that that is the precise thing that happened.

And He can change your personal destiny, too. Define what it is that you hope for, ask for it in His name, and no matter how impossible it may seem, the coming year is the year for your hope to start coming true.

Guideposts editor Jim McDermott in the days when he was Leuchten's best customer

SEPTEMBER 1983

Giving Good Measure *by James McDermott, editor*

The other day someone asked me who the happiest man I had ever met was. Swirling out of the blue, the name Max Leuchten came to mind. It puzzled me at first, but then I began remembering the scenes at Leuchten's Candy Store in Madison, New Jersey, during the 1940s and '50s. Max was a tall, angular man with an oval face, not much hair, great brown eyes and an enormous smile in which a number of gold teeth flashed. The smile was more or less perpetual, even when he was scolding us kids for unruliness.

Leuchten's was divided into three parts. On the left, as you entered, was a section of dark mahogany booths that was the invariable lunchtime denizen of the mayor, the chief of police, the editor of the Madison *Eagle,* and the local Ford dealer. In the middle was a rectangle of sparkling glass cabinets heaped with sweets—fragrant chocolates of every description, glittering ropes of rock candy and plump pastel petits fours. To the right was the gleaming black marble soda fountain section, featuring Leuchten's homemade ice cream, which

Max and his amiable staff would pack so overflowingly into takeout cartons that their tops barely fit on.

Max's smiling presence seemed everywhere at once. Clucking to the patrons at the mahogany booths ("Everything's all right, chentulmens?"), presiding over the inevitable gaggle of kids at the fountain ("Ruthie, give Jimmie an extra scoop; he looks skinny today!") and beaming from the candy counter ("Take a little free sample of this and tell me how you like it").

Max gave so much away that we always wondered how he prospered. But prosper he did, and, of course, the giving was his secret. Max's beaming happiness was my first lesson—and that of thousands of other youngsters who flocked to his marvelous store—in the law of giving. "Give, and it shall be given unto you; good measure, pressed down, and shaken together, and running over," Jesus told us (Luke 6:38). Why, it's almost as if He had been describing the way Max packed his delicious ice cream.

On January 20, 1981, when Kathryn Koob and her fellow hostages were released after 444 days of captivity in Teheran, she said immediately that she intended to thank God for sustaining her in her ordeal by speaking of His faithfulness to groups around the country. She kept her word, and also wrote a book about her imprisonment and spiritual growth, Guest of the Revolution. *Glance at the title of the book you're now holding and you'll see the key Bible promise that Kathryn relied on.*

APRIL 1956

The Magic of Three Days *by Patt Barnes*

It was a beautiful spring day, and a sense of peace stayed with me as I left the Cathedral on Easter Monday morning. I paused for a moment on top of the steps leading to the Avenue, now crowded with people rushing to their jobs. Sitting in her usual place inside a small archway was the old flower lady. At her feet, corsages and boutonnieres were parading on top of a spread-open newspaper.

The flower lady was smiling, her wrinkled old face alive with some inner joy. I started down the stairs—then, on an impulse, turned and picked out a flower.

As I put it in my lapel, I said, "You look happy this morning."

"Why not? Everything is good."

She was dressed so shabbily and seemed so very old that her reply startled me.

"You've been sitting here for many years now, haven't you? And always smiling. You wear your troubles well."

"You can't reach my age and not have troubles," she replied. "Only it's like Jesus and Good Friday..." She paused for a moment.

"Yes?" I prompted.

"Well, when Jesus was crucified on Good Friday, that was the worst day for the whole world. And when I get troubles I remember that, and then I think of what happened only three days later—Easter and our Lord arising. So when I get troubles, I've learned to wait three days...somehow everything gets all right again."

And she smiled goodbye. Her words still follow me whenever I think I have troubles... "Give God a chance to help...wait three days."

U.S. Diplomat Kathryn Koob, 1982

JULY 1982

Waiting, Yielded and Still *by Kathryn Koob, diplomat*

When we Americans were first taken hostage in Iran, we were terrified. We didn't know who our captors were, or what their demands would be. What were they going to do with us? Outside the embassy compound, the rage of the crowd added to the ugly atmosphere. Their screaming would go on until two in the morning, then start up again at six A.M.— mobs of people yelling their hatred, their triumph, their anger.

One time after I'd fallen asleep, I was awakened by the distinct impression that someone had sat down on my bed. I turned over quickly, expecting to see one of my guards. But no one was there. Instantly, I was reminded of the Holy Spirit, the Comforter. And with the sense of His presence came a very real knowledge that I had a source of strength that the students and mobs didn't have.

Then a hymn came into my mind, one I'd learned way back when I was a freshman in high school: "Have Thine own way, Lord! Have Thine own way! Thou art the potter; I am the clay. Mold me and make me after Thy will, while I am waiting, yielded and still."

How those words spoke to me! I knew I couldn't do anything to change my situation as a political prisoner. But when I accepted that fact, I could say, "Okay, Lord, here I am. I don't know what's going to happen in this situation. But use me. *While I am waiting, yielded and still.*"

As a diplomat, I was especially aware that my government could not give in to terrorists' demands in order to free us. I told my guards, "We may be here for the next fifteen years! And my job is to sit here and wait."

They couldn't believe I could take that attitude. But I did, and I set about ordering my morning hours in a kind of contemplative system for myself—Bible studies, prayer and meditation, reading.

I developed a morning prayer that went like this: "Thank You, Lord, for bringing me through the night. Thank You for giving me today. I give it back to You. Show me what You would have me do with it."

There were a lot of days when it seemed He wasn't having me do anything. But He was. He was teaching me to love, He was teaching me to accept, He was teaching me to try to be open to new ideas and to new understanding.

And that's something that can happen in anyone's life, in *your* life, if you let yourself be opened to His will—if you are "waiting, yielded and still."

*When she first wrote for Guideposts in 1954, Catherine Marshall
was the widow of the former chaplain of the U. S. Senate, Peter
Marshall (1902–1949). What was Peter Marshall's philosophy
of prayer? "We cannot see God's form," he would say to his
congregation, "but we can feel His presence. He knows all about
you—your hidden perplexity. He waits to speak to you comfortingly,
forgivingly. You may tell Him your needs in your own way."*

OCTOBER 1960

The Prayer of Relinquishment *by Catherine Marshall, writer*

Like most people, when I first began active experimentation with prayer, I was full of questions, such as: Why are some agonizingly sincere prayers granted, while others are not?

Today I still have questions. Mysteries about prayer are always ahead of present knowledge— luring, beckoning on to further experimentation.

But one thing I do know; I learned it through hard experience. It's a way of prayer that has resulted consistently in a glorious answer, glorious because each time power beyond human reckoning has been released. This is the Prayer of Relinquishment.

I got my first glimpse of it in the fall of 1943. I had then been ill for six months with a widespread lung infection, and a bevy of specialists seemed unable to help. Persistent prayer, using all the faith I could muster, had resulted in— nothing. I was still in bed full time.

One afternoon a pamphlet was put in my hands. It was the story of a missionary who had been an invalid for eight years. Constantly she had prayed that God would make her well, so that she might do His work. Finally, worn out with futile petition, she prayed, "All right. I give up. If You want me to be an invalid, that's Your business. Anyway, I want You even more than I want health. You decide." In two weeks the woman was out of bed, completely well.

This made no sense to me, yet I could not forget the story. On the morning of September 14th—how can I ever forget the date?—I came to the same point of abject acceptance.

"I'm tired of asking," was the burden of my prayer. "I'm beaten, through. God, You decide what You want for me."

Tears flowed. I had no faith as I understood faith, expected nothing. The gift of my sick self was made with no trace of graciousness.

And the result? It was as if I had touched a button that opened windows in heaven; as if some dynamo of heavenly power began flowing, flowing. Within a few hours I had experienced the presence of the Living Christ in a way that wiped away all doubt and revolutionized my life. From that moment my recovery began.

Through this incident and others that followed, God was trying to teach me something important about prayer. Gradually, I saw that a demanding spirit, with self-will as its rudder, blocks prayer. I understood that the reason for this is that God absolutely refuses to violate our free will; that, therefore, unless self-will is voluntarily given up, even God cannot move to answer prayer.

In time, I gained more understanding about the Prayer of Relinquishment through the experiences of others in contemporary life and through books. Jesus' prayer in the Garden of Gethsemane is a pattern for us, I learned. Christ could have avoided the cross. He did not have to go up to Jerusalem that last time. He could have compromised with the priests, bargained with Caiaphas. He could have capitalized on His following and appeased Judas

Catherine Marshall, 1914–1983

by setting up the beginning of an earthly kingdom. Pilate wanted to release Him, all but begged Him to say the right words—so that he might. Even in the Garden on the night of betrayal, He had plenty of time and opportunity to flee, but Christ used His free will to leave the decision up to His Father.

J. B. Phillips in his book on the Gospels *(The Gospels—Translated into Modern English)* brings Jesus' prayer into focus for us. "Dear Father, all things are possible to You. Please let me not have to drink this cup. Yet it is not what I want, but what You want."

The prayer was not answered as the human Jesus wished. Yet power has been flowing from His cross ever since.

I remember the agony of one attractive young girl, Sara B——, who shared with me her doubts about her engagement. "I love Jeb," she said, "and Jeb loves me. But the problem is, he drinks. Not that he's an alcoholic, you know. Yet the drinking is a sort of symbol of a lot of ideas he has. This has bothered me so much that I wonder if God is trying to tell me to give Jeb up."

As we talked, Sara came to her own conclusion. It was that she would lose something infinitely precious if she did not follow the highest and the best that she knew. Tears glistened in her eyes as she said, "I'm going to break the engagement. If God wants me to marry Jeb, He will see that things change—about the drinking and all."

Right then, simply and poignantly, she told God of her decision. She was putting her broken dreams and her now unknown future into God's hands.

Jeb's ideas and ideals didn't change, so Sara did not marry him. But a year later Sara wrote me an ecstatic letter. "It nearly killed me to give up Jeb. Yet God knew that he wasn't the one for me. Now I've met The Man and we're to be married. Now I *really* have something to say about trusting God!…"

It's good to remember that not even the Master Shepherd can lead if the sheep have not this trust and insist on running ahead of Him or taking side paths or just stubbornly refusing to follow Him. That's the why of Christ's insistence on the practical obedience: *And why call ye me, Lord, Lord, and do not the things which I say?* (Luke 6:46). Our pliability must be complete, from our wills right on through to our actions.

When we come right down to it, how can we make obedience real, except as we give over our self-will in reference to each of life's episodes as it unfolds? That's why it shouldn't surprise us that at the heart of the secret of answered prayer lies the Law of Relinquishment.

So Mrs. Nathaniel Hawthorne, wife of the famous American author, found as she wrestled in prayer in the city of Rome one February day in 1860. Una, the Hawthornes' eldest daughter, was dying of malaria. The attending physician, Dr. Franco, that afternoon had warned that unless the young girl's fever abated before morning, she would die.

As Mrs. Hawthorne sat by Una's bed, her thoughts went to what her husband had said earlier that day. "I cannot endure the alterna-

"A problem is an opportunity in work clothes." Henry Kaiser Jr. had heard his industrialist father say it before, but it always seemed to apply to business problems. Then Kaiser came down with a crippling case of multiple sclerosis. He went from doctor to doctor looking for help. Finally, it occurred to him, "Perhaps an illness can be an opportunity in work clothes, too" (Guideposts 1954). That thinking gave him the courage to undergo therapy, which gave him strength—and God an opportunity to help.

tions of hope and fear; therefore I have settled with myself not to hope at all."

But the mother could not share Nathaniel's hopelessness. Una could not, must not die. This daughter strongly resembled her father, had the finest mind, the most complex character of all the Hawthorne children. Why should some capricious Providence demand that they give her up?

As the night deepened, the girl lay so still that she seemed to be in the anteroom of death. The mother went to the window and looked out on the piazza. There was no moonlight; a dark sky was heavy with clouds.

"I cannot bear this loss—cannot—cannot…" Then suddenly, unaccountably, another thought took over. "Why should I doubt the goodness of God? Let Him take Una, if He sees best. I can *give* her to Him. No, I won't fight against Him anymore."

Then an even stranger thing happened. Having made the great sacrifice, Mrs. Hawthorne expected to feel sadder. Instead she felt lighter, happier than at any time since Una's long illness had begun.

Some minutes later she walked back to the girl's bedside, felt her daughter's forehead. It was cool. Una was sleeping naturally. And the mother rushed into the next room to tell her husband that a miracle had happened.

Now the question is: What is the spiritual law implicit in this Prayer of Relinquishment?

Fear is like a screen erected between us and God, so that His power cannot get through to us. So, how does one get rid of fear?

This is not easy when the life of someone dear hangs in the balance, or when what we want most is involved. At such times, every emotion, every passion, is tied up in the dread that what we fear most is about to come upon us. Obviously only drastic measures can deal with such a gigantic fear and the demanding spirit that usually goes along with it. My experience has been that trying to deal with it by repeating faith affirmations is not drastic enough.

So then we are squarely up against the Law of Relinquishment. Was Jesus showing us how to use this law when He said, *Resist not evil?*(Matthew 5:39). In God's eyes, fear is evil because it's an acting out of lack of trust in Him. So Jesus is advising: Resist not fear. (Note that He made only one exception to this: *Fear him*— [the Devil]—*which is able to destroy both soul and body in hell* [Matthew 10:28]).

In other words, Jesus is saying, admit the possibility of what you fear most. And lo, as you stop fleeing, force yourself to walk up to the fear, look it full in the face—never forgetting that God and His power are still the supreme reality—the fear evaporates. Drastic? Yes. But it is one sure way of releasing prayer power into human affairs.

What do iron products and people who go through severe trials have in common? In Guideposts (1984), actor Ned Beatty used these examples to explain. The famous Spanish sword known as "the Toledo blade" is subjected to white heat and hammering, and the result is incomparable durability. The 16th-century Spanish monk, John of the Cross, was subjected to a prison ordeal and a crisis of doubt, and found that his character and faith had been strengthened. Metal and mettle. The crucible improves both.

AUGUST 1961

The Secret of the Frying Pan *by Nanette Bailey, real estate agent*

I lay propped up on the sofa, pain keeping me from enjoying the autumn color outside my window. The house was cold and I had asked the new practical nurse (one of a long series; nurses didn't stay very long) to build a fire. Mrs. Harmon was silent as she brought in the logs, holding each one at arm's length from her stiff white uniform. Without a word she held a match to the fire and disappeared into the kitchen with my untouched lunch tray.

Mrs. Harmon's silence matched my mood. There was a kind of honesty in silence, an honesty, I reflected bitterly, that you seldom see anymore. I was a real estate agent. Not a very successful one, but I had learned to promote and hustle and maneuver. The world, I had long ago concluded, was run by the dishonest, and the rest of us had to defend ourselves. Each year I strengthened my own defenses, adding a little cynicism, a little indifference to my personality.

I was a little horrified, sometimes, at the hard, worldly-wise face that looked back at me from the mirror, but I saw little prospect that it would change. And now, to top things off, this crippling arthritis attack! For weeks I hadn't been out of the house, hadn't been free of pain. I could see no point to it: the lost sales, the enforced idleness, the suffering.

Then Mrs. Harmon entered, carrying the frying pan.

In the hours that followed, I watched a little drama that cast a sudden new light on my ill-ness, that lit my whole life, in fact, with hope. For I glimpsed, that fall afternoon, one of the uses God can make of suffering.

Mrs. Harmon held the frying pan far away from her, gingerly, as she had the logs. Here comes a complaint, I thought. And to make it worse, a complaint was justified. It really was an ugly old thing, made of heavy cast iron and thick with the baked-on crust of many years. I should have thrown it out long ago, but it had been Mother's. It reminded me of simpler, happier days. And I really had tried to get it clean. I'd scoured and scrubbed and scraped: hardly a day that I didn't worry away at it, without making a dent in that stubborn crust.

And now, I thought, I'm going to get a lecture on kitchen hygiene. Mrs. Harmon, however, said not a word. She carried the offending frying pan to the fire and, as I stared, stopped and laid it across the logs. Only at the door to the kitchen did she speak. "Ever watch fire clean a pan?" she asked.

The rest of the short October afternoon I watched as the fire went to work. First the old pan sputtered and smoked as if complaining at this ill-treatment. But after a while it grew silent. A faint glow, red first, then almost white spread through its body.

Then as I watched, transfixed, there was a tiny "ping." A piece of the ancient crust had popped off and dropped into the fire. In a few minutes, another piece came loose, and

When their six-year-old boy was kidnapped and murdered, John and Reve Walsh struggled with devastating grief (Guideposts 1984). Then they resolved to try to convince Congress to pass a bill that would allow FBI agents to help local police in missing-child cases. The Walshes lobbied relentlessly, day after day, for a year and a half. In 1983, due in part to their efforts, the bill was passed, proving once again that ordinary citizens can achieve extraordinary results—and find healing for themselves.

another. All afternoon the cleansing process went on until finally, as the fire died, the pan turned from white to dull red and then to black again. A glowing, lustrous black, like a new pan. No, more beautiful. Like an old pan shined in fire.

As the room grew dusky, Mrs. Harmon came in armed with a great stack of hot pads.

She reached into the fireplace and lifted the gleaming pan from the coals, inspecting it in silence. When she spoke, it was in a low voice.

"People go through fire, too," she said thoughtfully. "A nurse sees it all the time." She looked down at the pan. "I've seen men and women come out of it as shining and clean as this pan."

AUGUST 1977

The Lifeline *by Rev. William T. Murphy*

One of the members of my congregation was recovering from a brain tumor operation when I paid a call on him in the hospital. He lay in bed, curtained off from another patient who was desperately ill and in a deep coma. Quietly, I offered up a prayer for my parishioner, thanking God for His mighty healing power.

Several weeks later, I was making another visit to the hospital when a man on crutches called out to me. He hobbled over and enthusiastically reached for my hand. "You don't know me," he said, and indeed I had never

seen him before, "but you helped save my life." I was mystified.

Then he explained about the illness he had just survived, about the coma he had been in, a coma so deep that he had been unable to hear his wife or his son who spoke to him at his bedside.

"I *did* hear the soft words of a prayer, however," he said, and as he talked I realized that the words he heard had been mine. "Your prayer became my lifeline," he told me as I stood shaking my head at this new evidence of how prayer penetrates.

Chet Bitterman III

NOVEMBER 1982

A Story of Unexpected Thankfulness *by Chet Bitterman Jr.,*
independent scale dealer

The clearing in the Amazon jungle was hot and bright.

"I'm thankful it's not raining!" I said to my wife Mary.

"And thankful we've got these few minutes alone," I added as Mary and I stood hand in hand before the grave. There was writing on the headstone but it was in Spanish. "It's a beautiful setting, Mary. I'm thankful for that."

Then I heard the word I'd been repeating. *Thankful.* How could a man travel 3,000 miles to the graveside of his murdered 28-year-old son and find reasons to give thanks?

For me, the lesson in thanksgiving didn't start until I was 47 years old and facing the greatest crisis of my life. Up to that time, my reaction to things was often impatience. For example, a lot of Amish people travel the roads around our hometown of Lancaster, Pennsylvania. To get stuck behind one of those farm families in their slow-moving, horse-drawn buggy would set me fuming. Waiting was always the hardest thing in the world for me. When our first child was born, Mary was in labor 19 endless hours, while I raced up and down corridors and charged through doors marked "no admittance." Not being able to *do* anything—that was the worst. And then suddenly there he was, red, healthy and howling. We named him Chet Bitterman III.

And it was soon apparent that the third Chet was going to be just like the second, a guy who couldn't sit still. I think he broke his first bone at age five, jumping out a window. Or maybe the first was the cracked collarbone when he hit the ceiling bouncing on his bunk bed. If he remembered to take his glasses off before playing in a neighborhood football game, he'd sit on them afterward. At 20, he drove his motorcycle into an embankment, mauling his right foot, leaving permanent scars where the doctors pinned the pieces together.

He wasn't a wild youngster, he just threw himself all out into everything he did. He brought the same kind of total involvement to the church groups he belonged to. Church was central to us all. In fact, when Chet was eight I had offered myself for the mission field. But I had too little education, too many children (by now Chet had four younger brothers and sisters).

"Why not go into business," someone said, "and support the missionaries?"

This was how I came to open my own shop, installing and servicing the 60-foot-long scales used to weigh trucks along the highway, and the big industrial scales used by feed mills and stone quarries. It's supported a good many missionaries over the years, even while our family grew to include eight children. My shop is in our basement and that's where Chet started learning the business. ("There's only one way to verify a scale, son: Place a known weight on it.") Before long he was out on the truck with me, lugging those 50-pound standard weights from job to job. By the end of an average day he and I would each have lifted 32,000 pounds.

"Blessed are they that mourn." Thomas Dooley (1927–1961) was born into a wealthy St. Louis family with all that money could buy. And yet, when he lived with next to nothing, he found even greater happiness. In the mid-50's, the young doctor discovered his true vocation, healing the poor and sick in war-stricken Indochina. It was there that Dooley found out what the second beatitude meant. By mourning—by truly understanding the sorrows of the poor— he was blessed.

By his early 20s, Chet knew he wanted to go to the mission field in person. He married a beautiful girl named Brenda Gardner whose parents were with the Wycliffe Bible Translators, an organization extending literacy all over the world, translating the Bible into hundreds of languages never before written down. Brenda and Chet too joined Wycliffe and, after three years of linguistic training, were assigned to Colombia, where Brenda's folks were.

In May 1979, Mary and I saw them off from the International Departures area of the Miami airport. We were all a little subdued, realizing it would be two years before we saw one another again.

"Anna Ruth will be so big we won't know her!" Our little granddaughter was just two. "And the new baby!" Mary went on. "We won't know for days if it's a boy or a girl."

"Nonsense, Mother! We'll be in touch by radio from the base."

"And maybe," said Brenda, "when we reach our tribal area and get our house built, you can come and visit us in the jungle!" But that wouldn't be for at least a year and a half. First there would be more training at the Wycliffe base in Lomalinda, adjustment to the climate, food, and lifestyle of the Amazon rain forest.

In October the radio call came with the good news of the birth of another granddaughter.

The following month, November 1979, news from another part of the world was ominous. A group of Americans were taken hostage by revolutionaries in Iran. I fretted at reports of similar groups at work in Colombia.

"Don't worry, Dad," Chet wrote. "Our work has nothing to do with politics."

Saturday, January 17, 1981, I got home late because of the icy roads. "I just had a wonderful long talk with Chet!" Mary greeted me. "He and Brenda and the girls are in Bogota for a week." They had flown up to the Colombian capital for a final medical check before going into their tribal area far to the south.

It was a good weekend all around. On Sunday came the news that the Iranian hostages would be released.

Monday morning, Mary and I drove over to see her mother who had not been well. We got back to find my office manager, John Williams, waiting with an ash-gray face: "Wycliffe called. The guerrillas have kidnapped Chet."

Guerrillas? Chet? I heard the words but could make no sense of them. We spent the next hour on the phone, piecing together as much of the story as anyone knew. Before dawn that morning, January 19, a group of heavily armed masked gunmen—members of a revolutionary faction known as "M-19"— had broken into the house Wycliffe rented in Bogota.

Seventeen people were spending the night there, five of them children. All were herded sleepy-eyed into the living room. Mothers and children were permitted to sit on the sofa, the others made to lie face down on the floor. Eventually the intruders departed taking a single hostage—Chet—along with them. Why Chet? No one knew. Maybe because his Spanish was better than the others'. Maybe for no special reason.

Dr. Thomas Dooley with young patient

Before leaving, they allowed him to kiss his little girls, and go back to the bedroom for his contact lenses. Then they put him into a station wagon and drove away. Their price for his return: the withdrawal of all 200 Wycliffe workers currently in Colombia.

"You pretend to be missionaries, but we know you are spies for the Central Intelligence Agency." If Wycliffe was not out of the country in exactly one month, Chet would be shot.

The pointlessness of it, the pigheaded stupidity, made me want to pick up those 50-pound weights and start smashing something. Apparently the Colombian government was powerless, the American government equally so. "But there's got to be something we can do!" I cried.

"We can pray," Mary said. "And we can get others to pray."

Mary spent the rest of the day and night on the telephone, calling churches, prayer groups, missionary societies, Christian radio stations—every religious resource we knew of. Meanwhile, I paced—down to the basement, up to the kitchen for tea, back to the basement. This inaction— suddenly I knew what it was like. It was like those awful hours in the hospital, waiting for Chet to be born.

I wasn't going to sit twiddling my thumbs this time! I was going to do something! I'd get some guns and a bunch of buddies and fly to Bogota and take the place apart brick by brick until I found where they were holding my son.

I knew it was a fantasy. I also knew that if I couldn't find some outlet for the rage inside me I was going to have another heart attack or kill someone or do both. "Lord," I begged, "there's got to be something I can do!"

There is. Give thanks.

The thought couldn't have come from me. It was a million miles from where my head was just then. But neither would it go away. *Give thanks.* It just stayed there, facing down my own thoughts. I even recognized where it came from—and that was unusual too. I wasn't like Chet, who knew hundreds of Bible verses by heart. I'd never been able to sit still long enough to memorize much. But I knew this one—chapter and verse. First Thessalonians 5:18: *In every thing give thanks: for this is the will of God....*

But...why think of it now? "Every thing" couldn't possibly mean *this* situation. Not the kidnapping of a husband and father on the threshold of his life's work. You couldn't give thanks for *that.*

Give thanks. I couldn't! It wasn't human. I felt shocked, angry, frustrated—anything but thankful. Then I noticed that the verse didn't say anything about the way I felt. "Give thanks" was God's command, not "feel thankful." Thanksgiving was apparently—to start with anyhow— not a matter of the emotions but the will.

Was I *willing* then, to give thanks? No! I wanted justice. I wanted revenge. I didn't want to give up my righteous wrath. In my pacing I passed the weights, saw Chet lugging them out to the truck, sweat beading his forehead. "The way to check out a scale, son, is to place a known weight on it."

At Guideposts, we know that our readers believe in and practice prayer. But what about readers of other magazines? People *magazine—read by Americans of all persuasions—polled its readers in 1984 on their attitudes to prayer and faith. They found that: 7 out of every 10* People *readers regularly prayed at home; in the past 10 years, religious influence had increased for 45%; 54% had gone to religious services in the past week.* People *readers… Guideposts readers…in America, faith is surging!*

The Bible was that known weight to me, the standard that had proved itself trustworthy. And so at last, grudgingly, without an ounce of positive emotion to back it up, I mumbled, "Okay. I'll give thanks."

There's another thing that working with scales impresses on you: the importance of accuracy. My thanks would have to be honest thanks. Was there anything in this mess I could *truly* be grateful for?

Well…what about all those Bible verses Chet could recite? They must be a help to him right now. I could be thankful for his memorizing so much Scripture.

And…these weights! These thousands of pounds Chet had hoisted daily to give him a physique that could take just about any kind of strain. Thank God for Chet's strength.

Your strength, too, of course, Lord! Because You are with him—his whereabouts are no mystery to You. Thank You for Your presence with him. With Brenda and the children. With Mary and me.

The items were coming so fast now that I seized a piece of paper. Thank God we could be proud of Chet. Thank God he spoke Spanish…and made friends easily. Thank God he and Mary had that great talk two days ago. Soon, I had filled a page with things for which —in the midst of this situation—I could be genuinely thankful.

Something even stranger was happening. As I wrote, the tension and rage and anguish drained away. I felt light, I felt free, I felt— thankful! Feelings I could never have drummed up by straining for them had followed effortlessly this act of obedience.

As I say, Mary had turned to God naturally and gracefully in this crisis, praying and asking others to pray. Now, together, we asked God to help us show our trust in Him. And so He did. He used us with the reporters who descended on our house, with people who wrote and called from all over the country and beyond.

The deadline for the missionaries to leave Colombia was February 19. At no time did Brenda or Mary or I suggest that the organization capitulate. Not only would it negate 19 years of effort in Colombia, where Wycliffe translators were working in 35 previously unwritten languages, it would endanger thousands of Wycliffe workers all over the world.

And anyhow Mary and I and many of those praying for Chet had received again and again the assurance that he would be released. When February 19 came and went and the M-19 issued a new, extended ultimatum we all breathed easier. It was going to be Iran all over again. For the next few weeks rumors sped between Bogota and Washington. Chet was free. He was not free. The deadline had been extended two weeks. It had been re-extended 24 hours. Chet had been killed. Chet was alive.

On March 7, a local newspaper phoned. Was it true that Chet's body had been found in an abandoned bus on a side street in Bogota? Mary put them off. "There've been so many rumors." And yet with her incredible sensitivity Mary knew at once that this was not just another rumor. Our boy was dead.

Wycliffe called us to confirm the report. Chet had been shot once through the heart. I

Reflections by Antoinette Goethschius

When I am sore beset, I seek some quiet place,
Some lonely room or barren windswept hill,
And there in silence wait apart until
I see again the smile upon God's face,
Until His presence floods me like the dawn,
And I can hear His whispered, "Peace, be still,"
And know again the strength to do His will.
I turn to take my load and find it gone.

refused to believe it. I had God's word! At last I got Bogota on the telephone. George Gardner, Brenda's father, had been to the morgue.

"It's him, Chet."

"George, are you positive? Couldn't there be a mistake?"

"I even pulled off his sock to check that scar on his foot."

I grasped at the last remaining straw. "Which foot, George?"

"The right one."

The right foot…that old motorcycle injury …there was no mistake.

I moved through the next few days in a blur. Church next morning. People shaking hands. "We're so sorry." A letter from President Reagan delivered by an envoy. They flew Chet's body to Lomalinda and buried him in a jungle clearing there on the Wycliffe base. Afterward, Brenda and her parents and the two little girls came up to the States. Mary and I joined them for a few days of solitude in North Carolina. And it was there that life started coming back into focus for me.

But it was a focus from a different angle, a new one for me, the view from forever. I hadn't heard God wrong, Chet *had* been released, released into freedom and joy and service we could only dimly imagine. To wean us from an earthly perspective to a heavenly one, that's God's purpose from the day we are born. Chet sees that way now; I'm still working at it.

And the secret is the one I started to learn on a January day nearly two years ago. The key to seeing as God does is to give thanks in everything…

The nearest town to the Wycliffe base had a hospital, but no ambulance. Our neighbors in Lancaster raised money for one as a memorial to Chet. In April 1982, we went down to present it to the people of Villavicencio from the people of Lancaster.

After the presentation ceremony, Mary and I were flown farther into that sea of green trees, 15 minutes by small plane, to the Wycliffe base where Chet is buried. Which is how we came to be standing in that little jungle clearing.

Earlier, the words of the hospital administrator who accepted the ambulance had been repeated to us by a translator. Now they echoed in my ears. "You came with love instead of anger…"

Thank You, Lord, for doing this.

"Love never dies…"

Thank You for setting our sights on the eternal.

"*Gracias,*" said Mary suddenly, pointing to the word on the headstone. "Doesn't that mean 'thank you'?"

Gracias a Dios…

I don't know many Spanish words, but in any language these are all I need:

Thanks be to God…

A VERY PRESENT HELP . . .

At Home

How do we keep God in the center of our homes?

Norman Vincent Peale recalls a dinner party many years ago at the apartment of some dear old friends who, after 37 years of marriage—their children old and grown—had moved into smaller quarters.

"We are alone," they said, "and in an apartment again, but just as we have always done with our houses, we want to dedicate this home to Jesus Christ."

With that, there was a prayer, a reading from the Bible and all the guests held hands and sang, "Blest Be the Tie That Binds." It was a simple ceremony, this blessing of the home, but a significant one. People everywhere have found ways to invite God into their home. In Italy, in the spring, as the dust is shaken from musty rugs, a priest visits and blesses the homes in his parish...Jewish families often nail a tiny box called a *mezuzah* outside their front doors. Inside there is a miniscule scroll with passages of Scripture, a reminder that God's love blesses all who dwell within.

Mealtime, of course, provides a perfect opportunity for seeking God's blessing, and many people have developed their own distinctive ways of giving thanks. In Rick Hamlin's home (Guideposts 1984), his father's dinnertime prayer is whimsically known as "The six o'clock news" because Mr. Hamlin cites so many of those in need of God's good news that day—his family, the neighbor down the street, survivors of an earthquake half a world away.

In Ruth Ward's family in Pennsylvania (Guideposts 1975), a different member is prayed for each day of the week, with the name posted on the refrigerator door. Ruth found this custom particularly gratifying when she woke up one morning with the flu. She found her name up there on the door and knew she was blessed.

I stand at the door and knock, Jesus said. *If any man hear my voice, and open the door, I will come in to him, and will sup with him, and he with me.* (Revelation 3:20)

So now, open the door.

*Guideposts editor Grace Oursler (1900-1955),
with (from left) Leonard LeSourd and
Norman Vincent Peale*

AUGUST 1948

Desperate Enough *by Grace Perkins Oursler, editor*

The boy had fallen, running home after school, and skinned his left knee. It was no more than a scratch—there wasn't even a rent in his trousers—but by night the knee started to ache. Nothing much, he thought, being 13 and the sturdy son of a frontiersman. Ignoring the pain, he knelt in his nightgown and said his prayers, then climbed into bed in the room where he and his five brothers slept.

His leg was painful the next morning, but he still did not tell anyone. The farm kept the whole family relentlessly busy; always he had to be up at six to do his chores before school. And he must be thorough about them or he would be sent back to do them over again, no matter what else he had to miss. In their household, discipline was fair but stern.

Two mornings later, the leg ached too badly for him to drag himself to the barn. That was a Sunday and he could remain behind, while the rest of the family drove into town. School homework finished, he sat in the parlor rocker, examining and comparing the three family Bibles; one in German that held the records of all their births and deaths; another in Greek that was his father's proud possession and finally the King James version shared by mother and all the sons.

One night this week it would be the boy's turn to lead the family devotions. He could select his own passages from the Old and New Testaments and read them aloud and try to get a discussion going; sometimes they became exciting. But now the pain blurred his attention;

he put aside the Scriptures and dozed until his brothers returned from Sunday school.

Mom and Dad did not come home with them because Sunday was parents' day off; the boys did the housework and cooked the big meal of the week, while father and mother stayed on for church service.

But by the time dinner was ready the boy had climbed into bed. The shoe had to be cut off his swollen and discolored leg. Why on earth hadn't he told somebody? Go quick and fetch the doctor!

Mother bathed knee and foot and thigh, applied poultices and wiped the boy's sweating forehead with a moist, cool cloth. She was an intense and vital woman. Confronted with this angry infection, her manner remained serene. Mom had nursed her brood through accidents and ailments from toothaches to scarlet fever; one son she had lost, but that only made her calmer and more determined when she had to fight for the others.

Old Dr. Conklin examined the leg and pursed his lips. "It's not likely we can save it!"

The invalid sat up stiffly. "What's that mean?" he asked huskily.

"It means," explained the doctor gently, "if things get worse we'll have to amputate."

"Not me!" stormed the boy. "I won't have it! I'd rather die!"

"The longer we wait, the more we will have to take off," urged the doctor.

"You won't take any off!" The boy's voice broke with an adolescent crack, as his mother

In Guideposts' third year, Grace Perkins Oursler became its dynamic Executive Editor. Years before, Grace—a Roman Catholic—lost her faith, but regained it in a valiant spiritual struggle. "I love my faith and practice it with my whole heart," she used to tell us. "I assume Protestants and Jews working with Guideposts feel the same way about their faiths. And that is what I believe Guideposts should stand for and work for tirelessly."

turned away, shaken. But there was no adolescence in the eyes that defied the doctor's reproachful gaze.

Dr. Conklin stalked out, nodding to the mother to follow him. As he stood in the hallway explaining to both parents about what could and probably would happen, they could hear the boy calling for his brother: "Ed! *Ed!* Come up here, will you?"

The brother stamped in and then they heard the sick lad's voice, high pitched with pain: "If I go out of my head, Ed, don't let them cut off my leg. Promise me, Ed—*promise!*"

In a moment Ed came out and ran to the kitchen. When he returned his mother said, "Ed, what's your brother asking for?"

"Fork! To bite on; keep from screaming."

Then Edgar stood outside the bedroom door, his arms folded. Quite clearly he was standing on guard.

Ed looked straight at old Dr. Conklin. "Nobody's going to saw off that leg!" he announced.

"But, Ed—you'll be sorry," gasped the doctor.

"Maybe so, Doc. But I gave him my word." And nothing changed that.

If Ed had not stood his ground, father and mother might have yielded. They were not yet convinced that amputation was necessary; they were doubtful. The adamant attitude first of the sick boy and then of his brother was incredible, for defiance of parental authority was unknown in this household. Yet there was Ed, standing before the sickroom door.

"Guess we'll wait and see how he looks by tonight, eh, Doc?" said the father.

For two days and nights Ed stood guard, sleeping at the threshold, not leaving even to eat. The fever mounted, and the suffering boy babbled in torment, but the older brother showed no weakening of resolve, even though the discoloration of the swollen leg was creeping toward the pelvis, just as the doctor had predicted. Ed remained firm because he had given his promise, and also because he shared the frontiersmen's horror of being less than physically perfect.

The parents knew that their son would never forgive an amputation, and Ed's attitude continued to be decisive, time after time, when the doctor returned. Once, in helpless rage, Dr. Conklin shouted: "It's murder!" and slammed the front door. Nothing but a miracle could save the boy now!

Mother, father and watchful brother Ed shared the same thought, as their anxious eyes turned from the doorway. Had they forgotten their faith in the turmoil of their fears? Why, this sick boy's grandfather, that vigorous and inspiring old farmer-minister who had been leader of the River Brethren Colony in Pennsylvania, had always believed in healings wrought by faith. Now, in this desperate hour, the three went to their knees at the bedside.

They prayed, taking turns in leading one another. Father, mother—and at last Edgar—would rise and go about the farm work and rejoin the continual prayer. During the second night the other four brothers would kneel from time to time and join in the prayers.

The next morning, when the faithful old doctor stopped by again, his experienced eye saw a sign. The swelling was going down! Dr. Conklin closed his eyes and made a rusty prayer of his own—a prayer of thanksgiving.

During the Eisenhower administration (1953–1961), Bernard Shanley, special counsel to the White House, was asked if the President set down any hard-and-fast rules. "Yep, and they're very simple," said Shanley. They were: "I want everybody smiling around here.... Always take your job seriously, but never yourself.... Don't forget to pray." Good house rules for any house.

Even after the boy dropped into a normal sleep, one member of the family after another kept the prayer vigil.

It was nightfall again and the lamps were lighted when the boy opened his eyes. The swelling was away down now, and the discoloration had almost faded. In three weeks— pale and weak, but with eyes clear and voice strong—the boy could stand up.

And Ike Eisenhower was ready to face life.

MARCH 1960

The Man With 500 Bibles *by Elizabeth Sherrill, editor*

On a Guideposts editorial trip last summer, my husband and I paid a visit to a well-known American. It's surprising that more people don't think of him as a Bible student, as well as a statesman. More than 500 Bibles line his library shelves.

Shortly after his name became famous 15 years ago, a newspaper columnist wrote that this man had read the Bible through four times before he was 14 years old.

"He quotes from it, chapter and verse."

Almost as soon as the column appeared, packages of Bibles started arriving from all over the world.

They came from people of many backgrounds, as though the world were saying: No matter how different we are, we can agree in our respect for this Book. The man is a Democrat, but Republican friends such as Ezra Taft Benson sent him personally inscribed volumes. He is a Protestant, but he received Douay versions from many Catholic friends. And in his own handwriting is a note stuck in the front of an Old Testament: "Given to my mother by Rabbi Meyerberg during her last illness."

"But you know," he told us, "I think the ones that mean the most are from people I've never met. Total strangers—and yet they've sent me something very precious."

On and on the Bibles go. Magnificent gold-illuminated volumes and quarter paperback editions. We saw Bibles in Chinese and Navajo, in Lubalulua and Tagalog. He has Bibles in 120 different languages and dialects; Bibles with faded family pictures pasted in the fly leaves; Bibles that have been used so long that they are falling apart.

In 1951, the American Bible Society made him its honorary president. When he accepted the office, he said:

"Whenever I want to find something, this is where I look for it."

The man accepting the honor was at that time already president in another capacity: President of the United States, Harry S. Truman.

Precious time. In a busy home, it's hard to find time for devotions. As Dale Evans Rogers wrote in Guideposts (1958), "If your house is anything like ours, there really isn't any 'first thing' in the morning." Dale shared some of her solutions: praying in the car; reading the Bible at dinner time; and using a recipe box in the kitchen filled with scriptural passages to study. She called the box, "The Bread of Life."

JULY 1956

The Battle With My Sink *by Elaine St. Johns, editor*

My sink and I had been fighting a cold war ever since we met. Some rare souls seemed to enjoy the duties performed there. Myself, I never had. I felt resentment, self-pity, or utter futility every time the dishes I had put away gleaming turned up four hours later with dirty faces. Or, when I counted the endless pounds of vegetables I had peeled there and the mountain of them to come.

Besides, the sink had allies. My husband, my children, the cats—all seemed in league with it. Bits of eggshell from unscheduled meals, muddy paw marks that appeared mysteriously, or coffee grounds against which the drain rebelled.

I had prayed very earnestly about this. I tried practicing Psalms or memorizing verses from the New Testament while performing my distasteful duties, but to no avail. I could not make myself like it.

Then one afternoon I approached the front lines to peel my way a little further into that mountain of vegetables. Just outside the window over the sink, my ten-year-old daughter, Kristen, was setting up some experiment on the window ledge. There were two avocado seeds spiked with toothpicks suspended in glasses of water. In a shallow dish was the top of a carrot. There were lima beans in a pot of water and, in a jelly glass, a bare wand from a cherry tree with only tight brown buds on it.

My daughter was just placing a piece of bread in a plastic container beside them.

"There," she remarked with satisfaction. "That'll mold."

"It certainly will," I said in a fury. *"Look* at my kitchen. As if there weren't enough garbage...take that stuff out of here."

To lose my temper was a victory for the enemy. And in the end, in the inevitable shame that followed, I made peace with my daughter and allowed the dreadful assortment to remain.

Soon the avocado seeds split their hard shells and sprouted; the carrot stub slowly grew feathery leaves. The beans developed shoots, and the cherry wand turned its buds pink. The bread spun gray cobwebs in the plastic jar. All this, of course, was only "the miracle of nature." But I saw it for the first time.

I became so absorbed with these growing things, so filled with curiosity and admiration for their progress, that I found myself watching them closely, cheering them on. I forgot to fight my battle with the sink and instead fought with them and for them. And as they won, I won. Suddenly I realized that my dishes were washed, my potatoes peeled, quite effortlessly, while I marveled at the mystery of Growth of Life. I saw that it was at this altar that I, too, served—*we* served, my sink and I, privileged parties in the miracle of unfolding life.

She was always a writer, and a fine one—it's just that we weren't aware of it. We knew her as John Sherrill's wife and the mother of Scott, Donn and Liz. Then, one day, she submitted the story below. Ever since, Elizabeth Sherrill has been a Guideposts star, casting her gentle light on a throng of stories and books (often with John— theirs is a marriage that works). And when she's not writing or grandmothering or traveling, she's teaching. We've learned to pay attention.

AUGUST 1961

If He Came to Your House *by Lois Blanchard Eades*

When you saw Him coming, would you meet Him at the door
With arms outstretched in welcome to your Heavenly Visitor?
Or would you have to change your clothes before you let Him in?
Or hide some magazines, and put the Bible where they'd been?
Would you hide your worldly music and put some hymnbooks out?
Could you let Jesus walk right in, or would you rush about?

And I wonder—if the Savior spent a day or two with you,
Would you go right on doing the things you always do?
Would you go right on saying the things you always say?
Would life for you continue as it does from day to day?
Would you take Jesus with you everywhere you'd planned to go?
Or would you maybe change your plans for just a day or so?

Would you be glad to have Him meet your very closest friends?
Or would you hope they stay away until His visit ends?
Would you be glad to have Him stay forever on and on?
Or would you sigh with great relief when He at last was gone?
It might be interesting to know the things that you would do,
If Jesus came in person to spend some time with you.

Elizabeth Sherrill, 1954

MAY 1958

The Child Nobody Wanted *by Elizabeth Sherrill, editor*

Peter* was not a "lovable" child. Since his parents had died, he'd been shuttled from one family to another, not wanted, not belonging. Now, at age five, he was protecting himself from a world that didn't want him by hating that world. Peter wouldn't talk, he wouldn't smile, he hated everybody.

At the Brookdale Adoption Service, they'd just about given up finding a home for Peter. My friend Isobel Clarke is a caseworker there. She talked to me often about Peter. "It would take a miracle to make that boy risk loving someone again," she said.

And then one day, Mrs. Greene came to the Brookdale Adoption Service. Mrs. Greene told Isobel that she and her husband had waited 15 years for a child of their own; now they knew there wouldn't be one. Isobel hardly heard her; she was looking into Mrs. Greene's face, thinking she had never seen a face so full of love. And as she looked at her, Isobel was thinking, "Peter."

She told Mrs. Greene about him and saw her eyes shine at the idea of having a little boy of her own. "But I'm frightened," Isobel admitted to me, "Peter is such a badly hurt little boy. Mrs. Greene won't believe me when I tell her that he hates everybody. She hasn't seen him yet."

It was a long time before Mrs. Greene could see Peter. First there had to be interviews, medical reports, family histories—the Adoption Service puts "parents" and child together with infinite pains before they are ever allowed to meet.

But at last the great day came when Mrs. Greene was to see Peter for the first time. Peter was taken to the public park "to play on the swings." Mrs. Greene and Isobel were to sit down on one of the benches where Mrs. Greene could watch him without his knowing that he was being "considered."

As Isobel walked with Mrs. Greene to the park, her heart was pounding so hard she was afraid Mrs. Greene would hear it. She knew, as she'd never known anything before, that this woman and this little boy belonged together. "But, dear God, let them know it too," she prayed as they neared the gate. "Don't let her see just his silent, angry little face! Don't let this first meeting be so bad it spoils the rest!"

For there would be other meetings of course: another "chance" meeting next time with Mr. Greene as well, then a visit to Peter's boarding home, then...but so much depended on this first time!

They were through the gate now, and Isobel saw Peter a little way off, near the swings. He wasn't swinging, he was standing next to the fence, his eyes on the ground.

Isobel turned with an encouraging smile to Mrs. Greene, but she had forgotten Isobel was there. Her eyes were fixed on Peter.

*Names throughout have been changed.

*As a young girl, the lovely actress Esther Rolle was nicknamed
"Black Velvet" for her smooth nut-brown skin … until it erupted
with eczema (Guideposts 1981). For months she suffered,
wondering if she'd ever be "Black Velvet" again. Early one spring
morning, Esther went outside. The night before, the ground had
been bare but now it was covered with lavender blossoms. "You see,"
her mother said in words that Esther needed desperately to hear,
"God has the power to call beauty out of nowhere. When He's ready,
He'll call out yours."*

Then Mrs. Greene was walking, straight to him. No, no! thought Isobel, hurrying after her. This was all wrong! Peter must never guess that she was watching him! Mrs. Greene was almost running now. Peter looked up and saw her, and he too started running—not away, but straight to her.

Now they stopped, a foot apart, neither of them speaking, just looking at each other. Isobel caught up with them.

"Peter," she said, "do you know who this lady is?"

"Yes," said Peter. His eyes never left Mrs. Greene's face as he said, "She's my mother."

FEBRUARY 1971

A Bit of Being Needed *by Lucille Campbell*

I thought I was doing right when I took my Aunt Nell from a nursing home to live with our family. I thought being with my children would make her happy. But I soon felt I had made a mistake. Aunt Nell was as vague, forgetful and unhappy as she had been in the nursing home. She was also short and irritated with my children.

I prayed to God for a solution. A few days later, a neighbor asked me to keep her 18-month-old baby while she took her older children to the dentist. The baby was fretful and all morning I held him in my arms. When it came time to prepare lunch, I put him, crying, into his playpen.

I heard Aunt Nell chattering to him and he stopped fussing. Then she picked him up and cuddled him. They had a great time playing and singing nursery songs.

It was also the first time Aunt Nell had been content in our home. Was this God's gentle way of showing the solution to our problem? I meant to find out.

"Aunt Nell," I'd say, "will you please help me shell these peas?" Or it might be, "Would you please entertain Billy with one of your stories?" or perhaps, "Do you think you could help Robin make her doll a dress?" Aunt Nell was as pleased as a child.

One day, I had to be gone in the morning and told my daughter to give Aunt Nell lunch on time. Later when I returned, I asked, "Aunt Nell, has Donna given you your lunch?"

She hesitated, shook her head and smiled charmingly. "I don't just exactly remember," she confessed. "But if she did, it was delicious!" And with that attitude, we do love her. We do need her.

Eddie Albert and his wife Margo, with children Maria and Edward

JANUARY 1962

Someday, Maria *by Eddie Albert, actor*

Someday, Maria, someone is going to say a silly thing to you. "Maria," he'll say, and he'll be very solemn, "you must always be grateful to Mr. Albert for choosing you out of all those children."

And the trouble is, Maria, that you just might believe him. Because you are beautiful, because I adore you, because your hair is long and your eyes enormous, because you are seven years old and have me completely wrapped around your little finger, you might actually believe that I stepped into that orphanage, looked around at all the children and selected you. But I didn't, Maria. I wasn't the one who chose you at all.

It was three years ago that I had dinner in Paris with Art Buchwald. It was the first time I'd been away from Margo and young Edward, and I missed them terribly. Only one thing cast a shadow when I thought of my family—there wasn't enough of it! Margo and I never dreamed of having just one child. After Edward's birth, when no brothers or sisters came, we placed our name with adoption agencies all over the country. Years went by, but no child came to live with us.

That evening in Paris, I was sounding off to Art on the slow pace of adoption. He laid down his fork. "We have three adopted kids," he said, "and we didn't wait years and years to get them. We found one in England, one in France and one in Spain—and you couldn't ask for finer youngsters."

He leaned across the table. "It would break your heart to see some of those orphanages. Why, we saw one in Spain that had over two thousand children."

It was one of those strange moments when everything seems to make sense, even the language. Margo was born in Mexico and speaks Spanish fluently. I went to the telephone and talked to her in California. The next day I was bound for Madrid and that orphanage with its 2,000 children.

Once on the plane, the enormity of what I was doing swept over me. How was I going to pick the right child from 2,000?

Psychiatry, I thought. I'd pick a child who looked healthy and bright and then take him or her to a psychiatrist for tests. I lowered the seat back; I was tired.

But sleep wouldn't come. Suddenly I realized that psychiatry could not really define the special magic that makes one person belong with another.

I remembered what I'd learned long ago, that the only valid position for viewing a decision is eternity, that the only One who sees from there is God. I'd asked Him to guide me in lesser matters; why not in this one? Did I really have more confidence in myself than in Him? The children in the orphanage were His. He knew which one belonged with us.

But how would *I* know? How would I be shown His choice for our family? As soon as I

In actor Robert Young's home (remember him on T.V.'s "Father Knows Best"?), he made it a virtue to let his children choose their own church; he stayed at home. Then, one day, his eldest daughter joined a church and started to attend services regularly. One by one, the rest of the family followed suit—including Father—and it became part of their life. Perhaps the father who knows best, knows when he can learn from his children.

asked the question, I knew the answer. God's choice would be the first child I saw.

There in the plane I bowed my head. "Lord," I said, "I'll take that first child."

This time, I got to sleep.

Early the next morning, I was sitting in the office of the director of the great gray-walled orphanage.

"And what kind of child do you have in mind?" he asked in English.

"I would not be so impertinent as to say," I told him.

The director stared at me, then at the paper he'd been writing on. "You have one son, age seven. So I suppose you would like a girl?"

"A girl would be fine."

The director scrutinized me for a moment. Abruptly he picked up the phone and spoke a few words in Spanish. I wondered if he heard my heart pounding as we waited.

The door opened and a nun led in a little girl. I stared at her, gulped and closed my eyes.

"Lord!" I prayed. "You don't mean it!"

For there in front of me you stood, Maria—the toughest, most defiant, dirtiest four-year-old I had ever seen. You stood with your feet planted wide apart, your eyes on the floor.

I looked from you to the director. He was watching me nervously, apologetically, retaining the nun to whisk you away when the American exploded. I suddenly knew that this was not the first time you had been shown to a prospective parent. Suspicions stabbed me. You might be a behavior problem...

"How do we go about adopting her?" My words came quickly.

The director stared at me as if he hadn't heard right. Then he sprang from his chair so hastily he almost knocked it over and plunked you into my lap. And so, with your featherweight on my knee, I heard the director outline procedures—the Spanish government required certain papers; the United States, others.

I hardly listened. For—was I imagining it or—was there a gentle pressure against my chest? I leaned forward half an inch; the tiny pressure increased.

My proud Maria, before you responded to me you were testing me to see if I would respond to you. It was a kind of unspoken proposition with no loss of face. "I could love you if you loved me." My brave Maria!

I didn't see you again for two whole weeks, while the slow, legal part of the adoption got started. My first job was to tell Margo that we had a daughter. I'd call her and talk about mechanics—she would have to deal with the immigration authorities, find a welfare agency to sponsor us...Then there was Margo's voice from California, asking the one question I'd been pretending she wouldn't ask.

"Oh, Eddie, describe her to me!"

I suppose that was the longest pause ever run up on a transatlantic phone call. Then I remembered a photograph I'd once seen of Margo as a child, she was all skinny arms and legs.

"Honey," I said, "she reminds me a lot of you."

One day while we were waiting for final papers, the orphanage gave me permission to

Robert Young with editor Van Varner (on left)

take you out for lunch. At the restaurant you scraped your plate clean while I was unfolding my napkin. Then you ate my lunch, too.

In the taxi going back you sat close to me, studying my face. That is why you didn't see the orphanage until we had stopped in front of it. You looked at the gray walls, then back at me.

Maria! How could I have known? How could I have guessed?

Somehow, no one in the orphanage had explained to you that this was only a visit, only out to lunch. So many children, overworked Sisters, and no one to read in your eyes that you thought *this* was the day of adoption, the final leave-taking. And now I had brought you back!

You flung yourself, shrieking, to the sidewalk. And I, with my miserable lack of Spanish, could not explain. I knelt beside you, begging you to believe me. "I'm coming back! *Mañana*, Maria! Tomorrow!" When a nun came out to get you, we were both sitting in the middle of the sidewalk, crying our eyes out.

I did come back, the next day, and the next, until the unbelievable day when you were ours.

It was 24 hours from Madrid to Los Angeles. You sat on my lap the entire plane trip; you would not sleep.

We were a pretty groggy pair when we stumbled off the plane in California and into Margo's arms. She let loose a machine-gun volley of Spanish. The only word of which I understood was "Mama."

Going home, you sat in her lap, and for weeks afterward I was a lucky man if I got so much as a glance.

At home, Margo tucked you into bed. And still you would not close your eyes. You'd been without sleep 36 hours, but you didn't want to let Margo out of your sight. At last you pointed to her wedding band.

"Give me your ring," you said.

Margo slipped off the ring and placed it in your hand. "Now you can't leave me," you said. A second later you were asleep.

And Edward—how did he feel about this possible competition for our love? We soon found out. You had lungs that could summon the fire department, but whenever I asked you to speak more quietly, Edward would give me a look of deep reproach.

"Papa! Of course she shouts! There were two thousand kids making a racket; she had to yell to be heard."

Any correction you received had to be while Edward was out of the room. And you felt the same way about him. I'll never forget the day the school bully knocked Edward down and you knocked down the bully. They tell me you were banging his head on the floor when a teacher pulled you off.

I love the toughness in you. I love your loyalty. I love your quick mind. I even love your noise (but not while Papa's napping, all right, honey?).

I think you are the most beautiful little girl in the world, and sometimes, watching you, I think, *How in all the world did I find you?*

Then I remember. I didn't find you. I didn't do it at all.

John Glenn and his parents

JANUARY 1963

The World My Son Took With Him *by Mrs. John H. Glenn Sr., housewife*

Every mother knows that it isn't parents alone who raise a child—it's the whole community that surrounds him.

When our son completed America's first manned orbit of Earth, his father and I came in for some of the general congratulations, just by dint of having raised him.

Proud? You bet, but more than this I think we were grateful. Grateful for our town of New Concord, Ohio. Because for us, and for John and Annie, New Concord is not just a place, it is a way of life.

It's a family town. Fathers come home for lunch here. Children come home for fun and companionship. There are only 2,000 people in New Concord now, and when Johnny was growing up, there were even fewer, but these families put down deep roots; the youngsters playing in our yard today are the grandchildren of the friends we made when we moved here 39 years ago.

New Concord's way of life is also a church way. There are four churches in town and things seem to revolve around Sunday worship and midweek prayer meeting. "Are we going to church Sunday?" is probably the least-asked question in New Concord.

I don't mean that living here is a life without problems—only that trouble, when it does come, is somehow less defeating in these circumstances. We've had our share of grief like all families. John was not our first child, as the papers had it, but our middle one; our first and third babies died and we adopted our daughter after we learned we could have no more children of our own. But just the fact that these things were known by everyone brought its own kind of comfort.

Certainly we've had financial troubles. Herschel (I've always called my husband by his middle name) chose New Concord to settle in because it looked like a good place to start a plumbing and heating service. He bought an old brown shingled house on Main Street for his store, and then he built on a showroom in front.

Then came the depression. All new building stopped and the farmers put off modernizing their homes. Plumbing in those days was not the necessity it is today, anyway. I began to help out in the store by keeping the books, and at Johnny's nap time I'd fold an old Army blanket at the bottom of our display bathtub and Johnny would go to sleep.

In the evenings, I did the washing and ironing and cleaning at home. It was exhausting, but working side by side with Herschel had wonderful rewards. There was a closeness that most people never get a chance to know. I learned a lot too. I learned to recognize Herschel's skill, and to know just why he was concerned over a rise in the price of copper tubing. One day an old farmer remarked to Herschel, "That gal in your office sure knows her pumps." For me it was a real baccalaureate.

America's astronauts took more than just themselves into space. Ed White carried a cross, a St. Christopher medal and a star of David in his space suit. Buzz Aldrin celebrated communion on the moon. Edgar Mitchell carried copies of the Scriptures there. And on Christmas Eve in 1968, Frank Borman read from the Bible as he circled the moon, "In the beginning...." Even beyond this world, these men took their faith with them.

•

Of course, everyone in town was in the same boat during the depression, and there was a kind of brotherhood to hard times. Herschel and Homer Castor, town dentist and father of a little girl named Annie, who was already Johnny's best friend, were talking one day. "People seem willing to do without bathtubs before everything else," my husband remarked. "No, Herschel," said Homer, "they give up teeth first, then tubs."

A small town can help you keep your sense of proportion in success as well as in failure. I was never more aware of this than the day John came home after that first orbital flight. He'd been greeted by the President, applauded by Congress, showered with ticker tape in New York. Now he stood up in the school gym in New Concord and looked around at the people he had known all his life. "I know you teachers were pretty surprised to read about the straight A average some of the newspaper writers gave me," he began. "And you coaches who let me warm quite a few benches now discover you played all your key moves through me." He grinned at us. "Coming home can cut you down to size pretty fast."

Not that the town wasn't proud of him. But it was real pride, I thought that day, not hero worship. While the rest of the country was trying to idolize John, New Concord remembered the little boy who earned money for a bicycle by selling rhubarb from my garden.

But in the midst of my gratitude for the kind of childhood John had, I am aware that this type of environment is increasingly rare. For more and more families, home is a city of strangers, or a growing suburb with a lot of people moving in and moving out. Even in New Concord, we feel the push of the future. The stable, small-town world is not the world in which most parents are raising their families today.

Why am I talking about it, then? Is it only to mourn over it, or is it possible that we can bring what is fine and wonderful about small-town life into life wherever we are?

I think that we can. I think so from watching Annie and John raise what are, in a grandmother's eyes anyhow, two wonderfully balanced children, in surroundings that could not be more different from New Concord. On their 18th wedding anniversary, we figured up that John and Annie had moved 19 times. That's up to 20 now since their move from Arlington, Virginia to Houston, Texas recently.

Yet Lyn and David do not seem like children who have never belonged anywhere, but are at home wherever they may be. I think the reason for this is clear to see. Annie and John like the small-town way of life, and they simply take it with them wherever they go.

Two things, after all, make up the essential life of New Concord: family and church. Now, it takes a little more doing to maintain a close-knit family when the father is not only away for lunch, but may be away for months on end. Starting during World War II when they were married, through Korea, and the long periods of space-flight training, John and Annie have known an endless series of separations. They bridge the gap through the simple device of

*In 1978, we received a Writers Workshop entry from a woman in South Carolina. Busy with two children, a minister husband and a nursing career, she'd never had much time to write. Nonetheless, wouldn't we consider her for the Workshop? We read the woman's story and loved it—*The Boy With the Golden Hair, *which runs below. Since her Workshop debut, she's used her God-given talent to show us God's great power working in the gentlest ways. The writer— Sue Monk Kidd—has become one of our most prolific contributors.*

knowledge: Annie cannot work side by side with John as I did with Herschel, but she and the children can know each day where John is, why he is there, exactly what he is doing.

We ourselves had a chance to see the system work when we spent Thanksgiving in Arlington last year, after John knew that he would be making the three-orbit trip. He unrolled a flight map on the dining-room table and explained every detail of the flight. After the flight, neighbors told us they'd paced the floor and wrung their hands in suspense. We hadn't. With a map and a stopwatch in front of us, we had never been busier, never felt closer to John.

A father who is away a lot can find special ways, too, to let his family know they come first. A friend stopped by recently to tell us about a visit in Arlington. He had gone to John's house one evening to see him about an important matter. John himself had just got back from a trip and told the friend that he would be with him shortly. First, he had promised Lyn help with her schoolwork and then David needed a hand with a model kit.

Our friend told us, "I didn't mind the wait and it was good to see a father who puts first things first."

As for church, this, too, takes a little more effort in a complex society where Sunday morning worship is not the automatic habit. But its values, too, are all the more evident. John and Annie look for a church in any new home almost before they've unpacked. Annie plays the organ, which makes her doubly welcome.

When there has been no church where John is stationed, they've sought out like-minded people and started one. The church they helped found in Patuxent, Maryland held services in a theater, while Annie, John and the others threw themselves into a fund-raising campaign so they could build a real church. They built one, too, but John had been transferred by then.

People often ask them how they can spend so much time and effort in a given church when they know they'll soon be leaving. But here, of course, is the very heart of the secret: they may leave a town, but they never leave the church. The church extends beyond state lines and localities.

This, I think, is the reason why Annie and John are able to take New Concord's contentment with them: A close and affectionate family, drawing nourishment, support and belonging from the transcendent church—this is what makes lives joyous wherever we live.

Sue Monk Kidd, at home

NOVEMBER 1979

The Boy With the Golden Hair *by Sue Monk Kidd, editor*

I groped out of bed at 11 o'clock that Thanksgiving morning without a thankful throb in my heart. Sunlight hung in the bedroom in shafts of cold yellow. I slumped against the window by the bed and frowned at a group of boys playing a noisy game of baseball in a vacant lot behind our apartment.

Sandy and I had just married that summer. He was a first-year graduate student in theology and I was a college junior. Our apartment was cramped, we didn't have the money to buy a turkey and we were both bone-tired from heavy academic loads. I had never been apart from my family on Thanksgiving, but now I was 1,000 miles away.

As I edged moodily around the bed, which occupied most of our cramped bedroom, I could see Sandy hunched over a table piled with books. He smiled and said, "Good morning," but before I could mutter my own, the phone rang. I sat on the bed and answered.

"Hello, honey. Happy Thanksgiving!" It was Mom. I blinked back tears.

"Oh, Mom. I miss you all so!"

When I hung up, tears were coursing down my cheeks. I sat on the bed as the memories flooded back. Mom would be bustling in her steamy kitchen, counting out gleaming pieces of silver, setting out the ancient pilgrim candles that presided over our table each year. How I yearned to be a part of the celebration!

The kitchen by now would be filled with the sweet smells of all the good things to come.

Daddy would be bent over a turkey, tucking cranberries and pickled peaches around it in wreath. In between puffs on his spicy-smelling pipe, Granddaddy would be clucking at my teen-aged brothers wrestling on the rug. There would be the orange and brown quilt tucked around Grandma's knees, a serene smile lighting up her soft features. The long maple table would already be heavy with Mom's floral pattern china.

But these scenes, instead of comforting me, were a torment. Sandy rustled papers in the next room. I forced myself off the unmade bed.

I wandered to the kitchen and randomly opened the cabinets to find a large can of spaghetti, half a jar of peanut butter, six stale marshmallows, a dwindling bottle of catsup and four old potatoes sprouting leaves. The refrigerator was worse. Day-old tea, three apples and cheese with mold on one corner. Dismal!

"What's for dinner?" Sandy asked, when I appeared in the doorway.

"Maybe some kind soul will leave a Thanksgiving basket on our doorstep. Otherwise you're stuck with canned spaghetti and potatoes that look like potted plants," I said. Fleeing to the bedroom, I left him staring after me with a bewildered face.

I dropped onto the bed, certain a soldier in a foreign foxhole at Christmas couldn't have been more heartsick. I felt like a Thanksgiving Scrooge, hoarding my troubles like gold bars. I muffled my face with a pillow and sobbed.

"Oh, God," I whispered, "I feel so awful.

Guideposts offices in Carmel, NY, our home

Can You help me?" But nothing happened. There was only the silence of the bedroom and the raucous baseball game in the vacant lot out back. Staring out the bedroom window, the sun seemed to throw my own reflection back.

A small figure hobbled beyond the window, moving almost magically across my reflection. He created a strange double image, standing in my own mirrored reflection—a crippled boy, maybe nine or ten years old.

He stopped at the edge of the lot and seemed to contemplate how to cross a shallow ditch. A flash of light boomeranged from the silvery braces around his legs. Sunlight and shadows played in his blond hair.

He glanced over his shoulder at the boys in the vacant lot. Red and blue caps dotted their heads and mitts dangled from their hands. They stood motionless, watching the crippled boy who turned and searched the tall grass.

I glimpsed the top of a baseball peeping through the weeds, just inches past the ditch, beyond his reach. He must have discovered it at the same instant. He slowly sank one crutch into the ditch and leaned forward, his eyes fixed on the ball. He swung his lifeless legs. One landed against his crutch. Suddenly his right shoulder dropped. His crutches lunged forward and he sprawled across the ditch.

I gasped as he went down, seeing the embarrassed pain on his face. Lying on the ground, he looked backward once again at his friends, who waited patiently for him to bring the ball.

He had fallen almost on top of the baseball. With a smile, he wrapped his fingers around the ball and tucked it in his pocket.

Standing the crutches before him, he inched his body forward—up, up, ever so slowly, dragging his legs behind him. The struggle twisted his face until at last he stood erect.

He paused a moment to catch his breath, raising his head and gazing past the Texas pines. God's joy seemed to leap from his face. His eyes sparkled with gratitude for his contribution to his friends' baseball game.

He turned and swept his legs through the crutches. Up, out, down—the steel cages on his calves seesawed across the lot. In those moments, when my heart had reached out to him, I had ceased to see my own troubled reflection. Now, as I watched him go, my eyes refocused on my own image in the glass.

With the sun's warmth whispering from the window and boyish shouts in the distance, I wondered. Did God nudge me to this spot to glimpse a small boy, who was thankful for the chance to stumble after a baseball for his friends?

I turned and hurried to the kitchen where I climbed to the cabinet over the refrigerator. The silver wedding gifts, not yet used, hid under a cloud of dust. In minutes I had polished them to a sparkling sheen.

When I called Sandy to dinner, it was to a table glowing with silver, crystal and flickering candles. His eyes roved over the covered casserole dishes. I lifted the lids. Steaming spaghetti garnished with cheese, creamy mashed potatoes and baked apples glistening under marshmallow topping. It looked delicious!

"Where did you get this feast?" he asked.

"It was here all the time," I said. "But it took a little gratitude to find it."

In 1953, Guideposts moved its business offices to Carmel, New York. Carmel, like so many place names in America, comes from the Bible. It refers to the mountain where Elijah triumphed over the followers of Baal (I Kings 18). It is also a place of beauty, as in "Thine head upon thee is like Carmel" (Song 7:5). Salem, Canaan, Bethlehem, Nazareth, Philadelphia, Carmel, those Biblical names that blossom all over the United States are good reminders that God is with us wherever we make our home.

DECEMBER 1981

Bittersweet Christmas *by Madeline Weatherford, editorial assistant*

Christmas was the most special holiday of all for my father. Mother told me that he introduced me to my first Christmas tree when I was nine days old. It was a small tree, but every ornament, candle and strand of silver tinsel was meticulously hung in place, as only he could do it. When he had finally finished, he took me from my bassinet and held me up to see his handiwork.

Daddy lived long enough to decorate just four more Christmas trees—each one a little larger than the year before.

The year he died—after a short bout with pneumonia—Mother sat down with me for a talk about Christmas. "Madeline," she said gently, "Santa will be leaving gifts for you, but we won't be having a tree and decorations. It's just too much to do this year."

The morning of Christmas Eve arrived with no special arrangements for the next day, other than early mass and dinner at a relative's house. Just before noon the phone rang and Mother answered. After a pause, I heard her say, "That's very kind of you, but I think we'll spend the evening here together. It's the first since..." She recovered, thanked the caller again and hung up.

"Who was it?" I asked.

"One of our neighbors," Mother said. "She wanted us to come down this evening. I... I can't."

Mother was silent most of the day. Late in the afternoon, she changed her mind. She called our neighbor and told her we'd stop in for a few minutes.

"It's thoughtful of her," Mother said to me, "and we don't want to seem ungrateful."

When we rang the neighbor's doorbell, she kissed us and led us through the foyer. The living room beyond seemed dark with an odd-colored glow. She motioned us forward, and I stepped into the room and caught my breath. There, shining with colored lights and ornaments and gaily wrapped packages, was a magnificent Christmas tree. Seated around it, smiling broadly, were Mrs. Abrams, Mrs. Cohen, Mrs. Blount, Mrs. Dreyfus. "Surprise, surprise!" they chorused.

Today, I can close my eyes and bring back that scene at will. Many times it has sustained me when things have gone badly, when I have doubted the human heart. I can still feel the love of those neighbors—those Jewish women who ventured into an unfamiliar tradition so that one little Christian girl without a daddy could have a merry Christmas.

Sgt. James Lopez reunited with his family

DECEMBER 1981

How To Wait Through a Long Darkness *by Mary Lopez,*
housewife

Waiting. Nobody ever said it was easy. And it wasn't easy for me and my family, not for all the 444 days that our son Jimmy was held captive in Iran. I know now, however, that there are ways for people to learn how to wait through even the darkest nights.

And sometimes the nights were *very* dark. As if worrying about Jimmy's safety wasn't enough hardship, there were some cruel, unnecessary blows.

There were the crank phone calls, like the one from the extortionist who told us that for $10,000 he could secure Jimmy's release through "secret channels." There were the false reports, like the one that came over the radio saying that some of the hostages had tried to escape and had been shot. Knowing our 21-year-old's courageous nature, we were sure he would be one of them. There were the times when the spirit simply flagged. My husband Jesse, calm and firm through most of the ordeal, went through a particularly hard period of depression and anger.

But through all the long wait, there were three things that helped us, three things that could be adapted to any long waiting situation:

1. *The Scrapbook.* We called it the "Welcome Home Jimmy Packet." The idea was suggested to Jesse by an ex-P.O.W. as something constructive we could do as a family. We

collected pictures and souvenirs of birthdays, family get-togethers, school activities, anything that Jimmy was missing but would want to know about when he came home, right down to the ribbons that our daughter Marcie's rabbit won at school.

The scrapbook became a positive object of hope. It was a way we could tell ourselves that Jimmy was coming back, that one day the waiting would be over.

2. *The Candle.* The day the embassy fell to the militant students, Jesse and I went to our church, Holy Angels, to light a candle and pray for Jimmy. After we'd seen our priest, Father Maloney, we brought the candle home and placed it, glowing, on the fireplace mantel. That vigil candle became very special to us. The first week, the whole family slept within sight of it. And we still gravitated to the little flame to pray when we couldn't sleep. Jesse and I were always checking to see if it was time again for us to replace that candle. We were determined to keep it burning. It was a constant light in our long dark night.

3. *Our Talks With God.* We put our trust in God that He would watch over Jimmy, and all of us. Yet, on occasion, we found it necessary to turn to Father Maloney for help. This good priest pointed out to us that there would be times when we'd even feel anger and re-

Grace Coolidge (1879–1957) when she was First Lady

sentiment toward God because of things we didn't understand or couldn't control.

"You should talk with God the way Jesus did in the garden of Gethsemane," Father Maloney told us. "The Bible tells us that Jesus was strengthened by approaching God this way [Luke 22:41-43]." Then Father Maloney said, "There are two guidelines for anyone who is experiencing the agony of despair: One, tell God exactly how you feel. Two, accept the situation."

Putting that sound advice to work, we shared our feelings with God. We accepted His will.

God stayed with us in our trials, through all the weeks and months that we added to Jimmy's scrapbook and kept the vigil candle burning. And God was there on that glorious day last January when the long vigil ended and our son came back to us, safe at home at last.

MAY 1948

The Open Door

by Grace Coolidge, former schoolteacher

Grace Goodhue (Mrs. Calvin) Coolidge, widow of the 30th President of the United States, wrote the following poem after the death of her son, Calvin Jr., in 1924.

You, my son,
Have shown me God.
Your kiss upon my cheek
Has made me feel the gentle touch
Of Him who leads us on.
The memory of your smile, when young,
Reveals His face,
As mellowing years come on apace.
And when you went before,
You left the gates of Heaven ajar
That I might glimpse,
Approaching from afar,
The glories of His grace.

Hold, son, my hand,
Guide me along the path
That, coming,
I may stumble not,
Nor roam,
Nor fail to show the way
Which leads us—Home.

Teen drinking often leads to tragedy. No one knows that better than Kevin Tunell (Guideposts 1983). One New Year's Eve, after drinking with fellow high-school seniors, Kevin drove off and hit an oncoming car, killing the 18-year-old girl at the wheel. Instead of a jail term, the judge sentenced him to a year of telling his story to school kids. His effort, and that of others, helped bring about: a drop of 50% in the county's highway death toll; 12 new chapters of Students Against Drunk Driving in Virginia.

SEPTEMBER 1980

Runaway Mother *by Ruth Evans,* retail buyer*

That year when I went back to work, we really needed my extra income to help save for our daughter Joan's college education. My husband John had taken on additional work, too, which took him away from home a lot, and it was Joan who suggested that she could help out by doing more chores around the house.

I felt good about our family. We had a kind of team spirit. I believed we had understandings about our life together—such as having care and consideration for one another, sharing and bearing one another's burdens, respecting privacy, respecting our home and following certain guidelines of behavior so as not to hurt one another or the family. Then came summer. Joan's 17th summer…

It was a Saturday afternoon. John was away on a business trip. Joan was at a friend's house. I was down in the basement, looking for a can of paint to touch up some scratched woodwork in the kitchen. The light was poor, so I had a flashlight with me. The basement was a catchall for household tools, discarded toys, broken furniture, snow tires.

"What a mess," I muttered as I played the light around the walls and into the corners, remembering stacking up some old paint cans when we'd cleaned in the spring. The light fell on a dropcloth draped over a mound of something.

"Ah, there it is…" I lifted the cloth—and gasped.

There was a large pile of beer cans and wine bottles, all stacked so as to fit under the draped cloth. Stunned, I stared at it for more than a minute, then carefully replaced the cloth and went back upstairs.

The house was still. I sat at the kitchen table. My thoughts were a jumble.

Who put them there? Why? When? We just cleaned the basement this spring. They must have accumulated over the summer. Joan doesn't even drink. Does she? Has she been having people here without our knowing? She knows we don't allow that. She's never lied to us…

As I sat there in the silent house, I felt my confidence as a mother start to crack. *Does Joan lie to me? Has she deceived us? Who are her friends? What has she been doing?*

My fingers were shaking as I dialed John's hotel. *Maybe,* I thought, *he could come home early…*

"I'm sorry. There's no answer in his room. Would you like to leave a message?"

"No…No."

How could I find out the truth?

A dark dread accompanied me as I went up to Joan's bedroom. I stood in the doorway, my eyes darting about the room searching for clues among the posters, the records on the floor, the jumble of hair ribbons, brushes, lip gloss and acne cream on her dressing table. Her diary lay open on her nightstand.

I had never, ever, looked in anyone's diary. But that afternoon I did. I picked it up and sat

*Names throughout have been changed.

For days, Karen Borak had been scolding her eight-year-old daughter Lina for her messy room, loud music, tardiness at school and the way she neglected her homework to play with her guinea pigs (Guideposts 1984). But while writing a letter to a friend who'd asked for news of Lina, Karen found herself telling about her daughter's achievements in Brownies, skill in soccer and the prize she'd just won at school. And then, Karen wrote a second letter filled with affection and praise. A letter to Lina.

on the edge of her bed and paged through it, looking for some bit of information that would confirm my worst fears. I was trembling. I felt sneaky and unclean. But I did it.

There were entries about going swimming, and about books, and movies, and people she liked, and didn't like, and then…there it was.

"The kids came over again today. Some of them got drunk. Hope Mom doesn't find out."

She had betrayed us. Anger welled up in me that made me want to scream, to tear the little diary to shreds, to pull the posters off the wall, overturn the messy dressing table. Instead, I carefully propped the diary on her pillow for her to see, open to the incriminating page, and went to the living room to wait.

I sat, staring out of the window, thinking about all my years of motherhood, the financial struggles, the physical exhaustion, the sacrifices. Oh, yes, I remembered the happy times, too. *Better to have never had them,* I thought, *if this is the result.*

I felt terribly guilty about reading her diary. That I had stooped so low to discover the truth about my daughter compounded my feeling of helplessness. I hated myself…but I distrusted my daughter.

I heard Joan come in the back door and run up to her room. It seemed an eternity until she appeared in the doorway. Her face was white. Her shoulders sagged.

"You read my diary," she said.

I nodded. "I know. I found the bottles in the basement."

"Mom, I want to explain. It's not me. But I didn't know what to do…"

I looked at her, but I wasn't seeing Joan, my daughter. I only saw some stranger. How could I listen to her? What could I believe? *Who was this person?* I panicked, and something just snapped in me.

That's when I did it. I walked out.

The next thing I knew I was in the car, heading out of town. Tears of self-pity filled my eyes and I had to keep wiping them away so I could see to get onto the interstate highway.

My foot pressed harder on the accelerator as I sped on past the outlying farmlands. The wind blew hard against my face, drying my tears as fast as they flowed. I don't know where I thought I was going. I just knew I had to get away from Joan.

It began to get dark, so I pulled off the highway and stopped the car on the shoulder of a narrow country road. I laid my face against the steering wheel and closed my eyes. I hadn't really prayed for many years, yet there in the twilight the words came as effortlessly as when I was a child.

"God," I whispered, "I hurt so much. I don't know what to do. Please help me, God. Help me. Help me…"

I must have dozed, because when I raised my head it was pitch-dark and I saw lights from a village on a distant hillside. I started the car and drove toward the lights, thinking I might find some direction.

I don't know what had happened to me as I slept, but I felt strangely serene as I drove. It was as if someone were leading me. At a crossroads was a small, white clapboard church. I stopped the car. I had to strain to read its name, dimly

A Kitchen Prayer   by Klara Munkres

Lord of all pots and pans and things, since I've not time to be
A saint by doing lovely things or watching late with Thee,
Or dreaming in the dawn light or storming Heaven's gates
Make me a saint by getting meals and washing up the plates.
Although I must have Martha's hands, I have a Mary mind
And when I black the boots and shoes Thy sandals, Lord, I find.

illuminated by a nearby street lamp. There was no one about, so I got out of the car to get a closer look. Hand-carved gilt letters above the doors spelled the words: *The Church of the Covenant.*

Still feeling curiously calm, I sat on the church steps and stretched out my legs, breathing deeply, taking in the cool night air.

"Church of the Covenant," I said the words aloud.

"Covenant." It had a nice sound, a comforting sound...a familiar sound.

It reminded me of long-ago Sunday-school days and the stories of God's covenant with the children of Israel; how He had promised, "I will be your God and you will be My people...." He would never let them go. He would be faithful even when they were not. I smiled. Remembering.

"Covenant." Joan's white and frightened face appeared before me. "Poor baby," I sighed. Then I saw another face. A much younger face, soft, trusting, nuzzled against my own. "I need your nearneth," she'd lisp as I tucked her into bed...

Then I understood. I knew. There was no thunderclap, no bolt of lightning—just a sure and quiet understanding came to me as I sat there on those church steps. I knew what God wanted me to do. He had demonstrated it this very evening when I cried out to Him and He was there. In His faithfulness, He had led me and comforted me. Surely I could do the same for my child...His child.

Yes, I thought somberly as I got back in the car and headed down the winding road to the highway, *we have a lot of problems to deal with— the drinking, the lying, the kids in the house... reading her diary, my job, John's business trips. But maybe we can work them out if...and only if...*

Joan was sleeping on the sofa. Her face was puffy and blotchy, as it always gets when she's been crying. The table was laid for dinner. On the stove was a pot of spaghetti, congealed in a gluey white mass, obviously cooked many hours before. I sat on the edge of the sofa and took her in my arms.

"Where did you go, Mom?" she mumbled fuzzily, rubbing her face into my shoulder.

"I was running away from home," I said softly. She held me tight.

"You can't do that. What would we do without you?"

"I came back, Joan."

"Mom, I'm sorry about everything, and I need your help. But you read my diary, too, Mom..."

"I know. We both broke each other's trust. We have to start all over again. But we can do it, I know..."

I held her away from me and looked deeply into her eyes. The words came on my lips even before I had time to think. I spoke them as if they were my own.

"You are my people, Joan...I will never let you go."

"I won't let you go either." Now she clung tightly to me, and we were both crying.

"That's our covenant, God," I whispered. "That's our covenant."

I think of how they trod the earth, what time I scrub the floor
Accept this meditation Lord, I haven't time for more.
Warm all the kitchen with Thy love, and light it with Thy peace
Forgive me all my worrying and make my grumbling cease.
Thou who didst love to give men food, in room or by sea
Accept this service that I do, I do it unto Thee.

Next day we were able to confront each other, openly, across the dining-room table. Yes, she had let her friends come over. Then more who weren't her friends came and she didn't know how to stop them. No, she didn't drink. She'd tried it, but it made her feel awful. Yes, she had lied to me because she was afraid of upsetting me.

And I? Well, I had been so preoccupied with my new job that I'd neglected her need for guidance and attention. I hadn't taken the time to get to know her.

John came home. He was exhausted from the long weekend of work, but he listened with real concern to our retelling of the events of the past 24 hours. When we finished, there was a long silence. John's eyes were filled with tears when he looked long and hard at us. Then he got up and went to his briefcase.

"A covenant," he said thickly. "That's what we need." He returned to the table with a sheet of paper.

"First, I think we'd better pray," he said.

Awkwardly, he groped for our hands. We held tight as John prayed: "God, we've really wandered. Help us to keep our covenant with You and with one another."

Then he wrote at the top of the paper these words: *Because we are a family, brought together by God Himself, we do hereby make this covenant with one another…*

Well, that day we actually made a list of the things that each of us felt deeply about. Joan needed a commitment of time from John and me; I needed John's active participation in the day-to-day family decisions; John needed the assurance from us that we valued him far more than his income. Our list went on and on. What we actually wrote wasn't nearly as important as what we learned in the process of sharing—openly and honestly with one another…

All that happened over a year ago. Joan and I have been able to rebuild our trust in each other; John is around the house more now and that's a big help to me; Joan sings in the church choir; John and I are there every Sunday, too; soon Joan will be going to college; the basement is clean…again.

Our family covenant is taped to the refrigerator door. Every now and then we take it down, cross out some items, add some others. I suppose we don't really need it anymore, because we've come to know one another so well. But I like its presence. It's a daily reminder of the Someone Who has never let our family go. Who has been faithful, even when we were not.

On the Job

In the first summer after World War II, both Guideposts and Donald Seibert were just starting out. The young Seibert was singing and playing the piano in an eight-piece dance band on the shores of Lake Chautauqua in up-state New York.

The season began promisingly. Seibert, with his wife and baby daughter, rented rooms above a nearby restaurant, and soon "The Rhythmaires," with "The Romantic Vocals of Donny Seibert" caught on with the resort's many vacationers.

Then trouble. When a few severe summer storms followed each other in quick succession, business at the pavilion dropped off. After two weeks, the other band members fled, leaving Seibert with a difficult decision to make. Should he honor his word with the landlord and stay on, or should he sneak away too?

Seibert honored his word. It was tough. He cleaned cabins, changed beds, washed sheets and worked in a juice-processing plant twenty miles away—rising at 4:30 a.m. every work day. In the end, he paid his rent, fulfilling his agreement. He practiced a business principle that he would put to work again and again in his career: He kept his word.

The following year, Seibert went to work for J. C. Penney as a shoe clerk in Bradford, Pennsylvania. From there, he made a slow, but astounding, climb to store manager, department head and eventually chairman of the board of one of the nation's biggest retailers. As with so many who write about their jobs in Guideposts, faith wasn't something he left at home, or in church on Sundays. He took it with him to work.

The world has changed dramatically in forty years. Secretaries have gone from manual typewriters to electric ones and on to word processors. Farms that yielded 38 bushels of corn per acre in 1945 average well above 100. Checkbooks are balanced with pocket calculators and dinners are cooked speedily in microwave ovens. And the dance bands of today play a sound that Donny Seibert never dreamed of.

Since Guideposts began, a lot has changed about our work, but the faith that enables us to do our best remains unchanged.

We wouldn't leave home without it.

Ted Hustead and his soda fountain crew, late 1930s

JULY 1982

Wall and Water *by Ted Hustead, druggist*

"We might as well close up, Ted," my wife Dorothy said. "There won't be any more customers today. It's too cold out."

I knew that Dorothy was right, but I stepped out into the dusk, hoping to see someone coming our way.

It was December 1931. Dorothy and I had just bought the only drugstore in a town called Wall on the edge of the South Dakota Badlands. We'd been open a few days, and business had been bad.

I stood shivering on the wooden sidewalk. In this little prairie town there were only 326 people; 326 poor people. Most of them were farmers who'd been wiped out either by the Depression or drought.

When I went back inside, I turned off the light over the soda fountain and joined Dorothy and our four-year-old son Billy in our "apartment," a room we'd made by stretching a blanket across the back of the store....

I had graduated from pharmacy school in 1929, and after two years of working for other druggists, I knew that Dorothy and I had to find our own store. My father had just died, and he'd left me a $3,000 legacy. I'd work with that.

We were living in Canova, South Dakota, when we began our search, covering Nebraska and South Dakota in our Model T. As we searched, we were sure of two things: We wanted to be in a small town, and we wanted the town to have a Catholic church. In Can-

ova, the nearest parish was 20 miles away. We wanted to be able to go to mass every day.

In Wall, where the drugstore was for sale, we found both a small town and a Catholic church. And when we talked to the priest, the doctor and the banker, they all told us that Wall was a good place with good people and that they wanted us to come live there.

Dorothy and I were excited about Wall, but when we got back home and told our families about our plan, we found them skeptical.

"That town is in the middle of nowhere," a cousin said, "and furthermore, everybody there is flat broke busted."

My father-in-law was understanding, but even he said, "You know, Wall is just about as Godforsaken as you can get."

But Dorothy and I couldn't give up on Wall, so our families agreed that we should all pray about the decision. Led by two of Dorothy's aunts, who were Dominican nuns, we asked God's guidance.

In the end, everyone felt that it was God's will for us to go to Wall. But now that Dorothy and I were all alone here, we wondered if we'd heard God right.

The first few months went by and business didn't improve much. Once again, Dorothy and I sat by the stove and asked ourselves if we'd done the right thing.

"I don't mind being poor," Dorothy said to me. "But I wonder if we can use our talents to their fullest here in Wall."

What scars the Depression left on us Americans! We know, because a day doesn't go by that we don't receive a story looking back at Depression hardships. And yet, all these stories reveal other things about those days too: resourcefulness, persistence, courage, creativity. Giving when there is little to give; hoping when there seems little to hope for. And most of all, trusting in a protective God. Yes, these stories are about the struggles of the 1930s—by some valiant people who wear their scars like medals.

But the next minute Dorothy said, "We shouldn't get down, Ted. I'm sure we can use our abilities fully here. We *can* make this place work!"

Dorothy's optimism lifted me. I said to her, "Five years, Dorothy, that's what I think we should give to this store. Five *good* years, and if it doesn't work by then, well, then we'll…"

"Don't worry about then," said Dorothy. "We'll make it go. And just think, Ted, pretty soon that monument at Mount Rushmore will be done, and then there will be an endless stream of people going by. I'm sure they'll visit us!"

Over the next few years we drummed up enough business to pay our bills, but that was it. We weren't starving, it's true, and we'd begun to make good friends in Wall. Our pastor, Father John Connolly, had become a tower of strength, helping us keep our faith strong. And we had worked hard to serve our neighbors well. Filling prescriptions for a sick child or an ailing farmer made me feel that I was doing something good.

But all of this didn't seem to be enough. I still spent too many hours looking out the store window for customers who never showed up. I felt I was wasting too much of my life watching people pass by. Maybe, as Dorothy's father had said, Wall *was* Godforsaken.

By the time the summer of 1936 came around, our business hadn't grown much at all. Our five-year trial would be up in December. What would we do then? Along with nine-year-old Billy, Dorothy and I now had a one-

month-old daughter, Mary Elizabeth. What hardships was I putting them in store for?

I was lost in a dust storm of worries and doubts. I was ready to give up.

One hot Sunday in July, though, a great change swept us up. It started quietly, in the deadening heat of an early afternoon, when Dorothy said to me, "You don't need me here, Ted. I'm going to go put Billy and the baby down for a nap and maybe take one myself."

So Dorothy and the children headed off to a room that we had rented on the outskirts of town.

I minded the empty store. I swatted flies with a rolled-up newspaper. I stood in the door, and no matter where I looked, there was no shade, because the sun was so high and fierce.

An hour later Dorothy came back.

"Too hot to sleep?" I asked.

"No, it wasn't the heat that kept me awake," Dorothy said. "It was all the cars going by on Route 16A. The jalopies just about shook the house to pieces."

"That's too bad," I said.

"No, because you know what, Ted? I think I finally saw how we can get all those travelers to come to our store."

"And how's that?" I asked.

"Well, now what is it that those travelers really want after driving across that hot prairie? They're thirsty. They want water. *Ice* cold water! Now we've got plenty of ice and water. Why don't we put up signs on the highway telling people to come here for free ice water? Listen, I even made up a few lines for the sign:

There are certain themes that have appeared in Guideposts over the years, such familiar maxims as "Bloom where you're planted," or "You can, if you think you can." But there are six words probably most pertinent to the success of Guideposts, six words that Dr. Peale feels are the root of success to any venture. Those six words? "Find a need and fill it."

"Get a soda
Get root beer
Turn next corner
Just as near
To Highway 16 & 14
Free Ice Water
Wall Drug."

It wasn't Wordsworth, but I was willing to give it a try. During the next few days a high-school boy and I put together some signs. We modeled them after the old Burma Shave highway signs. Each phrase of Dorothy's little poem went on a 12- by 36-inch board. We'd space the boards out so that people could read them as they drove.

The next weekend, the boy and I went out to the highway and put up our signs for free ice water. I must admit that I felt somewhat silly doing it, but by the time I got back to the store, people had already begun showing up for their ice water.

Dorothy was running all around to keep up. I pitched in alongside her.

"Five glasses of ice water, please," a father called out.

"May I have a glass for Grandma?" one boy asked. "She's in the car."

"Say, good sir," one traveler said in a Scottish brogue, "we're going all the way to Yellowstone Park. Would you mind filling up this jug with your water."

"Hey, this free ice water is a great idea," said a salesman, sidling up onto a stool. "How about selling me an ice-cream cone?"

For hours people came pouring in, all hot and frazzled. For hours we poured gallons of ice water, made ice-cream cones and gave highway directions. When the travelers started on their way again, refreshed and ready for new adventures, they gave us hearty thanks.

When the day was done, Dorothy and I were pooped. We sat in front of the store, watching the sun set, feeling a cool breeze come in off the prairie. In the summer twilight, Wall looked radiant. It looked like a good place to call home.

"Well, Ted," Dorothy said to me, "I guess the ice water signs worked."

They surely did work and we've never really been lonely for customers since then. The next summer we had to hire eight girls to help us, and now that the store is in the good hands of my son Bill, Wall Drug draws up to twenty *thousand* people on a summer day.

Free Ice Water. It brought us Husteads a long way and it taught me my greatest lesson, and that's that there's absolutely no place on God's earth that's Godforsaken. No matter where you live, you can succeed, because wherever you are, you can reach out to other people with something that they need!

And when you give people what they need, you've helped them in a good Christian way; and maybe that's why when you help others, you'll find that you end up helping yourself as well. That means more than good business. It means a good happy life.

Who says it can't be done? In Guideposts (1968), we told about a prank that General Electric engineers used to play on newcomers. "Frost the inside of a light bulb," they'd tell them. It was thought to be impossible. Then, one day, along came a novice engineer named Marvin Pipkin who went right to work on this "impossible task." He came back several months later…with a light bulb frosted on the inside. No one had let Marvin in on the joke.

FEBRUARY 1975

Hurry, Before the Ice Cream Melts *by Thomas Carvel, ice cream maker*

Back in the summer of 1934, I was 28 years old and at a dead end. I was living in New York City then, bouncing from one thing to another….Nothing seemed to work for me.

Eventually I scraped together enough money one summer to build a small house trailer, which I hitched to a Model A Ford. I had planned to take the trailer out of the steamy city and sell ice cream, hot dogs and soft drinks.

On a Friday afternoon, I set off for Kensico Dam, north of White Plains, New York. There I would try to cool off picnickers and passersby—at a profit, I hoped.

As I made my way along Central Avenue in Hartsdale, New York, one of the trailer tires blew out. I was out in the middle of nowhere, without a person in sight. I had no tools to fix the tire and no money to have it fixed. On top of all that, the ice cream in my trailer was melting—and it represented my entire savings.

Feeling absolutely at my wit's end, I sat on the Ford's running board and prayed: "Dear Lord, I dream of running my own business someday. But I can't go anywhere with that tire. What am I supposed to do?"

When I finished praying, I felt a little better, but the tire was still flat and I didn't notice anybody coming to rescue me. I did notice, though, a little pottery shop across the road from where my trailer sat. Venturing over, I was greeted by a burly, gray-haired man.

"Trouble?" he said.

"Yes, my trailer broke down," I said, going into a recital of my woes.

"Look," the man said, "I'll help you bring your trailer over to my yard here, and you can hitch it up to my electricity."

Thus, began a new turn in my life. Pop Quinlan let me hook up his lights to my trailer and I was open for business both day and night. I paid Pop when I could and helped him sell pottery when I couldn't.

Gradually business picked up. I discovered the advantages of selling from a stationary stand. I learned the refrigeration business there, too—and in my spare time I worked in the back of the pottery shop on a mechanical device to dispense ice cream. Eventually I patented the inventions I had worked out.

A few years later I began to market my own ice cream in Carvel stores—and that pottery shop became the chain's pilot plant.

Some may call what happened to me just plain good luck. I see it a bit differently.

I believe that if you work hard enough at something, God will see your struggles. He'll see your tears and your sweat, and He'll care. And if you'll just open yourself up to the possibilities—which often lie hidden—things *will* change for the better, often beyond your wildest dreams.

Your worst day could be the beginning of something very good. That's the way it was for me.

Carole Melson in one of her Brumby rockers

DECEMBER 1980

The Dream That Wouldn't Die *by Carole Melson, factory owner*

The day after my husband's funeral, I had to get away, so I drove into the quiet Georgia countryside alone. My heart was too full of grief to do anything but think about the terrible events in the last week that left me a widow at 37 with three children.

As I drove, my mind veered sadly from one thing to another…Frank's courtship, our wedding, the children, the fun we had, the big dream we shared—and then his fatal and totally unexpected heart attack.

Without really knowing where I was or what I was doing, I finally pulled up in front of the long, low building that once held our dream, a site of bustling activity only a few days ago.

For five years Frank and I had dreamed of reviving the famous Brumby Rocking Chair, and we planned to start making them in this building. The Brumby family had long manufactured this much-loved bent-oak rocker but had retired from business over a quarter-century ago. Since then, the famous rockers had become collectors' items, loved heirlooms passed down from one generation to the next.

Mother had raised her babies in one, as had so many other women. When it came my turn to have children, I longed for one of those exquisitely made, beautifully balanced rockers, which were virtually untippable, allowing a mother to rise safely with baby in one arm.

Luckily, friends had a Brumby and they loaned it to us. All three of my children were nursed in that chair, rocked when colicky,

reassured and lulled to sleep in it when nightmares came. There was something almost mystically soothing about a Brumby, something pacifying and tranquilizing about that rhythmic creaking in the still of the night.

The inner peace that resulted had made it easy for me to encourage Frank and share his dream of recreating the beauty of the old Brumby rockers. Mine was the dream of providing mothers of new generations with a chair that would give them and their children an unforgettable link of love.

For five years Frank had struggled to make our dream come true: from entering into a royalty agreement with the Brumby family to searching the country for the original unique machinery that had been sold at an auction when the company closed in 1944.

My hand gripped the steering wheel as I thought of how—on the very day Frank suffered his heart attack—he had happily bought the last piece of equipment.

Wiping my eyes, I pushed open the car door and walked into the deserted building. I came upon a shipping crate containing one of the old Brumby machines Frank had bought to bend wood for the rockers.

Putting my hand on the crate, I thought that my husband's hand had rested there just a few days before when he was excitedly anticipating the work ahead. Now it was all over.

"Why, God?" I asked, slumping against the crate. Tears of self-pity ran down my face.

Sometimes opportunity knocks in surprising ways. Margaret Rudkin became an entrepreneur...unexpectedly (Guideposts 1952). Her son had asthma; so, following the advice of a doctor, she made him fresh homemade bread. She'd never baked much before, but gradually she learned how to make excellent bread. Her neighbors suggested she sell it, which she did; and that was the beginning of a vastly successful firm called Pepperidge Farm.

"What am I going to do with this?" I cried in sudden anger, slamming my fist against the crate. I had no manufacturing experience, I knew nothing about making furniture. Suddenly, the whole scheme seemed farfetched.

For two months I pondered my options. Well-intentioned friends and our family attorney advised that taking on the rocker plant would be too much for me. How could I hope to launch a brand-new company with all its complexities and pitfalls?

But rising above these negatives was Frank's dream. You can't live with someone for years and see him put all his heart, thought and energy into something and then just slam the door and walk away.

Frank's dream meant too much to me to be abandoned. In October 1971, I found myself trying to get things off the ground. As I sat nervously in my office that first day, I prayed for the Lord to guide my decisions. I knew I couldn't handle everything on my own—I just wasn't wise enough, experienced enough or strong enough. I needed someone who was all three.

Prayer seemed to make me calmer, and as I looked out into the piney woods outside my office window, an idea came. It was so simple. But then, isn't God simple? It was as if He said: "If you want to know something, find somebody who knows."

But the Brumby plant had closed 27 years ago, I thought. *Surely no one would be left by now?* Even so, I inquired around town. To my surprise, I learned about a local man, T. S. Smith, who had been the last shop superintendent at

the old rocker plant. T. S. was 65 but still working. A friendly, lanky man who stood straight despite his years, he said he'd be glad to come out to the plant the next day after work.

"No problem at all, Miz Melson," he said cheerfully. "Besides, I'd kinda like to see those old machines again after all these years."

As it turned out, T. S. was a godsend. To my surprise, he insisted on coming back after work the next day—and the next. Before long he was coming out regularly in his spare time to supervise things. When he couldn't figure something out, he'd tell me that so and so "worked on this machine for more'n twenty-five years. Why don't you call him?"

In a short time, I had a group of retired Brumby old-timers, employed part-time or acting in advisory capacities.

Hammer and wood chisel in hand, I began working side-by-side in the shop with T. S., learning by doing. I began to see why my husband had loved woodworking. I enjoyed the look and feel of freshly lathed wood, the clean pungent smell of shavings underfoot and the aromatic sawdust that clung to arms and hair. I finally reached the point where I could, if the need arose, assemble a Brumby rocker.

Learning to construct them was one thing, getting the wood was another. The type of solid red oak needed was very difficult to find. Finally we located a tiny sawmill in the Alabama hills and had its two-man crew cut the rich red oak to our specifications.

When we finally had a stock of wood and began manufacturing, some of the back posts

Marva Collins bravely gave up 14 years' tenure as a public-school teacher and cashed in her pension check to found a ghetto school that has helped "uneducable" children reach extraordinary academic levels (Guideposts 1981). Where did she get the courage to start Chicago's Westside Prep? She and her husband "believed that if God wanted us to do it, He would take care of us." On both counts, God did.

split in the crucial steam-bending process. I was heartsick.

"What are we doing wrong?" I asked T.S.

"It's the wood, Miz Melson," he replied, picking up a piece and running his thumbnail along it. "Something's wrong with it."

Together we found that we had mistakenly used kiln-dried wood in which the grain fiber is already set. We had to use naturally air-dried wood, which is more limber. I learned that over half of the wood in the chairs would have to be slowly air-dried. "How long will it take, T.S.?" I asked.

"Well, ma'am, the posts are two and a half inches thick; they'll take 'bout eighteen to twenty-four months," he replied matter-of-factly.

I was stunned. "I don't have that kind of time!" I cried.

He scratched his head a moment. "Well, we could saw them into smaller pieces close to pattern size," he said. "Then it needn't take more than six to eight months."

When we thought all our problems were solved, the antique machines began to break down to a screeching, smoking halt.

I was almost hysterical.

After a hurried inspection, T.S. came up to me. "It's the babbits, ma'am."

"Babbits?" I screeched. "What's babbits?"

"Bearings, ma'am, bearings. You see, these old machines were made to run off old-fashioned pulley belts from a central source like steam or water power. But now that each has its own electric motor, the lead babbit bearings just can't take that direct-drive thrust and have to be replaced more often."

"Where can we get them?"

"We can't, ma'am. We have to melt the lead and pour them ourselves."

I gasped and stared at the ceiling.

"Beg your pardon, Miz Melson, but it seems you're fighting this thing too much. And trying to fight it alone. You do have folks who want to help you, if you'd let 'em."

I had to admit that T.S. was right. I had thought I had to prove myself—and do it all on my own. And so, from T.S., I even learned how to pour and mold babbits.

It took a good six months to get into production, and we opened the doors in March 1972. I dubbed the revived company The Rocker Shop, and people began calling me The Rocking Chair Lady. We sell our rockers on a direct first-come, first-served basis to people who write or come to call.

Taking Frank's dream and seeing it through, despite the dire predictions that a woman who knew nothing about manufacturing would fail, has been very gratifying. Yet I must confess that I get the most pleasure hearing from people of all ages who appreciate the workmanship, comfort and pleasure my husband knew they would find in this lovable rocker.

Sometimes when the line is shut down in the evening, I'll walk through the quiet factory alone. As I stand there looking at the long lines of rockers in various stages of completion, I almost feel Frank's hand on my shoulder and hear him saying, "I knew you could do it, honey. With God's help, I *knew* you could do it."

Marva Collins and pupil, 1980

MARCH 1961

The Tools That Wouldn't Stay Stolen *by Leonard E. LeSourd, editor*

Sid Thompson stopped his car at the side of the road. He took several deep breaths, hoping to dissolve the knot in his stomach.

Ahead was the delivery platform of the maintenance building of his company. He could see Pete, the guard, checking equipment. It was Friday, November 6th, 1959—the day Sid had dreaded so much.

Momentary panic seized him. Was he about to lose the best job he ever had? "I don't have to go through with it," Sid said to himself.

But he couldn't turn back now. He had committed himself to a principle; he would stick to it regardless of what it cost him....

Sid Thompson is a tinsmith at a large industrial plant in northern New Jersey. He is no crusader. An easygoing, balding man of 55, Sid, in fact, had no spiritual direction until early in 1959 when he and his wife, Evelyn, started to participate in a fellowship group at Marble Collegiate Church in New York City.

There was much talk about moral problems and facing up to Christian standards. "A better world begins with me," was a phrase that impressed Sid.

And then one night Sid was forced to look deep inside his soul. He was never the same again.

It happened during a talk by a visiting speaker: Rajmohan Gandhi, grandson of the late Mahatma Gandhi of India. Young Gandhi told how several years before he had been challenged to measure his life by Christ's four standards: love, purity, unselfishness and honesty.

"I wasn't doing very well with any of these four," he told the group, "especially honesty. During my college days, I had found a way to steal rides on the local trolleys. I tried to run away from the memory, but it ate into my soul.

"Finally, I knew I had to make restitution. So I paid back to the trolley company the money involved. Newspapers heard about it and ran stories of how Gandhi's grandson was a thief. It was unpleasant, but something I had to do to start a new life."

Then young Gandhi went on to tell of his work with Moral Re-Armament, and the adventure he had found in working for a better world.

When he finished speaking, Sid Thompson sat motionless in his seat for several minutes. Later, back in his New Jersey apartment, Sid went down to his workshop. For a moment he looked around at his equipment: pipe fittings, electric switches, tools and even a big brass pump, all sneaked out of his plant over the years. Everyone does it, he had rationalized.

Sid found his wife in the kitchen, drinking coffee. He sat down beside her. "Like young Gandhi, I feel like a thief too," he said.

"What do you mean?"

"I have a workroom full of assorted stuff that belongs to the company. Do you think I should return it?" he asked, deeply concerned.

"It's up to you," Evelyn said, uncertainly.

Neither voiced their inner fear, namely, that

Walt Disney (1901–1966) grew up in Marceline, Missouri, where his father, Elias, built the church and was a deacon of the congregation. In Guideposts (1949), Walt acknowledged his reliance on God and the practical value of religion. "It helps ... keep you attuned to the Divine inspiration. Without inspiration, we would perish." Now, who would know that better than the creator of Mickey Mouse, Donald Duck and Disneyland?

Sid couldn't afford to lose his job. They were deeply in debt and needed a steady income.

Another very practical concern bothered Sid. He had been a leader in a union reform group that had unsuccessfully protested a contract negotiated with the company. Their appeals to the N.L.R.B. had infuriated union leaders as well as Joe Willoughby,* the plant manager.

Sid Thompson could imagine their triumph if he returned the stolen property. The reformer who had to be reformed: what a laugh!

"I have other faults to correct," Sid said to himself. "This problem can wait a while."

But in the months that followed, Sid had the strange feeling that God was nudging him on.

In growing desperation, Sid tried to think of alternatives: find another job and then ship the tools back...return them anonymously... move away. But it was no good. Like Gandhi, he knew what he had to do.

He shared his anguish with Evelyn. They began morning prayers, asking God to give Sid courage.

Finally, Sid Thompson set Friday, November 6th, as a deadline.

Meanwhile, Sid's memory began to work overtime. There were eight New York City parking tickets he had ignored, on the knowledge that as a New Jersey resident he could not be summoned. There was a library book he had never bothered to return. With a sinking heart, he recalled some company equipment he had used while installing electric fixtures in his mother's house.

If he were going to set things right, he reasoned, he might as well go all the way. Reluctantly, he figured the value of the fixtures at $100. The traffic tickets at another $40.

That night Sid wrote a letter to the New York Traffic Bureau, enclosing the eight parking tickets and $40. The following morning, he went to the company credit union office and borrowed $100. Wednesday night, he returned the library book.

Thursday at work he used a coffee break to tell Pete, the maintenance guard, of his plan to return company property the following morning. Pete was dumbfounded. "You're out of your mind, Sid. Don't do it. You'll lose your job."

Sid looked steadily into the eyes of his incredulous friend: "It's something I've got to do."

That night, Sid Thompson wrote a letter to his company president. It took most of the evening. It said:

"Some weeks ago while listening to a talk by Rajmohan Gandhi, I began to re-examine my past activities in light of a more complete understanding of honesty...I found many small things, and a few not so small, taken from the company...these I have returned, but there are some items I cannot return...in my prayer for guidance the figure came to me as $100....Enclosed is a check for $100...I give it now, gladly, as a witness of my trust and faith in God that these dollars are the best investment in my future I can possibly make...."

Friday morning, Sid sat at the breakfast table feeling like a man awaiting execution. By

*Names of plant personnel have been changed.

Walt Disney

the curb outside stood their 1948 sedan—its trunk stowed with the equipment. The letter was ready to be posted.

"Don't look so scared," Evelyn whispered as she kissed him good-bye. "Remember, God is in this too."

When Pete saw him drive up, he began shaking his head. "Don't do it, Sid."

Sid smiled wanly, began unloading the trunk of his car.

The stockroom clerk was even more nervous and apprehensive. "Why are you sticking your neck out, Sid? This junk isn't worth getting fired for." And then, hopefully, he suggested, "Look, Sid, I'll stick it over in the corner, and when they find it, nobody will know where it came from."

A tempting moment!

But Sid drew a deep breath and told the clerk that he would explain the whole situation to Mr. Rogers, the stockroom supervisor.

Sunday evening, the Thompsons went to the fellowship meeting at Marble Collegiate Church. In a simple ten-minute talk, Sid reported his experience of restitution. Spiritual power flowed from him that evening. Not until months later was the extent of this power realized.

Thompson was summoned to Willoughby's office the following Wednesday. "Sid's gonna get it now," fellow workers predicted. A few minutes later Sid came out feeling a little dazed. Willoughby had been ill at ease. Showing neither approval nor disapproval, he returned the check, suggesting it might be sent to a charity (later this was done). Then, with an odd, unfathomable look on his face, Joe shook hands with Sid and the session was over. One can only speculate on the dilemma that must have faced top company executives as to how they'd handle Sid's letter and his return of company property.

A year has passed. Sid Thompson continues at his job. On the surface, things look much the same, but there is something different. It is reflected in the genial way Willoughby speaks to Sid now when they meet in the maintenance shop. It is in the way Sid's friends look up to him in small matters.

Most important of all is the chain reaction effect of Sid's decision. Attending the fellowship meeting the night Sid spoke were others who had taken "a few little things" from their employers. One person later returned some textiles, another turned in to police a $3,000 pearl necklace found on the sidewalk. Still others are in the process of making restitutions—at cost to themselves.

Morality *can* be as contagious as immorality. In a confused and corrupt world, this is a heartening sign.

*Annamae Cheney was a "workshopper," a participant at the first
Writers' Workshop in 1967. That workshop, and all the ones that
have followed, evolved from a conversation between Dr. Peale and
Catherine Marshall. "What could be done to improve the
quality of Christian writing?" they asked themselves. "Where can
Guideposts find more writers?" "How can we find more stories?"
And then the answer came—it was surprisingly simple: "Why don't
we turn to our readers?" And they did.*

NOVEMBER 1982

That Impossible Man! *by Annamae Cheney, legal secretary*

"No! No! No! It has to be perfect! Do it over!"

I snatched the report from my boss' hand, quickly scanning the pages for the insignificant changes he had made this time. It was hard to believe that this tall, quiet Texan could become such a tyrant when he stepped into his law office.

Spotting some red pen marks, I forced my best smile and said, "I'll take care of this right away." But deep down I was seething, not so much because I had to retype the lengthy legal papers, but because I was stuck in this degrading, good-for-nothing job.

It had been so different when I had started this job fresh out of high school. I'd attacked the memos and legal pleadings with enthusiasm, hoping to impress the man everyone in our small California town knew and admired as Judge, the stately, proper Southern gentleman lawyer who was never seen in public without his Stetson.

But in the office, he seemed like a different man. No matter what I did, or how hard I tried, Judge would find something wrong with it. A small smudge on the paper or a title off-center by one character would send him rampaging toward my desk, his white hair flying, his voice at a fever pitch.

"Why should I put out for him?" I fumed one night. "All he does is complain. It's worthless to work for him."

I knew I couldn't quit—there were no other openings in our town, and I needed the money—so I simply quit trying. I typed only fast enough to get the memo done in time, filed just often enough to keep the piles small, completed the legal pleadings just well enough to keep my job.

One morning I turned in a pile of finished pleadings. In less than 10 minutes Judge was back out at my desk, cursing, his ruler pointing at some mistakes on the page. "Why don't you have your mind on your business?" he roared. Turning on his heels, he headed for his office. Stopping short, he turned back. "And, Annamae, what have you done to your hair? It looks terrible,"

I just glared at him as he closed the door to his office—how dare he say that! And the next day when he came at me with some more redos, I couldn't take it any longer. "Find yourself someone who doesn't get sick, make any mistakes or mind your terrible language. I'm leaving in two weeks."

"One will be sufficient," Judge responded coldly.

I cried myself to sleep that night. It was a relief to know I wouldn't have to put up with that impossible man any longer.

I got to the office late the next morning and found Judge frantically pawing through a pile of papers on his desk.

"What are you looking for?" I asked.

first Guideposts Writers' Workshop, 1967, with Annamae Cheney seated farthest right

I was shocked when he looked up at me. His eyes were bloodshot. For the first time I could remember, he looked old beyond his 70 years. "I'm leaving for the East. My mother died last night," he said, his voice breaking. "Get your pen—I'll tell you what needs to be done."

My pen flew over a notebook as Judge dictated instructions. His voice was shaky; there were cracks in his granite exterior. "I'll be gone for two weeks," he said as he headed out the door.

I ran after him down the hall. "Would you like me to stay until you get back?" I offered.

"Yes, I'd appreciate that." And he was gone.

I completed the urgent business by noon—but the rest of the typing could wait. I couldn't imagine anything better than using my afternoon to do some reading.

After a quick trip to the local drugstore's magazine rack, I settled in for a pleasant afternoon. Quickly flipping the pages, I found my favorite section—the monthly mystery feature. Ironically this month's story was about a lawyer trying to save his business. Eagerly I began reading, devouring every word. Silently I cheered on the lawyer, and especially the secretary he couldn't do without. And when the lawyer and secretary teamed to score a major legal victory, I felt goose bumps all over, as if it had happened to me.

The telephone jolted me back to reality. It was a lawyer whom Judge knew well. "Judge will be out of the office for two weeks," I said. "May I leave him a message?"

"Oh, no!" he responded. "It's very impor-

tant that I get some information on a case right away. Could you check some files for me?"

"Well…" I hesitated. "I'm not sure I can help, but if it's so important, I'll try."

He told me the files he needed, and as I went to find them, I began to feel like that secretary in the story. By the time I pulled the last of the files, my heart was beating quickly.

"Here's the information," I said. "I also pulled a few other files I remember Judge said might be helpful to this case."

"Thank you, ma'am," the lawyer said, obviously relieved. "This is a great help. I sure am glad he has a legal secretary who cares about her work. Good-bye."

I swallowed hard at the last statement. For so many months I had simply done what was asked of me, nothing more.

Slowly I walked through each room of the empty office, past shelves and shelves of dusty law books. With each step, my emotions seemed to swell. "I want to do this job, and do it well," I finally prayed. "But, God, can I ever be forgiven for the way I've acted?"

My fingers flew over the typewriter keys the rest of that day. In subsequent days I began to acquaint myself with files, draft documents and put the office in order. Instead of disinterest causing poor work and more disinterest, my new determination improved my work, which only heightened my interest.

I no longer dreaded going to work—I'd discovered it could be fun. But I did dread the day that Judge would return. I'd be out of a job then.

How did Guideposts achieve its huge circulation? With lots of help! From the beginning, employers have given it to employees, grandparents to grandchildren. Conrad Hilton, the famous hotelier, was an early supporter—ordering thousands of copies for his hotel guests. To this day, there is a motel chambermaid in Florida who every year orders 40 subscriptions as a tithe—for all the rooms she cleans. As a gift, as a tithe, Guideposts gets around. Good news, when it's about His Good News, travels fast.

He walked through the door three days early. "Good afternoon," he said sharply. He walked quickly into his office and shut the door.

Shortly before five he called me into his office. My mind panicked. *What if he tells me not to come in tomorrow before I get a chance to change his mind?*

"What's been going on here?" he said immediately, pointing to his desk.

I managed a weak smile. I had used some of my extra time to reorganize his desk. The mail was opened, dated and stacked in order of importance. Long yellow sheets of typed drafts and completed documents were neatly arranged across the front of the desk. "I—I got everything done that you left, so I tried to organize the notes on your desk."

"You did this by yourself?"

I nodded.

With a puzzled look on his face, he thrust two wills at me. "Due in final form tomorrow —no changes." And he dismissed me.

Friday came all too quickly. I had been waiting for a good time to ask if he might let me stay on, but none seemed to come. And suddenly, there he was, signing what would be my last paycheck. "Okay, Annamae, now tell me why your attitude has taken a 180-degree turn," he said as he handed me the check.

"It's my fault we haven't gotten along," I said, speaking very tentatively. "I haven't cared enough about you, the business or the clients. But that's not what I want anymore. The last few days, I've taken a real interest in law, and I think my work reflects that. I know I have an awful lot to learn, and I'd like to learn it from you, if…well…if you think…you can forgive me and…um…let me stay on."

Judge searched my eyes for a long time, saying nothing. My palms were moist as I stood before his vast desk, pleas of petition to God running through my head like a deer through a forest—quick, darting prayers. *Please, let him understand.*

And then Judge smiled, a smile that seemed to transform his tired features. "Okay, darlin'," he said. "Let's get to work."

Work together we did—for the next five years. During that time, the business tripled, Judge developed a seemingly bottomless well of patience, and I developed a new respect for myself and the work I could do.

When I moved to another town, I began interviewing for other law jobs. After reading my résumé, the lawyer in charge of one office remarked, "Your qualifications are impeccable, and you do good work. How did you learn all this?"

The answer was easy. "Because I cared."

I got the job.

Like Sgt. Plouffe in the story below, Jack Loizeaux has a dangerous job. He dynamites condemned buildings in such a way that they "implode," bursting inward and falling into their own basements. In Guideposts (1977), he explained that he does his work calmly because he invokes the power of God before he releases the power of the dynamite. Just before he pushes the detonator button, Jack and his crew join hands and pray for a safe, successful demolition. What a wise way to begin any kind of work.

SEPTEMBER 1961

My Walk With Eternity *by Sgt. Leo Plouffe, bomb squad officer*

Very few of us, I suppose, think constantly about death. I do, regularly—as part of my job.

I am the detective-sergeant in charge of the Emergency Unit of the Montreal Police Department. One day I may have to climb to the top of a bridge and talk a would-be suicide back to the ground; the next I'll open a door and face a mad butcher wielding a cleaver; and the next, as happened March 8, 1957, I will be called on to disarm a man with dynamite strapped all around him.

That particular day I got a call to rush to the St. Lawrence Street branch of the Bank of Toronto-Dominion. St. Lawrence Street was slushy from a recent snow, and empty, though it was three in the afternoon. Empty, that is, except for a handful of uniformed police outside the bank. Inside, I knew, were a dozen employees, eight customers and a madman.

The madman was trying to rob the bank. A plastic mask completely covered his head. In one hand he held a pistol, in the other he held a cheap electrical switch. Sewed inside his jacket was a homemade corset that he had stuffed with dozens of sticks of dynamite. Unless the manager handed him all the money and let him walk out free, he was going to throw the switch, blowing himself, the bank, and the customers to dust.

Suddenly, as I approached, there was a shot and a shattering of glass.

"Allons! Vite!" I yelled, and ran forward to join the group of policemen rushing into the bank. One of the officers, Joe Perron, still held a smoking revolver in his hand. Inside the bank, slumped over in a chair, was the body of the madman. He was not dead, the shot had paralyzed him. Quickly, even before we could clear the bank, I forced the electrical switch from his hand. Then I took the detonators out of each stick of dynamite. There were 39 sticks in all, strapped to his body. One by one I made them harmless.

With the danger past, the reaction from pent-up emotions hit everyone at once. People were going up to strangers, repeating what had happened.

"You should have seen the manager, how brave he was."

Someone took off the bandit's mask. A young girl teller looked at him. "Such a nice looking boy, too. Do you think he'll die?"

"There's no way of knowing, Miss," I said. "How does any of us know? It just shows we should live in a state of grace."

The young man did die soon afterward, but not before he gave a confession that later sent me, for a second time in one day, walking deliberately toward death.

When I left the bank afterward, I thought my day's work was done. I headed home.

"You look exhausted," my wife said as I walked through the door. I told her about the

*The bomb that destroyed Hiroshima, August 6, 1945, changed
our lives. Never before had man commanded such awesome power.
"But we have another power, greater and stronger," Edwin L. Jones
wrote in Guideposts (1949). Jones was a building contractor who
had constructed part of the atomic-testing plant in Oak Ridge,
Tennessee. "We've had the power of Life for 2,000 years, and
we've been afraid to use it. I mean the spiritual power as revealed
to the world by Jesus Christ."*

handsome young man with the matted hair and the dynamite sewed around his body, and how one bullet alone had stood between us and death. My wife suggested that I lie down. But I couldn't. I was too keyed up to rest.

None of us knows, from one heartbeat to the next, when death may come. The only difference between me and another man is that by the nature of my work I am more aware of this possibility. And it is, I suppose, because of this awareness that I consciously try to live in a state of grace.

To be in a state of grace means letting nothing stand between you and the love of God. A person who knows he is going to die tries to achieve this state so that at his death he will not be separated from God, and will go straight to heaven. Every once in a while, after confession and communion, when I feel clean and close to my Maker, I can sense what it would be like to die then. There would be nothing to fear.

The telephone rang in the back of the house. I heard my wife's voice answer, "Yes, I'll tell him." She appeared in the door. "They want you back downtown, Leo. That madman from the bank left a bomb in Central Station."

I quickly discovered that the wounded man had regained consciousness for a brief moment in the hospital. He asked what time it was: he had set a bomb, he said, to go off at five o'clock. Then he lost consciousness again.

Where had he left that bomb? In his pants' pocket the police found a key, on which was the number 362. Every telephone at the

Department was pressed into use: calling hotels, clubs, schools, the bus depot, asking if they had a locker with the number 362 on it. Finally, Central Station answered yes. The locker was opened: inside was a brown leather briefcase. From the briefcase came the unmistakable sound of a timing mechanism. They sent for me.

I shook the slush off my rubbers as I walked into the high-vaulted waiting room of Central Station. Far off, at the opposite end of the room, for the first time cleared of commuters, I could see the wooden bench with the innocent looking briefcase resting on it. The clock above it said 8:32. Why was the explosion three and a half hours overdue?

There was a death-like silence in the waiting room. It was deserted except for police officers and one news photographer. I took off my coat and rubbers. Any moisture would increase the chance of accidental explosion.

"Good luck," one of the detectives said.

I started the long, lonesome walk across the station. My footsteps clicked hollowly. *Oh my God! I am heartily sorry for having offended Thee* ...The prayer raced through my mind as I walked forward....*I firmly resolve, with the help of Thy grace*...I wanted to feel the Presence of God beside me....*to amend my life, Amen.*

There was no doubt what was waiting for me if I made one faulty move. I leaned down and listened.

Tick. Tock.

I bent closer. Now I could distinguish two tickings, one louder than the other. Tick, *tick*,

Eleanor Roosevelt's (1884–1963) luminous faith in mankind and her tireless work for such causes as racial equality and human rights grew out of her faith in God. In her purse, wherever she went, she always carried the following prayer (Guideposts 1968): Our Father, who has set a restlessness in our hearts and made us all seekers after that which we can never fully find . . . keep us at tasks too hard for us, that we may be driven to Thee for strength.

tock, *tock.* The two sounds seemed to race each other, and my own pulse kept time with the faster.

"Better examine it closely, Plouffe," I said. "Why hasn't this bomb gone off? You've got to open it up. Take the two edges of the top and— there now—easy! Open her up!"

Tick, *tick,* tock, *tock.*

Several packages, wrapped in Christmas paper: a bottle of hair tonic, an alarm clock, and then another alarm clock, with wires soldered to its hands. "Why two clocks, Plouffe?" I asked myself. "Ah—of course: so that if he is stopped by a policeman, he opens his bag and shows the innocent clock. The man's clever, yes, clever enough to rig up a booby trap— easy now…where are the wires? There, leading out of that box. Shining, clean, well-soldered wires. Perfect job. Where do they go, Plouffe? Down into the bottom of the bag. What are you waiting for, *mon beau,* an invitation?"

Perspiration poured into my eyes. "Easy now, Plouffe," I said to myself. "Reach in with the left hand. Grasp the wire firmly—no slip-ping. Now the right hand…*I firmly resolve with the help of Thy grace…*

"Now, pull!"

Silence.

Except for the ticking of two clocks, silence. I wiped my eyes, looked deeper into the brief-case and pulled out five sticks of dynamite, wired to one of the clocks. Three tiny strands of cotton—absorbent cotton that was supposed to deaden the sound of the ticking— three tiny threads of cotton had been picked up by the clock hands and were wedged between them and the contacts, insulating them so that the bomb had not exploded at five o'clock.

Two thousand people had been in Central Station at five o'clock. Two thousand people separated from death by three strands of cotton fiber. There is a thinner line between life and death than most of us realize. It just goes to show the importance of being ready.

Before I turned back to the little group of officers, I wiped my eyes again. But this time I was wiping away tears of gratitude.

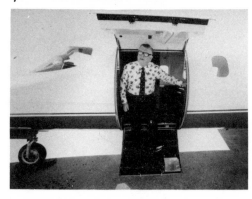

William Lear (1902–1978) and one of his jets

NOVEMBER 1975

Moment of Decision *by William P. Lear, inventor*

The phone call came while my wife Moya, our children and I were at dinner. "Bill," one of our company men reported anxiously, "another one has crashed."

It was the second Lear Jet to crash under mysterious circumstances within the month. People had died in each of the crashes. After getting the details, I slumped at the table, staring at my plate and wondering, *Why? Why?*

The planes were as much a part of me as my hands and brain. A new concept in private aircraft, the Lear Jet was an eight-seat 560-mph airplane of revolutionary design that offered the business world fast and economical executive travel.

Priced much lower than similar jets, our high-performance craft had received much favorable worldwide publicity.

But now those mysterious crashes.

The first had seemed unexplainable. It had happened shortly after the plane had taken off. There was no word from the pilot, no hint of what had happened. Pilot error seemed to be the only answer, yet something deeper within me couldn't accept that.

And now this news of a second crash. I got up from the table, my food uneaten.

"Moya," I said, "there's only one thing to do. Ground every Lear Jet until we can find out what's wrong."

She looked at me with concern. "You mean announce that openly?"

I nodded.

"But are you sure it's a fault in the plane?"

"I don't know, but we have to find out."

"Well," Moya said, "there's going to be an awful lot of fireworks among the company executives."

She was right.

"Bill Lear, you're out of your mind!" went the chorus of my associates. "Do you want to wreck the company? If you tell all the owners to ground their ships, you'll lose everyone's confidence. We're under no obligation to do that; there's absolutely no evidence it's a design or structural fault."

"Of course," they continued, "we can quietly launch a crash program of our own to investigate the situation. But we're under no obligation to make a public announcement. For heaven's sake, think it over!"

I did think it over. I went out into the hangar one night and sat down in the cockpit of my own Lear Jet. As I stared out of the sweptback windshield, I meditated on everything that had led up to the creation of the plane. My mind went back to my boyhood days in Chicago.

I remembered the countless Sundays I'd spent at the Moody Tabernacle in Chicago where I'd start at church school in the morning and end up in the evening listening to Paul Rader preach in the tabernacle. He had a way of making Biblical characters come alive. And stressed all through his talks were the courage and honesty that God expects of us.

In 1958, David Sarnoff, Chairman of the Board of RCA, told our readers about three things he'd asked his scientists to perfect for his company's 50th anniversary: a magnetic tape recorder for television, an electronic amplifier of light and an electronic air conditioner without any moving parts. "A cockeyed dream," they thought. And yet, in five years' time, they'd invented all three. As Sarnoff said, "Whatever man conceives in his heart or mind can become a reality."

As I sat in that dark, quiet jet, I faced my decision. From a business standpoint, my associates were right. It certainly wasn't good business to admit publicly that something might be wrong with our plane, especially if we did not have to. We were all convinced that it was the finest aircraft of its kind in the world.

I thought of the years of struggle it took us to achieve this new concept in aircraft. People were forever telling us that our ideas were too advanced, that our dreams couldn't become realities. But when experts argued that a certain thing couldn't be done, I'd laugh and point to the RAF's 500-page treatise on why the jet engine would never replace the propeller.

Now, after all the battles were fought, everything could go down the drain; needlessly perhaps, if we went ahead with our announcement.

But then I weighed the alternative. What if another Lear Jet went down? What if more lives were lost? Could I live with myself? Was *anything* worth that?

I stood up and stepped out of the plane. There was only one thing to do.

We contacted every Lear Jet owner and advised them to ground their planes until we could complete our investigation.

In the meantime, I set to work. I lay awake all night trying to figure out what had happened. I had taken my own jet apart inch by inch, studying every piece for a clue. Finally I decided to take Sherlock Holmes's approach. Perhaps now was the time to employ the great detective's famous principle of unraveling a mystery by looking for common denominators. What common factors were involved in both crashes?

It didn't take long to find that out. Both planes had taken off in a warm rain, had climbed rapidly to 24,000 feet, then leveled off. Suddenly, as their speed increased, they disappeared from the radar screen. It all seemed to have something to do with rain, altitude and speed.

There *was* an answer. I had to believe that. As I prayed, I thanked God for that answer whatever it might be. For, as I had learned at the tabernacle, one must believe God *will* answer before anything will happen. So, fired by this expectation, we worked on.

Again and again we went over the similarities—rain, a fast climb (no plane had climbed as fast before), the altitude of 24,000 feet, then the leveling off and acceleration.

Again I went over the plane. For some reason I was drawn to the plane's elevators, the movable part of the tail assembly that makes an airplane climb or dive. I studied them carefully, noting the usual drain holes in them.

Something tugged at me. Could those drain holes have something to do with it? I analyzed them in ratio to speed, aerodynamic pressure, rain, altitude—and suddenly I had an insight.

I went over my computations again. An ominous pattern was beginning to build before me. Normally the rainwater would drain. But at 24,000 feet and at high speed, the trapped water could freeze, the weight of it changing the center of balance of the elevators.

As a result, when the plane leveled off and

When R. G. LeTourneau (1888–1969) was deep in debt, he was asked to make a pledge to his church. "Lord, how can I?" he said. And yet, he did, trusting that the matter was in God's hands. Sure enough, his business soon turned around, eventually growing into the mammoth earth-moving equipment company that bears his name. "God," he explained in Guideposts (1945), "will not be any man's debtor."

increased speed, the unbalanced elevators might then flutter, throwing the plane out of control.

All of this could happen only under unusual circumstances, but still....

So far it was only a theory. Now there was only one thing to do—take the Lear Jet up myself, under the same conditions. And, to duplicate the rain aspect, we arranged tubing in front of the elevators to spray them with dyed water.

I went up. When I landed, we checked and sure enough, the interiors of the elevators were stained with dye.

Now to prove the final, and deadly, effect. We fastened two-ounce weights to the back of each elevator, duplicating the effect of the frozen water. Again I took the ship up myself. The jet shot into the blue like a bullet. At 24,000 feet I leveled off and began to accelerate.

The airspeed needle swung over to 450 mph, 500 mph, 550 mph. Suddenly the plane exploded into a vibration that almost sent me sprawling at the controls. It was all I could do to hang on to the wheel. Gauges flew from the instrument panel.

I immediately cut speed and was just barely able to bring the ship level. Breathing hard, I headed back to the field and landed. As I taxied down the runway, I knew I had the answer to the problem. It involved a simple change in the elevators. A small airfoil in front of the drain holes would prevent the situation from ever happening again.

Teams of company men went into action, rushing around the country and making the changes on our planes. Within three days all Lear Jets were flying again.

It took a year before we fully gained back public confidence in Lear Jets. But it did come back, perhaps more than it would have if we had avoided making the announcement. Not only did all the companies that had canceled their orders come back to reorder, but the plane also increased steadily in popularity.

The other day I happened to find myself in a commercial airliner. As we lumbered off the runway and lifted into the air, I noticed a small sweptwing white jet with a rakish, high, scorpion tail, climbing past us. It was like watching one of my own children. And, as I watched that Lear Jet disappear into the distance, I smiled and seemed to hear Paul Rader preaching again in the old Moody Tabernacle about the peace and satisfaction the Lord gives through a clear conscience.

Sgt. E.L. Allen

DECEMBER 1972

The Day Christmas Broke Into Prison *by Sgt. E.L. Allen, correctional officer*

The six correctional officers under my command in the huge California prison stared at me as if I had lost my mind. I didn't blame them. But I needed their help to carry out the proposal I had just made. As the silence lengthened, I breathed a short prayer. Then I waited—and waited—and waited.

For the past 11 years I have been an officer in a California Adjustment Center, which is a police term for prison. My colleagues and I are responsible for 65 inmates in a prison population of over 1,400. Ours is a dangerous and thankless task. Of the 65 prisoners in our charge, 50 are known killers—that is, they have killed someone (some have killed several times) or else they have tried their best to do so.

When desperate men are caged, enormous emotional pressures build up. For a few there may be hope, but for most there is nothing but today and tomorrow, today and tomorrow, with nothing on the other side of tomorrow. Despite all the locks and bars, despite all the searches and precautions, inmates sometimes manage to fashion crude weapons—a knife from a strip of steel torn from a metal grille, a dagger from a piece of bedspring, or a screwdriver stolen from the woodworking shop. All too often they use them. One of my officers has been stabbed five times, another has been slashed twice.

If you are a Christian—and I try to be—you should be able to put your faith to work wherever you find yourself. In a prison, this is not easy. When a prisoner goes berserk, you have to control him. When he attacks you, you have to defend yourself. I have had to do this on several occasions, and always the question comes into my mind, "What would Jesus do in a situation like this?" I'm not sure that I know the answer. Perhaps He would *love* the man into submission. All I know is that when the episode is ended, I always go back to the prisoner and tell him that I'm sorry that it was necessary to use force. And every time the prisoner has said, in effect, "It's okay, Sarge. I know you had to do it."

One day last December, while I was on duty at the prison, a thought flashed into my mind. I had been doing some research on inmates' backgrounds, talking to them, asking them questions. A depressingly high percentage never had visitors. They never received mail. No one cared about them. "What would happen," I said to myself, "if we tried to give these men a Christmas party?"

I almost rejected the idea out of hand, because prison regulations prohibit grouping more than six of these people together at any time. But the idea refused to go away. The dayroom, off the tiers of cells, would hold about 25 people. What if we divided our inmates into three groups of about 22 men and let them into the dayroom one group at a time? That way, they would still outnumber the

Guideposts has consistently told stories about people who take a stand on the job to help others, sometimes at great personal risk. As Hurricane Camille headed for the Gulf Coast, Ray Butterfield was convinced it would be worse than predicted. Early on, he broadcast warnings from WLOX-TV, Biloxi (where he was general manager). "Get out!" he urged. He stayed on until the last minute, and deserved much of the credit for keeping the fatalities low in one of the worst hurricanes ever.

guards more than three to one. Would they try to take advantage of such a situation if I did manage to get the rules suspended? What would happen to my job if they did? Who would pay for such a party, anyway? The whole thing seemed preposterous.

But still the idea would not go away. When I proposed it to my superiors, they gave me a reluctant green light. Now I was proposing it to my own officers. I explained that I had official permission. "If you want no part of this," I said, "I won't blame you. But here's how I feel. For three hundred sixty-four days out of the year we control and dominate these men. On this one day I would like to serve them a good meal, give them a gift, offer them a kind word as fellow human beings. To do this, I need your cooperation. Not only that, I'll have to ask you to help me pay for the party. Will you do it?"

The silence seemed to go on forever, thick and heavy and long. Finally the officer who had been stabbed five times cleared his throat. "Well," he said, "maybe I could form a singing group. Some of these Mexicans are pretty good with a guitar." Another officer looked dubiously around him. "Do you think we could decorate *this* place?" "Sure," said a third. "I'll bet we could even dream up a Christmas tree!" "What about food?" said a fourth. "We'd have to get it from outside." I felt my throat grow tight as the voices went on and on, each man offering his time and his money and his help.

During the week that followed, an enthusi-

asm was generated between officers and inmates that had never existed before. Black, white and Mexican singing groups were formed. The officers decorated the dayroom with sheets on which they had lettered "Merry Christmas" and "Happy New Year." Somebody made a marvelous Christmas tree out of a mop and streamers of green paper. We improvised a stage.

At one point, I learned later, a rough prisoner let it be known that he was planning to disrupt the party if he were let out of his cell. Shortly, a delegation of four other prisoners called on him. If he caused any trouble, they told him, there would be a great deal more trouble—for him. "What's the matter with you guys?" snarled the prisoner. "We're all cons, ain't we?" "You're a con," the leader of the group told him scornfully. "The rest of us just happen to be here!"

When news of what we were planning filtered into other sections of the prison, some people thought I was losing my mind. Our supervisors allowed plans to proceed, on condition that tear gas was available outside the unit. However, we all agreed that when the big day arrived, all tear-gas guns and handcuffs would be left in the security room. I was sure this was the right decision. Even so, I didn't sleep too well on Christmas Eve. I kept wondering where an ex-grocer with 11 years of custody experience would find another job.

On Christmas Day, instead of "keying" each inmate out separately and locking the cell door

In our Prayer Fellowship, we often hear from prisoners. In 1983,
Carl S. Holt sent us this poem, written for his wife Brandi.
I walked along an alien path with eyes that would not see.
I raged and cursed and fought against an unseen enemy.
Anger and sorrow, pain and fear—all paved my tortured road,
Until, at last, I prayed to God to ease my weary load.
A light came shining from His heart, a light to help me see.
My enemy came into view: the one I fought was me.

behind him, we let 22 men out at a time and didn't lock the doors. They came out warily, almost as if they were afraid it was some kind of trick or trap.

As each one came into the dayroom, a guard handed him a tray of food completely different from the drab prison fare: cold cuts, ham, salad, cakes and cookies, punch. (We ran over our food budget, but the caterer absorbed the loss.) Each inmate was given two packs of cigarettes. The men in the upper tier each got a gift-wrapped T-shirt; the men in the lower unit got socks.

At first there was some constraint—it was so strange and different for all of us. But then the first singing group sang *Silent Night* and we all joined in. Then they sang more carols and some popular songs, and soon everyone was talking to everyone.

Only once did I feel a twinge of real apprehension. That was when I saw an inmate considered to be extremely dangerous slowly approaching an officer he had stabbed only a few weeks earlier. Quickly I moved into a position that would allow me to aid the officer if he were attacked, but to my amazement I heard the inmate say to him, "I never received a Christmas gift from anyone before in my whole life. I can't repay you, but if you can find it in your heart to forgive me, I will never again take up a weapon against you or anyone else."

Finally the long day was over, but the singing continued late into the night and all my men stayed overtime. God had answered my prayers: We didn't have a single incident of any kind. As I was preparing to leave for home, I was handed a note signed by 65 "hard-core" prisoners:

"We no you had gas out side but you did not need it some of us praid and you had god as a corecsional officer have a good crismas"

Still inmates, yes. Still prisoners, yes. But men who now, because of His birthday, had something to hope for—on the other side of tomorrow.

In Worship

How do we worship God?

Each of us has a personal relationship with the Almighty, and the ways we find to praise Him are infinite. Christ said, "Where two or three are gathered together in My name, there I am among them," and ever since, Christians have known the great power generated when they gather together in "congregations." For years, Guideposts has been exploring and celebrating the various ways in which present-day congregations worship.

In 1978, Guideposts gave its annual Church Award to a remarkable little church in Hastings, Iowa (population 150). The century-old United Methodist Church had been in danger of closing. With an average attendance of 12 each Sunday in this small farm town, few seemed to care if the church survived. One night, a group of nine concerned parishioners met to talk.

"If we have to lose our church," they said to one another, "at least we ought to know why."

The Hastings Nine went out to their neighbors. They didn't ask for help and they didn't ask for money. They wanted to see what the people's needs were.

There was Joe Hall, for instance, who was sick in the hospital in Omaha. The pastor drove there right away, and later baptized the ailing man. There was the widow Frances Larsen who couldn't get to church because of a broken hip. So they started bringing tapes of services to her.

There was also the troubled mother who had all but given up on her teenage son who was in prison. The Hastings Nine prayed for her and her son. The pastor visited the youth. And when the mother began to feel the love of the church people, a new hope, a new faith, arose in her.

Little by little, weekly attendance at Hastings Methodist began to climb—until on Easter Sunday, 1978, there was real cause for joy. The solid-oak pews were crowded with 90 worshippers! The white clapboard church rang with alleluias.

Why did the Hastings church not only survive but flourish after coming so close to extinction? Because its tiny congregation went out as *Christians*, not *asking* for help, but *giving* help. They found the strength that a fellowship of Christians always provides.

Betty Banner at the time she wrote this story

JANUARY 1976

Farewell, on the Mountainside *by Betty Banner, former WPA caseworker*

Snow had fallen all night and the mountain was a fairyland of whiteness. I was 21 years old and expecting my first baby in the spring. All my life until the past ten months had been spent in a fairly good-sized town, and the deep, narrow valley between the tall mountain and ridge where I was living with my husband and his mother, was a constant source of interest and new experiences for me. The mountain folks I had come to know and the many customs of the "old folks" that they still cherished had formed a new world for me.

During the previous summer I had insisted that we attend the little white Methodist church about two miles down the valley, and even though the circuit-rider preacher only came once a month, I had helped organize a Sunday school for the in-between time.

This particular morning was Monday and "washday" by an infallible rule of the mountain community. Snow or no snow, we washed, and I hummed a tune as I helped my mother-in-law fill the zinc tubs on the glowing kitchen range and sorted the clothes for washing. My thoughts were of the coming baby, and the warm kitchen, accentuated by the white coldness seen through the windows, gave me a feeling of security and snugness. In thinking of my own happiness, I talked with my mother-in-law about the pity we felt for a young couple, who, we had been told, had lost their three-week-old baby during the night just the

day before. We were still speculating as to what might have caused such a death when a knock at the back door gave us both a start.

Opening the door, we were even more startled to see the very same father of the dead child we had just been discussing standing there. His name was John and he seemed hesitant to come into the kitchen and stood twirling his cap in his hands and staring at his feet. All of a sudden he took a deep breath and blurted out, "Betty, we was aimin' to bury our baby today, and now this snow an' all, and the preacher can't get acrost the ridge, and from the way hit's snowin' can't reckon when he could get here." Then, as we started to sympathize, he said, "My Maude...she's right smart tore up, and ain't able to git outta bed this mornin', but she says we just can't put our baby away 'lessen we have a service over her, and you're the only one I knowed round here I thought could do it."

It was a moment before my stunned brain could take it in that he was talking to and about me. I couldn't believe he was asking me to do the service. I started to stammer that I couldn't possibly preach a funeral, and besides we couldn't get the car out of the shed even to go two miles down the valley. I might have saved my breath, for he stood there with such grief and stubborn determination in his eyes that I felt like I was butting my head against a brick wall for all the progress I was making.

Prayer can cover great needs—and distances—as Ruth Stafford Peale explained in Guideposts (1983). She told of a mother who sought God's help for her son, a problem drinker living many miles away. With loving thoughts, the woman joined the young man as he rode the bus back and forth to work each day, praying him past a particular bar that tempted him. After several months of this, she learned that he'd stopped drinking. As Mrs. Peale pointed out, "Prayer is a vehicle that can get you there."

Then he said quietly, "How'd you feel if it was your young'un?" That did it. I had no answer for that, so I dumbly wiped my wet hands on my apron and began to untie it. I don't remember another word spoken as I pulled on rubber boots and coat and muffler. All I could do was pray frantically over and over, "Dear God, give me words to help. Help me to say what will comfort them...."

Leaving word about where I was going for my husband who was feeding cattle, I set out with John for the long cold walk to the church. Slipping, sliding, often wading drifts, with no conversation between us, the silent white flakes of snow pounding in our faces, we reached the church at last and went in. My heart came up into my throat. In spite of the snow, the little chapel was filled with mountain folks, and the little homemade coffin rested under a wreath of crepe-paper flowers in front of the rough altar.

Such a small, crude little chapel, with its oil lamps hanging on the walls, yet in that moment it seemed to me as vast and awesome as St. Patrick's Cathedral, which I once visited. I thought I'd never reach the front and as I stumbled down the aisle, my frantic brain could only repeat the same prayer. "Dear God, help me, help me. Let me say the words that will help them feel Your presence."

When I turned to face the silent congregation, I had to grip the pine pulpit tightly to keep from just going down. It hit me, too, that there was not even a Bible in front of me and I had not thought to bring mine!

As I realized that, I thought, *Well, this is it. I cannot go any further.* And then my eyes fell on that pitiful little box. Then and there God worked a miracle for me, just as surely as if He had reached out and touched my mind and lips. From somewhere unknown, the words came, disjointed as to correctness of quotation I am sure, but essentially those I had heard from early childhood on similar occasions. "I am the resurrection and the life..." "Casting all your care upon Him for He careth for you." "Suffer the children to come unto Me...for of such is the kingdom of heaven." On and on the words came, as if a scroll were being unwound before my eyes. Last of all came a prayer—and that was mine, for as I felt my own unborn child stirring within me, my petition for a grieving mother in a log cabin on that lonely mountainside found the right words for the final commitment of "earth to earth" at the tiny graveside.

I am now a grandmother, and through the years I have faced many trials and crosses where I have felt like giving up before I started. But always the memory of "my miracle" comes to me and I go on, for surely the loving God who could give an ignorant 21-year-old girl a funeral service can guide a more mature woman through any difficulty. Always, too, in such a crisis I seem to see John's face and hear the simple words he spoke as I turned from that grave toward home.

"Thank you—I knowed you could do it."

evangelist Billy Sunday, 1862–1935

MAY 1977

Billy Sunday and the Banker *by Lon Woodrum*

There never was a more colorful Christian evangelist than Billy Sunday, the onetime baseball player who rose up out of middle America in the teens and twenties to stir great throngs wherever he went. The stories about his exuberant, unorthodox ways of bringing people to the Lord abound to this day, and one of them was told to me years ago by the vice-president of a bank in Pennsylvania, Wallace Byrd.

Byrd was head teller in the bank at the time Billy Sunday came to town to conduct his crusade. Huge crowds gathered to hear him, but Byrd did not attend. He wanted no part of religion—especially that of itinerant evangelists.

But by some quirk of fate, Billy Sunday arranged for an account to be set up in Byrd's bank.

Day after day, Byrd watched Billy Sunday's account grow. And as it grew, so grew his animosity toward the evangelist.

On the Monday after his crusade ended, Billy Sunday came into the bank to settle his affairs. Among the checks from the previous night's collection was one for five dollars. That gave Byrd a chance to loose some of his resentment.

"Sir," Byrd said, "we can't honor this."

"Why not?" Sunday asked.

"The woman who wrote this check has less than five dollars in her account," he replied. "She is a widow, and very poor."

Sunday frowned at the check, and Byrd saw the opportunity for an extra harpoon. "Actually, sir, we are holding a mortgage on her home for fifteen hundred dollars. We'll have to foreclose very soon."

That, Byrd thought, *should hit this money-grabber where it hurts!*

Sunday responded by tearing up the widow's check. A moment later he laid a slip of paper in front of Byrd and said, "Will you honor this one?"

Byrd looked down to see a check for $1,500. "For the widow's mortgage," Sunday said.

"Why are you doing this?" Byrd asked.

"Friend," Sunday answered, "have you never read in the Great Book what a person of means is supposed to do about orphans and widows?"

After the evangelist left, Byrd was shaken. Again and again he thought about what had happened. He began to wonder how many other times Sunday might have done something similar, and he began to revise his thinking about evangelists. He thought, too, about the widow. Had she, by giving in faith out of her tiny possessions, been rewarded by this gift?

That was the turning point in Wallace Byrd's life, the event that led to his becoming a Christian. As Wallace Byrd told me, he never heard Billy Sunday preach from the pulpit. Sunday's only sermon to him was a signature on a personal check.

Just before World War II, Bishop Sheil of Chicago attended a pro-Nazi rally. As he attempted to change the group's thinking, an angry woman walked foward and shouted at him, "I'm a Catholic, but you're not a Catholic bishop. A bishop! Ha!...Rabbi Sheil," she called out, spitting in his face (Guideposts 1953). The ugly crowd yelled, but the bishop calmly turned his cheek. In the silence that followed, the bishop said, "Rabbi? That is what they called our Lord."

MAY 1952

Ten Men and a Prayer *by Fred Schiller, free-lance writer*

I was a buck private attached to Company C of the 846 Signal Photo Battalion. Sitting next to me in the station waiting room was a lieutenant of the much-decorated Third Infantry Division just back from European combat. It was early 1945.

When we started casual talk, I discovered that his name was McBride and that he was going home to Indiana on furlough. He told one experience with moving simplicity, then left to catch his train. His story is still so vivid in my mind, even after seven years, that I have an almost irresistible compulsion to relate it...

Italian hill "46" was finally abandoned on orders one bleak spring day back in 1944. As the weary GIs filed back toward the little Italian town of San Pietro, behind which American artillery answered the enemy, Sergeant Frazer began counting the costs of this mission.

"How many men left in their squad, Murphy?"

"Four, countin' myself."

Frazer then moved down the thin line of troops toward Max Halpern, a grizzled, flint-eyed Corporal, who carried a light machine gun cradled in his arm like a baby.

"Rosy got his right after the jump," said the Corporal. "Best squad leader I ever had." "Rosy" was Sergeant Rosenberg.

The remnants of the platoon then moved into the shattered village. The rest of their company had gathered beside a small church

with only three walls and half roof left. The section leaders were conferring with Lieutenant McBride beside the torn wall of the church.

"We'll wait here till the battalion assembles," said the officer. "Have your men ready to move out again in half an hour."

Corporal Halpern signaled his men to relax and, still cradling the machine gun, walked into the cool shadows inside the church. He didn't want to talk to anybody just then; he was feeling too keenly about his buddy, "Rosy," who had touched off the mine explosion that had cleared the way for the rest of the squad's advance.

Halpern looked wearily around the quiet, littered pews. But the cross above the altar remained in place and in the aisle, in front of the pews, knocked from its pedestal by the concussion of shell fire, standing upright, stood a statue of Christ. Glass and plaster fragments were everywhere, even on the altar and chancel floor.

For the first time in three days the knots inside Halpern began to loosen. He realized how tired he was. And the loss of a buddy overwhelmed him. Corporal Halpern lifted his eyes toward the altar and the sky above the shattered roof.

"Oh, God," he thought, "why—"

Suddenly Halpern laid his machine gun in a corner and walked outside to Lieutenant McBride.

In a small German town, at the end of World War II, amidst the rubble, there lay a broken statue. According to Tony Weitzel in Guideposts (1960), several American soldiers volunteered to fix it. After much diligent work, they still hadn't found two missing parts...and when the mended statue was unveiled, there stood Christ—without any hands. But at His feet there was a sign: "I have no hands. Won't you please lend me yours?"

"Lieutenant, while we're waiting, I want to round up ten fellows of our faith and say a prayer for Sergeant Rosenberg."

"Sure, Corporal. But why ten?"

"It's the Jewish prayer, 'Minchah.' According to Hebrew ritual it requires ten Hebrews."

The Corporal went off up the street among the rubble heaps and the little groups of men. When he returned, some minutes later, with a group of fellow GIs, the lieutenant was standing inside the church.

"Found them okay, Corporal?"

"No," said Halpern, "I'm short one man. Been through the whole battalion, but the rest are either killed or wounded. Don't know what I can do without the tenth either." The Corporal looked from his friends to the lieutenant.

"I don't think the Almighty would mind too much if one were absent," said Lt. McBride.

Corporal Halpern glanced toward the altar of the church and then up through the torn roof.

"I'll manage, Lieutenant," he said. "Come on fellows." The Corporal led the way down the church aisle and in silence arranged the eight men and himself in a circle before the chancel.

The lieutenant, at the back of the church, uncovered his head and then looked in surprise as he saw what Halpern was doing.

The Corporal gently lifted the statue of Christ and placed it in the circle between two of his buddies.

"Jesus was a Jew," he said softly. "He makes us ten."

Then he took out a little prayer book. "Repeat after me," he said to the quiet circle of his Jewish comrades. The prayer of "Minchah" rose solemnly...Sergeant Rosenberg would not be forgotten.

*Union Station, Washington, D.C.,
during World War II*

JUNE 1958

The Invasion *by Charles E. Wilson, former president of General Electric*

Thousands of people crisscrossed back and forth through Washington's Union Station that morning back in 1944. The high-ceilinged central waiting room was alive with a tense excitement that was reflected on the faces and in the quick footsteps of the wartime commuters coming to the capital. There was a sense of expectancy in the air. For weeks, months, one word had been in people's minds. It hung in the air, just out of reach: *Invasion.*

I stood there on this morning of June 6, 1944, waiting for a friend and scanning the faces of the commuters as they poured out of their trains and into the station. There was no announcement on the loudspeaker, no Extras were shouted, there was no visible source of the news: but suddenly the scurrying and the criss-crossing stopped, the loud hum of a thousand conversations ceased, the news passed from friend to friend, from stranger to stranger:

"What is it? What's happened?"

"The Invasion's begun...they're landing in Normandy."

A hush fell over the waiting room. I was aware of little things—the soft tread of the few people still walking, the stream of sunlight that fell into the waiting room as it does in a cathedral.

While I stood watching, it began. First it was a woman who, right there in the station, dropped to her knees and folded her hands; near her, a man knelt down. Then another, and another, until all around me people knelt in prayer before the hard wooden benches of Union Station.

What were we praying for that morning of the Invasion? For Jim or for Franz, or for Giovanni—or just for peace. Perhaps for no reason at all, except that in the hush we felt the need to pray.

The quiet lasted for no longer than a few minutes. Then, slowly, the woman rose to her feet. The man next to her rose, too, cleared his throat and walked off rapidly as if he felt a sudden embarrassment. Within seconds the station was alive with movement and talk again. But for those of us who witnessed the hush, Union Station will always have a special meaning: we were there on the day the railroad station in Washington, D.C., became a house of worship.

Why go to church? In an early Guideposts, a famous American gave some good reasons: To "cultivate the habit of feeling some responsibility for others"; to "listen to and take part in reading some beautiful passages from the Bible"; to "take part in singing some good hymns." The writer, who had achieved great fame on the battle field and in high office, concluded that a man should join a church "for the sake of showing his faith by his works." Who was the writer? Our 26th President, Theodore Roosevelt.

DECEMBER 1965

Black Sheep in the Flock *by Delorr Hayward, social worker*

His sermons were long and rambling and I don't believe he was much of an administrator. Until the crisis in our church, I'm sure that most of the congregation considered the Reverend Seth deJohn* a good and rather sweet man—but ineffectual.

When trouble nearly split our congregation, however, Pastor deJohn surprised a lot of us.

Millerton, Wisconsin—at the time of this story—was a small lumber town of a few thousand people. Community life centered about the church. The trouble started with the superintendent of our Sunday school who was a big boss at the mill. Next door to him lived a woman who was head of our Sunday school primary department.

A friendship developed between the two that caused a lot of talk as both were married and had families. Eventually, a delegation headed by Roger Barclay, the church finance chairman, came to see Pastor deJohn. I can just see the pastor, his face peaceful and serene, quietly greeting this group of determined men. Barclay opened the discussion.

"Reverend, there is an illicit relationship in this church...." He then detailed the situation.

"Haven't you come to some pretty strong conclusions on a very small amount of evidence?" the preacher asked calmly.

"You'll not get much evidence in a case like this," Barclay continued. "What matters is that parents in this church are scandalized. They'll

*Names throughout have been changed.

not send their children to Sunday school unless both parties are removed from the church."

"Asking them to resign their Sunday school responsibilities is one thing," replied the preacher. "Insisting that they leave the church is something else."

"We're here to tell you that the congregation won't tolerate their presence," snapped Barclay.

Pastor deJohn rose and walked to the window of his sparsely furnished church office. He looked outside for a moment, then faced the men.

"This is God's house," he said firmly. "As long as I am minister here no one will be denied entrance regardless of who he is or what he has done." Then his voice softened. "God will remove this problem in His own good time and in His own way, and no one will be hurt. We just have to be sure that our hearts are right, and to pray."

Barclay and his cohorts walked out and soon spread the word that the pastor was being "wishy-washy." The next Sunday, church attendance was half of normal. Meanwhile Seth deJohn was saddened when neither of the accused Sunday school officials sought him out nor appeared at church. The pastor was worried about this obvious declaration of guilt.

Before his sermon, Seth deJohn invited the members of his church to join him on Monday evening "to pray for the people and needs of this church."

Just as the sun rises every day, so do Guideposts readers raise their spirits in daily worship. Many make Daily Guideposts *part of this daily devotion. In 1977, a Guideposts editor, Fred Bauer, wrote the first collection of devotionals, one for each day of the year. In 1979, Marjorie Holmes, Arthur Gordon, Sue Monk Kidd, Dr. and Mrs. Peale and many other noted authors also began to write for* Daily Guideposts. *It continues to be a popular offering…this book containing 365 little stories of God's great goodness.*

Criticism of the minister was growing but, out of curiosity, nearly 20 people appeared. "I find no place in the Bible where Jesus said that we would be able to eliminate sin and trouble in this world," Pastor deJohn began. "He does say that He is the way and the light. We have a situation that is splitting our church. So I am asking you to join with me every Monday night to pray specifically for the people in our church."

The pastor reached into his pocket. "I have here a list of the members of our church—150 in all. These are people who have taken vows of allegiance to Jesus Christ. They belong to Him. Yet none of us is perfect. We make mistakes. We forget our vows. We envy; we hate; we gossip; we sin in so many ways. Yet despite our weakness, God loves us.

"I feel that God is here with us tonight. And where He is, there is power. For the rest of this hour I am going to read aloud, slowly, the names of the members of this church. Let us pray for each one in turn. Let us pray that God's love will surround him—or her—that good comes to each person."

He began the reading: "Mr. & Mrs. Harvey Allen....Harvey was out of work for two months recently and his son Ted has a bad case of asthma." And so every person in the congregation was prayed for including the two Sunday school officials.

In the three weeks that followed, more and more people appeared at the Monday night gathering. But Barclay, as head of the opposition to Seth deJohn, was indignant.

"We have a do-nothing pastor!" he said to his friends. "Prayer is not enough. Unless he takes stronger action, Seth deJohn will have to go. If our church board won't demand the resignation of these Sunday school officials, then they will have mine." Barclay knew that at least 50 others would follow him.

Roger Barclay decided to bring the situation to a head at the monthly board meeting. But if Pastor deJohn sensed the impending crisis, it was not apparent in his face the night of the meeting. He spoke warmly to each of the members as they entered. Then he opened the meeting with a prayer.

"Lord, we have much to be thankful for in our church," he began. "We have dedicated men and women who have a deep desire to serve You. I am grateful for Roger Barclay and the keen financial mind he brings to our affairs…and for John Stowe and his fine singing voice in our choir...."

The pastor offered up each member present by name to the Lord in a prayer of praise and thanksgiving.

The meeting proceeded quickly through routine matters to new business. Roger Barclay cleared his throat and rose to his feet. He looked at the pastor. Seth deJohn looked back with warmth, yes, even with affection. The two men faced each other. There was a total silence in the room. A very strange silence.

"There is a matter concerning the church that has disturbed me very much," said Barclay. "When I came to the church tonight I was prepared to ask for some drastic action. But

Rev. Raymond Knowles of Liberal, Kansas, remembered his grandfather well (Guideposts 1961). Every Sunday morning, rain or shine, the old man would attend services at the local Baptist church—even though he couldn't hear a word. He'd grown deaf with age. Knowles once asked him, "Grandpa, why do you keep on going to church when you can't hear what the preacher says?" "Because," the old man replied, "I want people to know whose side I'm on." That was his witness.

perhaps you just don't handle problems in church the same way you would in business. What I'm saying is that I have concluded that being a Christian is a lot harder than I once thought it was."

Then Roger Barclay sat down; the power of love and prayer had brought about a change in him. And from that moment the church was stronger and more united than ever.

Weeks later, the Sunday school superintendent was fired from his job at the mill. He took a lesser job in another town and moved his family there. The other family involved later

moved away, too, but the families were kept intact; another answer to Seth deJohn's prayer.

This story occurred some years ago, but I have used the principle involved many times— at business, in my home, among friends, with neighbors. And when I hear about the bitterness and divisiveness in so many churches today, I want to tell them about Pastor deJohn and frame for them his words as a guide for church disputes:

"If our hearts are right, God will remove this thing in His own good time and in His own good way, and no one will be hurt."

FEBRUARY 1967

How To Get More Out of Church *by Norman Vincent Peale, editor-in-chief*

1. Go with a sense of anticipation. Have a smile ready for everyone. Church should not be a place of gloom.
2. Plan to arrive at least 15 minutes early so that you will enter church relaxed, with time for some meditation.
3. Avoid conversation.
4. Pray for the needs of all those about you: family, friends, strangers, ushers, choir, the minister.
5. Try to eliminate any feelings you might have of criticism, ill will or resentments. Such emotions block the flow of spiritual power.
6. Go, expecting to find the answer to some

need of your own. Be ready to find it in the words of the hymn, the Scripture, a prayer or the sermon.
7. If it is hard for you to focus on God, think of a beautiful and peaceful scene of nature. God created it. How great and wonderful He is! To make God seem more personal, picture Jesus looking at you with outstretched hands of love and welcome.
8. Expect something exciting to happen to your spiritual life—or to someone else's— every Sunday morning. If you believe it will happen and pray for it to happen, it will happen.

Do you see people at church whom you don't really know? Are there parishioners whom you might be able to help in some way? Then it's time for a Recognition Day (Guideposts 1983), a day set aside—perhaps one Sunday a month—to single out individual members of the congregation. Just pin photos, along with brief descriptions of these folk in a central place—like the vestibule. Then watch as your church family draws closer!

SEPTEMBER 1951

The Mystery of the Crumpled Notepaper *by George H. Straley, journalist*

The sexton of the big city church was frankly puzzled. Every week for several months he had been finding a sheet of blue-lined notepaper, crumpled into a small tight wad, lying in a corner of the same lonely rear-row pew.

For some time he had attached no significance to the find; people were always leaving odd things in a church—handbags, spectacle cases, chewing gum. Once he had found a pair of unused theater tickets for a not-quite-proper show.

But one Monday morning he smoothed out one of the little wads of paper and read several pencilled words, written one under the other like a shopping list: Clara—ill; Lester—job; this month's rent.

After that, the sexton began looking for the paper wads. They were always there, after every Sunday morning service. He opened them all and read them. Then he began to watch for the person who sat in that particular corner of the pew.

It was a woman, he discovered—middle-aged, plain but kind-faced, unassuming. She was always alone. The sexton sought out the rector, told him what he had observed, and handed him the collection of note sheets. The rector read the cryptic words thoughtfully, furrowing his brow.

On the next Sunday he contrived to greet the woman at the church door as she was leaving, and asked her kindly if she would wait for him a moment in the vestry. In the privacy of that room he showed her the creased pages of blue-lined notepaper, and inquired gently if they had any meaning for the church.

Tears welled in the woman's eyes. She hesitated, then said softly:

"They have meaning for me. You'll think it's silly, I guess—but sometime ago I saw a sign among the advertising posters in a streetcar. It said, 'Take your troubles to church with you.' My troubles are written on those pieces of paper. I wrote them down during the week and brought them here on Sunday mornings—and left them. I felt that God was taking care of them."

"God is taking care of them," the rector said softly, "and I shall ask Him to keep on doing so. Please continue to bring your troubles here."

On his way out of the church the rector paused to pick up the freshly wadded note that had been left there that morning. Smoothing it out, he saw that it contained three words: "John—in Korea."

Why Don't We…do as Marilyn Morgan's church does on Balloon Sunday? (Guideposts 1984.) Once a year, helium balloons are handed out after the Sunday service. Each person composes a prayer on an adhesive tag and then attaches the tag to the balloon string. Singing, the congregation heads outside and together lets the balloons go. Heavenward, the prayer balloons fly. As Marilyn says, "It's a simple ceremony, reminding us in a vivid way that God needs to receive messages from us, His children."

SEPTEMBER 1977

The Fern *by Isabel Champ, writer*

There were hundreds of other ferns in the area, each rooted and nourished by the rich forest loam. But I noticed only one. Not because it was lacelike and exquisite and freshly green and trim—although it was all of these.

But because it was clinging to a bare, craggy rock that stubbornly jutted a frowning and sullen face at the wooded area around it.

I suppose I noticed this particular tender little fern because I'd been thinking about Lillian and it reminded me of her. "Such a sweet little lady. I can't understand how she puts up with that husband of hers. And Bill is just like that rock—stubborn and frowning and sullen."

And just as hard…

I'd said to her once, "Lillian, why don't you accept the fact that Bill will never be interested in spiritual things. Wouldn't it be easier if you gave up that dream of yours that he'll sometime sit beside you in the pew?"

"No…" she answered. "I think quietly loving—like God does with me—will eventually win him over. Now don't worry about me. I'll just 'hang in there' in the meantime."

"'Hang in there' is a good way to put it," I said to myself. "Bill's giving her about as much nourishment as that rock is giving that fern."

While I rested on a moss-covered log nearby, I kept thinking about the woodland plant with its new tendrils uncurling like fiddle necks. "It's so tender, I could bruise it with a touch. I just hope Bill's attitude doesn't bruise Lillian and leave her scarred. But she and the fern are alike…they're both getting strength from an unseen source."

I wasn't the only one who had such feelings about Bill. Hundreds of others, rooted and nourished by rich church fellowship, often said of him, "He's the hardest man we know."

Before continuing my woodsy walk, I took a last look at that hard, jagged rock. It wasn't until then that I noticed…

The little fern had cracked that rock.

Why Don't We…do as many churches have done, enacting the parable of the talents? In Guideposts (1984), Rolf Gompertz told of a California church where each member took $10 from the Sunday collection plate—$2,000 in all—and was charged to multiply these "talents." Members then put the money to work by making and selling homemade items. Three months later, the disbursed $2,000 was returned as $8,000! God's house had profited and, in turn, parishioners had expanded their personal talents.

NOVEMBER 1977

And I Almost Didn't Go *by Ruth Heaney, teacher*

I didn't want to go to church last Sunday. Something was amiss with me, but I didn't know what.

At the last minute, though, I dragged myself there only to find that I was sitting two pews behind the Schubert family. I knew the Schuberts casually, but everyone in town was well aware of the tragedy in their lives. Most of us already had donated money to the Jeanne Schubert Fund, for the medical costs the family was faced with were crushing. Many of us were praying daily for the little girl.

In my own prayers I always pictured Jeanne as she had been only a year before. I had been on my way to the compost pile with some vegetable parings when the sturdy nine-year-old had swooped into my driveway on her two-wheeler. Her cheeks were flushed from pedaling, and the contrast of that pinkness against her fair skin and dark hair was striking.

"Hi," she called out. "Do you have a baby?"

"Not anymore," I answered. "They're all grown up. Why?"

"I just love babies. I was hoping you would have one I could play with." With a wave of her hand, Jeanne whirled away again, leaving me feeling as though I'd just had a visit from Rose Red of my fairy-tale days!

Now, a year later, Jeanne was there in church with her family. The left side of her body appeared to be paralyzed; her neck could scarcely support her head. The dark hair was beginning to grow in after brain surgery.

My eyes filled with tears as I watched the little girl sag against her father. Cradling her in one arm, he stroked her hair and whispered to her softly. Once, he pulled a handkerchief from his pocket and tenderly touched the corners of her mouth where saliva had formed. From time to time, Jeanne's brother and sister peeked at her with loving concern.

The sermon that morning was a strong one, but I found my eyes returning again and again to the Schuberts. Why had this shadow come over such a wonderful Christian family?

The ushers passed the offering plates and carried them to the altar. The congregation rose for the doxology, and that's when Dot Schubert caught my attention. While I fought back tears of despair, Dot was standing erect, between her two younger children, singing clearly and firmly, "Praise God from Whom all blessings flow, praise Him all creatures here below…"

I looked more carefully at the Schuberts. This was not *tragedy* I was witnessing. This was triumph. Their God—and mine—was with them. They knew it and they were grateful. But I, on the other hand, who had so many blessings in life, could only express gratitude when things went well. The minute things went wrong I started questioning God.

Had I been drawn to church last Sunday for a reason? I don't know. I do know that by being there I was blessed. I not only heard a beautiful sermon from the pulpit; I saw one in a pew.

Prayer Fellowship at Guideposts was not the product of an executive decision or committee recommendation—it was simply always there. Right from the first day, we have prayed. We pray for one another, for our work, and for you out there. At 9:45 A.M. each Monday, we continue to meet in our offices in New York City and Carmel to pray about any special needs that you might have. If you or someone you care about has a problem, write to us: Prayer Fellowship, Guideposts, Carmel, New York 10512.

JULY 1968

A View of Glory *by Annette Daniel, Sunday school teacher*

Each Sunday morning in the primary and kindergarten departments of our church school, we allow about 15 minutes for "free-wheeling" after the children have heard the Bible story and recited the memory verse. The youngsters help themselves to crayons and paper, modeling clay, scissors and garden magazines, or they take turns painting with water colors at the easel. We make no effort to direct them or to suggest any subjects, and we reserve our compliments until the work is completed.

Tommy Fleming, a six-year-old, is a young artist whose thoughts are long, long thoughts. One Sunday, after we had studied the memory verse, "And the glory of the Lord shone round about them," I watched—without appearing to—as Tommy drew a picture of a church. People were going in and out. Tulips bloomed all along the front of the building. The church steeple was high, and from it came brilliant rays of gold, orange and red. When the picture was finished and I dared to ask what the rays represented, Tommy answered, "Well, this is God's house a'course, but you can't see God. All you can see is His glory."

Guideposts Prayer Fellowship, 1951

JUNE 1978

Our Friend the Trapper *by Van Varner, editor*

He came into our lives as thousands of people do each year, through a letter addressed to our Guideposts Prayer Fellowship.

"I would like your prayers," he said in a letter on lined yellow paper from Belleville, Pennsylvania, in February 1976. "I live alone on a little place along the foot of the mtns. in a beautiful valley of the Amish country. I see horses and buggies every day and mules and horses on the farms and roads. You see, my Amish farmer friends live the old-time way. I have not been well and have had several falls on this ice. I've also had some trouble getting extra income, as I get a disability check and it is not enough with everything so high in price. I tithe every amount that I am able to earn by hunting, fishing, trapping. If any of you hunt, fish, or trap, I wish you the best of luck.

A Friend,
Eugene Renninger"

That was our introduction. On Monday mornings after that as we sat around the long prayer table reading through stacks of prayer requests, we'd all stop if anyone said, "Ah! here's a letter from our friend the trapper." Then, here on the twenty-third floor of our Manhattan skyscraper, we'd put down our letters and listen, and let our friend the trapper take us away with him to a little farm where he and his parents and his grandparents before them planted crops "in signs"—signs of the zodiac. His letters were so descriptive that we could feel with him "the first snap of autumn," and go along with him "to hunt wild fox grapes for jelly" or "visit the old folks home to check on some groundhog trouble in their garden." Dozens of times we must have sat beside him in his car as he "hauled" his Amish farmer friends "to the eyeglass doctor" or "to the mule sales" or "to the vets for some stock medicine." Some of our voyages together took us back to the distant days of his boyhood when cattle were belled in the springtime and let loose to roam the free range. Then we'd wander back with him to the late fall as he "and an old uncle and his boy went out to find the lost cattle, walking the tops of mtns., and listening for the cowbells in the valleys and hollows and gaps..."

Advice from our friend the trapper came free and freely. "Ditney tea," he told us once, "gets the kidneys started. It is found only in the mtns." As for diarrhea: "Take two cups of raw cow's milk—must be right from the cow." And incidental information came bountifully. "Today I was lucky to find some fresh wild ginseng. It's a herb. You dig the roots and dry them, then sell. They are now about $80.00 a pound. Scarce in the mtns. and a dangerous job because of the rattlers and copperhead snakes. But it is a *thrill* to hunt out, and a healthy job..."

Though every morning he prayed to God after his Bible-reading, our friend always

Prayer Fellowship, 1983, including staffers (from left) Jack Haring, Naomi Lawrence, Eleanor Sass and Madeline Weatherford

made us feel that it was *our* prayers that were really doing the work for him:

"Fri. 20th had a cold, and my disability was bothering me. Have some back and spine trouble, you know, from accidents. This morning I was reading your booklet and all at once I had a strange feeling, so I looked up at the clock and it was a little after 15 to ten a.m., so I knew your prayers were getting through to me.

"Mon. 29th after dinner things started to change for me. I thought of your prayers for me. I was able to locate and buy two good milk goats very reasonable from a fine Christian farm girl. One looks like a show goat, a beautiful spotted goat, and fresh the first time May 17th. This goat gives around five qts. of milk a day, the best I ever heard of for a young goat first time fresh. Thank you. By the way, read Proverbs. Chapt. 27, verse 27."

We did. "And thou shalt have goats' milk enough for thy food," the Bible said.

"The old timer who told me about that verse," he added, "was a Forest Ranger in the beautiful mtns. of Licking Creek and Black Log. I used to meet him and his Dutch helper when I was bounty trapping. I would stop and eat my lunch with him, mostly beside a sand spring. The sand boils up out of these cold clear pure springs. I wish you Folks could drink of these wonderful clear cold pure waters. It makes me thirsty for a drink just thinking about it."

Sometimes our friend presented his problems to us. "For many years I brought all the coons and foxes in alive (unhurt) and sold them for re-stocking in places where there

were no farms. There was a lot of damage to the farmers—sweetcorn patches, also fruit crops, chickens, gardens. But last fall everything was protected, even the varmint and wild animals. I could not live trap or sell any. Did help two farmers, but had to turn all animals loose in the mtns. (no pay). So pray that we will again have laws fair and honest to all, this coming year, 1977."

And sometimes he asked for our advice. "I do not smoke. Don't drink and I never seen any dope and I don't gamble. But for some time I've had an urge to buy a 50-cent Penna. lottery ticket. The I.G.A. store owner, a young fellow, says it is for a good cause. And if I won I could buy the mtn. farm I've always wanted. What do you think?"

We can't recall what we wrote back, but perhaps our prayers were more effective than we ourselves realized, for his eventual lottery purchases, netted him "three lucky ones to mail in for the million dollar drawing and a $5.00 cash, lucky ticket, so I thought it was time to stop."

Lottery or no lottery, win or lose, there was to be no mountain farm. The time to stop was coming closer than he or any of us knew.

Four days before Christmas last year, a letter came in bearing his holiday greetings to us all, and, as always, his thanks for our prayers.

"Well, we had four inches of snow Sun. night. Mon. morning it was beautiful in this mtn. farm valley. The trees, bushes, everything was covered with a wet snow. Wish I could have

Worship Service—A Prayer by Alma Hendrix McNatt

Merciful Heavenly Father,
When there is a need for teaching, teach through me.
When there is a need for a message, speak through me.
When there is a need for love, love through me.
When there is a need for understanding, listen through me.
When there is a need for counseling, advise through me.
Whenever prayer is needed, pray through me.
When a helping hand is needed, reach through mine.

had a picture of it for you city Folks. A friend called me in the forenoon and asked if I wanted to go for a sleigh ride. Of course I said yes. Well, he come with a nice driving horse in the sleigh. He is an Amish boy, and we put my string or strap of big brass sleigh bells on the horse. We took an eight-mile ride with lots of sleigh bell music. These old brass bells of mine must be around 150 years old, and loud and clear ringing; 25 brass bells and all a different tone. It sure was a wonderful ride. Brought back memories of the good old days when all the teams and horses had bells on in the winter. When I was young there used to be all bobsleds and sleigh travel in the winter and all used bells. (I had a bobsled ride on Wens. 14th).

"Well, I had a bad sick spell from early Oct. till around Thanksgiving. I lost a lot of weight, was awful weak, but live alone, so had to keep going. Got my kidneys started with mtn. Ditney tea and was able to go to the Doc. Doc told me the whole body was infected and poisoned. I had a close call. Things are pretty wild here. We have seven bears and a bobcat on the mtn. Am getting ready to trap foxes and coons in Jan...." Then, from McVeytown, Pennsylva-

nia, we received this letter written on January 26, 1978.

"Dear Friends. I am writing to let you know about my brother Gene Renninger. He was sick all fall but did some trapping. He ate Christmas dinner with the neighbors and helped do the barn work, went home, was sick all night and went to the hospital about 2:45. As soon as they laid him down he died. Thought I would write to tell you.
                    Mrs. Evenlyn Brunner"

It is now Monday morning again. The clock says that it is a little past 15 minutes to ten. We're here, as usual, secretaries and editors and art and copy people, all gathered around the long table high up in our New York skyscraper. Sure, we're city folks mostly, but luckier ones than most, for we still hear the music of big brass sleigh bells, still taste water bubbling up from clear cold sand springs, still feel the dangerous thrill of finding wild fresh ginseng in rattler territory.

We have these things because you gave them to us, old friend. Does it please you to know that we're still praying for you? Because we are.

In Times of Trouble

Earthquakes, floods, hurricanes, fires—such disasters are often written about in the pages of Guideposts. The reason for presenting these often violent stories, however, is not just for their exciting action; it is to show that in times of trouble, no matter how small or great, there is always a greater Power present. And one person who certainly knows this is Lois Main.

Lois is a middle-aged housewife who lives in the small mid-California town of Coalinga, situated at the edge of the San Diablas Mountains. On one peaceful Sunday in May, 1983, she'd just returned from a stimulating three-day spiritual retreat, during which she'd become certain that praying for other people was her gift and her calling. That very night, she had a terrible premonition. "Pray for My children," she seemed to hear God tell her. Lois knew what she had to do. She must pray for the people of Coalinga.

She rose from her bed, dressed and walked through the town's deserted streets. In front of every house she passed, in front of every store, she prayed for the occupants. For hours she walked, stopped, prayed.

The next day, May 2, at 4:42 p.m., an earthquake jolted Coalinga. Walls collapsed, roofs came down, whole buildings crumbled. Much of the town lay in ruins. Lois Main's own house was virtually destroyed.

And yet, in this town of 6,757 people, there was not a single fatality. Clearly, God had been present.

At Guideposts, we try to look deeper into the meaning of the disasters that are visited upon us from time to time. We always hope that these true stories will excite the reader, and that in every one of them there is a lesson to be learned: Even in earthquake, wind and fire, God's voice can be heard. In the aftermath, His love can be felt.

Elaine St. Johns, 1955

NOVEMBER 1953

The Story Behind the Story *by Elaine St. Johns, editor*

The terse voice of my city editor came over the phone, waking me from a deep sleep. "A little girl has fallen into a well:...Get up there quick."

So I left my small daughter, tucked safely between white sheets, and drove across the dark city of Los Angeles to San Marino. It was more than 48 hours later before I kicked off muddy shoes in the city room of the *Los Angeles Mirror* and faced my typewriter.

I had all the facts, yet I had a stubborn feeling that something else was there—but I couldn't find it in my notes. Then I made the newspaperman's prayer: "God, give me the vision to see what had actually happened. Give me the wisdom to report it accurately."

For hours nothing came. It is hard to clear a vision that is blinded by emotion and tears...

At 4:45 on a Friday afternoon in April 1949, a laughing little three-year-old child was playing with her small friends in a vacant lot beside her home. Suddenly, she disappeared; she had fallen into a long-abandoned well. Fifteen minutes later, her mother called the police and reported that her daughter was wedged in the rusty old shaft. Half an hour later, firemen were pumping oxygen into the opening. At the end of an hour, efforts to raise Kathy with a rope failed and at six o'clock power equipment began digging a parallel hole.

During this brief time, the girl called back bravely to the familiar world above her. She answered those she loved, always with courage. "Yes, I'm all right." She wanted to please.

"Will you try to grab hold of the rope, Kathy?"

"I am, *I am!*" Then her voice ceased, but she had spoken long enough to convince those above her that she was unhurt by her fall.

By the time I reached the lot, it was no longer vacant. Under a blaze of lights, men and machines had begun to battle with Mother Earth. Men by the hundreds began to volunteer their help. Circus midgets, living in the vicinity, arrived and risked being lowered by their feet into the crumbling old shaft...there were Boy Scouts, long thin men, acrobats and engineers, firemen and contractors. There were men with dark skins, with red hair, with fierce accents and waving hands. All were drawn by the human drama, wanting to help.

By daybreak, people throughout the world were invisible spectators. Newspapers, radio and television put aside war and international news to headline the story of a desperate rescue attempt.

Bill Yancey, 38-year-old contractor, was one of the Navy's underwater demolition men who cleared the water of mines on the fortified beaches long before the first troops attempted landing. Bill was the first man into the rescue shaft, the last man out. At one stretch he sweated five back-breaking feet of earth out of that hole in an hour and a half.

Elaine St. Johns was a cityside reporter for the Los Angeles Mirror *when she sent her first story to us in 1950. She's been our West Coast Editor ever since. And true to family tradition, this daughter of newspaper woman and author Adela Rogers St. Johns, is an indefatigable writer. Once, two of her books were on the best-seller list at the same time and another,* Prayer Can Change Your Life *(written with Dr. William R. Parker), remains a constant favorite.*

An ex-sand hogger and boilermaker left his home in the San Fernando Valley the minute he heard of the accident. In spite of the stabbing pain of a hernia this man, Whitey Blickensderfer, stayed at his dangerous job until he collapsed and was taken to the hospital.

The father of five children, 25-year-old Clyde Harp, sneaked out of his own home to volunteer his help. "I didn't want to worry my wife," he said, "but I have five good reasons at home for lending a hand at the digging."

There were so many more. The parallel hole reached the 57-foot level early Saturday morning and a lateral tunnel was started. By Saturday night, a steel casing had been completed in the new shaft but workers hit a sand pocket and water flowed into the tunnel. Pumping began desperately.

Seldom had so much prayer power been focused on one person and on one rescue. Exhausted men continued their dangerous work against water, sand and cascades of rock. And what was happening around the world?

Men on a lonely watch on a ship far at sea followed the progress and took up a collection. Hard-coal miners in Denver had offered their help. A neighbor brought a chocolate cake— the only offering she could think of—to the family. One unidentified man brought over 700 gallons of hot coffee and stacks of doughnuts for the workers.

Meanwhile, sitting side by side, in a parked car during most of these frantic operations were the girl's white-faced mother and father. Beneath the giant machines and rigging, the bright lights, the microphone booming directions, lay a tiny figure whom none of these gallant rescuers had ever seen. Was all well with her? Was there water where she lay? Did she still know moments of consciousness and fear?

Fifty-three hours following the accident— after a total expenditure of a quarter of a million dollars—Bill Yancey was lowered into the rescue shaft on a bucket fastened to the end of a cable. The trapped girl's own doctor, young Robert J. McCullock, clad in a blue jacket, aviator's cap and dungaree trousers, began his descent, while the world above waited.

Then the answer came up. Men had lost. Kathy Fiscus, a little girl whom the whole world came to know, was dead. She had gone shortly after she last spoke. And that was all of the facts I had to report.

But not the end of the story. I knew there was something that would explain the frantic, futile fight.

I looked around the city room. There were the usual reports coming in: wars, strikes, families in trouble, racial problems.

And suddenly I saw the contrast.

There on the vacant lot, in San Marino, the whole world had united, for a few hours, over the life of one child.

Men had not lost. A little girl got people to loving one another. No distinction of color, race or creed, rich or poor, rose to mar the efforts of men and women who fought to save one made in His image.

That was the story. That was the miracle of Kathy Fiscus.

Headline—January 10, 1953:

Helpless Enterprise Drifts After Towline Efforts Fail

Rough Weather Interferes —List Grows Worse

JANUARY 1957

Storm Lashed Prayer *by Mrs. Kurt Carlsen, housewife*

Our Christmas joy came to an end abruptly on December 25th, five years ago. Until then we'd had a happy season in spite of the fact that the children—Sonia, 11, and Karen, 7—and I were all alone. The day before, my husband had sent us a Christmas message from his ship, the *Flying Enterprise,* and we were content. Shortly after church, however, the telephone rang.

"Have you heard about the storms, Agnes?" a friend asked me.

"No. What storms?"

"In the Atlantic. The *Flying Enterprise* is in trouble."

I thanked her and hung up. Then I called directly down to the owners, the Isbrandtsens, and learned that it was true.

"What's the matter, Mother?" Karen wanted to know when I hung up again. I explained, and I tried to tell her everything was going to be all right; but it's hard to keep children from knowing how you really feel.

I was worried. And I felt helpless. I turned on the radio and learned that Kurt was in the worst December storm the North Atlantic had known in 22 years. Waves were 60 feet high. The *Flying Enterprise*'s hull had been damaged. No details. The ship carried 50 passengers and crewmen. That was all.

The word spread rapidly. Friends came over to our house. Newspaper people began to call. The telephone rang constantly.

Some of the calls I welcomed, like the times

friends telephoned to say they were praying for us. It gave me a warm feeling, and I was reminded of the Danish expression *Enighed gör staerk,* which means "In unity there is strength."

Enighed gör staerk. I didn't think much about the words again until later that night after my friends had returned to their homes. I was alone, and yet I was not alone. My friends weren't with me; and yet I could feel their support. They had left, and yet I was still united with them and took strength from them.

Almost immediately, the feeling of helplessness left me. There *was* something I could do for Kurt, out there in the storm. I could support him, just as my friends were supporting me.

That night I began a special prayer.

"Enighed gör staerk," I prayed. "In unity there is strength, Kurt."

I pictured myself in the storm with Kurt, and I prayed that I could lend him my strength. I felt myself with him, giving him encouragement as he had to make his decisions, and I had the strong feeling he was being helped by my presence, 3,000 miles away!

The next morning, I asked friends to join me in this support of Kurt and his fellowmen aboard the *Enterprise.* The storm continued to rage, and the *Flying Enterprise* began to take water into her number three hold. She listed heavily to port. Kurt sent out an S.O.S. When the rescue ships arrived, he asked them to

The prayer bond between seafaring men and the Lord has always been strong and in the historic seaport city of Gloucester, Massachusetts, it is acknowledged in a public way. On the last Sunday in June, a crowd gathers around the waterfront statue of a fisherman to ask God's protection for the port's seafarers. The Archbishop of Boston leads the people in prayers, then tours the harbor in a police boat, blessing each fishing vessel. Why public prayer? "Where two or three are gathered together in my name…"

come in as close as they could. Then, on December 29, he took one last survey of the cracked hull, of the water in number three hold, and he made his decision. He ordered passengers and crew to abandon ship.

During that day, each passenger and each crewman aboard the *Enterprise* stood at the rail, took his turn, and jumped overboard. One by one they were hauled out of the sea, cold and weak from the shock and the exposure. By nightfall there was only Kurt left. The Coast Guard called over to him to jump, too. Kurt's answer immediately became front-page news.

"My duty is with the ship," he said. "I'll stay with her and bring her in. Or I'll watch her go down."

Kurt's decision was deeply rooted in maritime law. If the *Enterprise* were abandoned, but were later salvaged, Kurt's company would have lost all claim to her. If she were never completely abandoned, Kurt's company would always have a claim to her. Kurt felt it was his duty to stay with the ship until he was sure there was no chance of salvage.

Overnight, Kurt became a world-known figure. People watched as his ship listed at 60°. They waited eagerly for news about the storm. The *Enterprise*'s rudder now stuck helplessly out of the water. She was tossed at will by the waves. Her cargo shifted. She lost her generators. Kurt was without heat and light. He warmed his hands over a candle. He slept, when he could, cramped up against a bulkhead so he wouldn't be washed overboard. He had no food, except some soggy pound cake and tea. He was always wet, always cold, always in imminent danger of death.

Kurt remained like that for six days. Then, on January 2, the sea calmed. Three hundred miles away, in England, a salvage tug, the *Turmoil*, decided to make for the *Enterprise*. Hopes rose. On January 4, the *Turmoil* reached Kurt and drew up close alongside. A young man named Kenneth Dancy jumped aboard the *Enterprise*, and together the two men tied a cable on to the stern of the old freighter. The *Turmoil* began the long, slow, awkward trip back to port.

Then, on January 8, when the *Turmoil* was only 57 miles from port, the headlines said new storms brewing off the coast of England.

By now the *Enterprise* was almost on her side. She listed 80°, and any big wave would roll her on over. Pictures showed Kurt holding on to the side of the ship with such a precarious grip that our prayers were not, now, to bring the ship to port, but just to keep the men from harm and to give Kurt the strength to do what he felt he had to do.

Once, we were glad we were out there with him—when the radio told of a wave that broke over the stern and hit Kurt and he disappeared from sight. A moment later, he came up smiling and dripping and holding on for dear life to the bulkhead that was now a deck.

It seemed clear to me, now, that the *Enterprise* was not going to make it. I only wished Kurt would leave the ship before it was too late, and on January 9, fate stepped in to make matters still worse.

The tug's towline broke.

The day America prayed…May 19, 1780. As the Connecticut State Council met one morning, the sky turned black. Many members panicked, seeing this as the onset of Judgment Day, fulfilling Amos 8:9: "I will cause the sun to go down at noon, and I will darken the earth in the clear day." But Colonel Abraham Davenport prayed, then halted the flight, saying, "The Day of Judgment is close at hand, or it is not. But if it is, I wish to be found at my post of duty!" In prayer he knew, as we know now, God's assuring love.

Kurt and Kenneth were once again adrift in the open ocean on a sinking ship. The storm was getting worse. They knew the end was near. They crawled out slowly onto the funnel.

They waited yet awhile. Water inside the *Enterprise* was mounting and compressing the air that was still inside the ship. Then, suddenly, the door to the bridge exploded open. Kurt knew the time had come. He stood poised. Water rushed down the funnel. There was a great sucking, slurping sound. The old freighter gave one last shudder.

Kenneth and Kurt jumped.

They were in the water only a few moments before the *Turmoil* picked them up. Together they stood on the tug's deck and watched. Slowly the *Flying Enterprise* settled into the water. A reporter tried to interview Kurt right then. "I cannot," Kurt said. "Please do not ask me too hard. I cannot tell you how I feel at seeing her go."

It was over.

On January 12, Kurt returned to New York. There were parades for him up Broadway and in our hometown of Woodbridge. We were all there, Kurt, Sonia, Karen and myself. It was exciting, but we wanted very much to get back home where just the four of us could see each other without having a thousand people around.

Hours later, we closed the door on the final visitor. We were alone, just the four of us. I fixed a little dinner, and we all sat down. It was our Christmas: late, but unusually happy. In the distance I heard church bells tolling, and suddenly tears came to my eyes because I thought how the bells could have been tolling for another reason. Kurt looked up and saw the tears.

"There's no need," he said. "We're together now."

"Yes," I said. "We're together."

"Sometimes I did not know where the next strength was to come from," he said. "But it was always there."

"Yes," I said, and listened for a moment to the church bells tolling.

And the tears came again. *Enighed gör staerk.* It had been our own Christmas miracle.

Alaskan earthquake, 1964

APRIL 1965

That Bad Good Friday *by Mrs. Lowell Thomas Jr., writer*

It began as such a happy day, Good Friday one year ago. The snow, which had been coming down for two days, let up suddenly; which meant that my husband Lowell could fly to Fairbanks, and get back in time for us to have all of Easter weekend together.

The children and I waved good-bye as he drove off to the airport, then shut the door quickly because it was still below freezing outside. About five o'clock, feeling lonesome for him, Anne, eight, David, six, and I went upstairs to watch TV. Anne and David were wearing blue jeans and cotton T-shirts; I had on a wool dress and nylon stockings. We took off our shoes so we could sit on the bed.

It was half an hour later that I heard a rumbling sound. Although we frequently hear a similar roaring—the firing of guns at a nearby Army base—I knew instantly that this was the sound of an impending earthquake.

I leaped up, called to the children to follow, and raced for the stairs. By the time we reached the front hall, the whole house was beginning to shake. We ran outside into the snow, David crying, "Mommy, I'm in bare feet!"

We were about 10 feet beyond the door when the world around us fell apart. We were flung violently to the ground, which was jolting back and forth with unbelievable force.

The hallway through which we had just run split in two. We heard the crashing of glass, the sound of splintering wood. In front of us, a great tree crashed full length onto the ground. Our garage collapsed with a sharp report.

Now the earth began breaking up and buckling all about us. Suddenly, between Anne and me a great crack opened in the snow. I stared in disbelief as the trench widened, apparently bottomless, separating me from my child. I seized the hand she stretched out to me in time to pull her across the chasm to my side.

By now the whole lawn was breaking up into chunks of dirt, rock, snow and ice. We were left on a wildly bucking slab; suddenly it tilted sharply, and we had to hang on to keep from slipping into a yawning crevasse. Though sobbing, Anne had the presence of mind to hang on by herself—thank God, for I was holding David with one hand, our bit of ground with the other.

Now the earth seemed to be rising just ahead of us. I had the weird feeling that we were riding backward on a monstrous Ferris wheel, going down, down toward the water (our house had stood on a high bluff overlooking Cook Inlet). When the worst of the rocking stopped, I looked around and saw that the entire face of the bluff had fallen to sea level. A few feet away, at the water's edge, lay the roof of our house.

All I could think of was that the water would rise as earth tumbled into it and we would be trapped. The cliffs above us were sheer, with great sections of sand and clay still falling.

Guideposts has always been family-minded, even with its authors.
Take the Lowell Thomases. Lowell Senior, was a Guideposter from
the very start, and we seemed to grow up with his son. As a college
student, Lowell Junior, wrote about a historic trip to Tibet with his
dad (1950) and, later, a year-long flying adventure in Asia and Africa
with his wife Tay (1956). And Tay herself continued the saga with
an account of the devastating earthquake that destroyed their home
in Alaska (1965). See below.

The children both were hysterical, crying and saying over and over, "We'll die! We'll die!" I realized we'd have to find a way up that cliff but the children were too frightened to walk.

I suggested that we say a prayer asking Jesus to take care of us and guide us. Both children stopped crying, closed their eyes and fervently pleaded with Him to come and help us. This had an extraordinary effect on them and on me, and we set out with the first real stirrings of hope.

The next 20 minutes were one great nightmare as we clambered up and down the great slabs of earth and snow, our bare feet aching and raw in the cold. I found a large tree leaning against the cliff and thought for a few moments that we might be able to shinny up it, but we gained only a few feet. We kept moving to the right: trying to avoid holes, which opened at our feet, and rubble still falling from the cliff.

Suddenly a man appeared above us. "Help!" we called to him. He shouted down that he would hunt for a rope, then disappeared. As we waited we were aware for the first time that we were soaked to the skin from lying in the snow; the children were shaking and their lips were blue.

At last, six or eight men appeared at the top of the cliff. One of them, a stranger to us, started down toward us, finding one less steep spot. The children threw their arms around him as he reached us. He took off his black wool jacket, put it around Anne, then boosted David into his arms and led us all back up along the rope.

At the top there was a steep, sheer rim, which I doubt I could have scaled by myself. But willing hands hauled us up and tucked us into a waiting car. When I turned to thank our rescuer, he had gone.

We were driven to the home of friends who lived well away from the devastated area. They wrapped us in blankets, but there was no heat in the house nor any way to make a hot drink.

The children were offered beds but refused to leave my side where I huddled with the others over the portable radio; they finally curled up in sleeping bags on the floor. Sleep for me was impossible until two questions were answered: had Fairbanks, where Lowell was, felt the quake, and how could we get word to him that we were all right?

The radio reported all the homes along our street destroyed, and it listed tremendous damage in the downtown area. We, living in Anchorage, watching it grow day by day, had felt personal pride in each new building that rose. Now the tally of damaged schools, stores and office buildings mounted by the hour.

There was a continuous stream of "Tell John his parents are at the Stewarts," or "The Johnson family wants to know the whereabouts of daughter Ann." It seemed an eternity to me before radio contact was reestablished with Fairbanks and we learned that it had felt merely a strong jolt. Planes were arriv-

Mrs. Lowell Thomas Jr. and children, 1964

ing from there with doctors and supplies, and I knew Lowell would be aboard one of them.

Then suddenly the announcer's voice said, "If anyone knows the whereabouts of Mrs. Lowell Thomas and family, please contact us immediately." I ran to the telephone and was so overwhelmed to find it working that I could hardly talk to the person who answered. But I got the essentials through, and just half an hour later, Lowell walked through the door.

Words cannot describe our reunion. The kids and I were tremendously relieved, but Lowell's emotions were those of a man who had not known for many hours whether his family was dead or alive.

Next morning, Easter Sunday, Lowell, Anne, David and I rose early. We put on the same clothes we had been wearing for two days: Anne, the coat provided by our unknown rescuer, far more meaningful to her than any Easter bonnet; David, a pair of pants too small to button; some men's corduroy trousers for me.

Many in the Easter congregation wore similar outfits and the air in the heatless church was so cold that our breaths hung white above us as we sang "Hallelujah!" But it was an Easter service to remember.

At the rear of the church, the minister had pinned two sheets of paper, one to be signed by the "haves"—those who had clothing and household goods to contribute—and one where the homeless could write down what they needed. At least 20 families there that morning had lost everything, yet as we left the church I saw that not one person had signed the "have not" list.

For what was there that we did not have? We had new gratitude for the gift of life and for the fact that, in one of history's worst earthquakes, loss of life had been as small as it had. We had a state to rebuild, with a new love for the word "Alaska" born the night we watched our neighbors rise to heroism. Above all, we had the Easter message ringing in our hearts.

For the first Christians, too, lived through a sorrowful Friday, a Friday when their dreams collapsed, their hopes lay in ruins, when by every earthly standard they had lost everything. And then on Sunday morning they were the first to whisper the news that has transformed every loss from that day on, the news that love had won, that God had the final word, that death was overcome, that He had risen.

Headline—March 30, 1973:

U.S. Forces Out of Vietnam; Hanoi Frees the Last P.O.W.

JULY 1973

The Secret of Our Survival *by Capt. James E. Ray, former POW*

"P*ssst.*"

I struggled upright on the damp pallet in my solitary cell to hear better. It had sounded like a whisper.

No, I must have been hallucinating. I slumped back, wondering how long it had been since my 105 Thunderchief had been shot down as we bombed a railroad bridge on the Hanoi–China supply line.

That was May 8, 1966. I tried to forget the weeks since, the endless interrogations, the torture that left me screaming in agony.

Now I wish I had gone down with the plane. Anything would be better than the desolation, the awful sense of guilt at writing a confession under torture, the aloneness.

There! I heard it again. Now an unmistakable, "Hey, buddy?"

I scrambled flat on the floor and peered through the crack under the door. I was in one of the many cells facing a walled courtyard. The whisper had come from the next cell. I whispered back. He introduced himself as Bob Purcell, another Air Force man. We waited as the guard passed and then began to converse.

Soon all the prisoners on that yard were whispering. We started by learning about each other, where we were from, our families. One day I asked Bob what church he went to.

"Catholic," he said. "And you?"

"Baptist."

Bob was quiet for a moment, as if my mention of church evoked deep memories. Then he asked, "Do you know any Bible verses?"

"Well, the Lord's Prayer," I answered.

"Everyone knows that."

"How about the twenty-third psalm?"

"Only a little."

I began whispering it. He'd repeat each line after me. A little later he whispered the entire psalm back to me.

Other prisoners joined in, sharing verses they knew. Through these contacts a fellowship grew among us. The others said that I shouldn't feel bad about "confessing" under torture. "We've all done it," they assured me. I didn't feel so alone anymore.

As the number of prisoners grew, two of us shared a cell. My first roommate was Larry Chesley, a Mormon from Idaho. Though we had a few differences of belief, our common denominators were the Bible and Jesus Christ, and we were able to share much Scripture.

For by now it had become vital to our daily existence. Often racked with dysentery, weakened by the diet of rice and thin soups, our physical lives had shrunk within the prison walls. We spent 20 hours a day locked in our cells. And those Bible verses became rays of light, constant assurances of His love and care.

We made ink from brick dust and water or drops of medicine. We'd write verses on bits of toilet paper and pass them behind a loose brick at the toilets.

It was dangerous to pass these on. Communication between cells was forbidden and a

freed POW James Ray on his way home, 1973

man unlucky enough to be caught passing a note would be forced to stand with his arms up against a wall for several days, without sleep.

But the urge to share developed inventiveness. One night I lay with my ear pressed against the wooden wall of my cell to hear *Thump…thump* as somewhere on the wall, cells away, a fellow POW tapped out in Morse code: "I will lift up my eyes unto the hills, from whence cometh my help." (Psalm 121:1)

He tapped out his name—Russ Temperly—and passed on the seven other verses in that psalm, which I scratched on the concrete floor with a piece of broken tile.

By 1968, more of us were squeezed together and for two years four of us lived in an eight-by-eight-foot cell. In this close proximity, even minor personality rubs could flare into violent explosions. For instance, one guy liked to whistle. Talk about getting on your nerves! Some of the verses that helped us bear with one another were from Romans: "Every man among you is not to think of himself more highly than he ought to think…." (12:3–5)

Only by following Christ's teachings in constant forgiveness, patience and understanding were we able to get along together. The whistler? We recommended a schedule for when he should whistle.

Two and a half years went by before I could write my parents. A year later, I was allowed to receive my first letter. In the meantime, we subsisted on letters written 2,000 years ago.

By late 1970, almost all of the American POWs had been moved to Ha Lo, the main prison in downtown Hanoi. Newspapers later called this the Hanoi Hilton; we called it Heartbreak Hotel.

Some 50 of us lived, ate and slept together in one large room. Thanksgiving came shortly after we moved in and we held a brief service. We all were surprised to find how many of the men knew Scripture, learned from those verses passed along in whispers, bits of paper and wall thumpings. We immediately made plans for a Christmas service. A committee was formed and started to work.

Bits of green and red thread decorated the walls, a piece of green cloth was draped like a tree. Our crèche was made of figures carved from soap rations or molded from papier-mâché of moistened toilet paper.

We pooled the verses we knew and we now had a "consensus Bible," written covertly on bits of paper. It was the only Bible we had. As we sat in silence, the reader began: "In those days a decree went out from Caesar Augustus that all the world should be enrolled…." A six-man choir sang *Oh Little Town of Bethlehem.*

He went on: "And she gave birth to her first born son and wrapped Him in swaddling clothes…." "Away in the manger no crib for His bed, our Little Lord Jesus lay down His sweet head…." sang the choir.

Once again, I was a youngster in Sunday school at the First Baptist Church. Time had rolled back for all of us grizzled men in prison pajamas as, with eyes shining and tears trickling through beards, we joined in the singing. Glinting in the light from the kerosene lamp was a cross made of silver foil.

Occasionally, the guards would knock on

American POWs leaving Hanoi, 1973

the door, ordering us not to sing; but they finally gave up. Our program continued into a communion service led by Air Force Lt. Tom Moe. A Lutheran, he sang his church's chants as Episcopalians, Methodists and men of other denominations bowed their heads together.

Later that night, after many months of our asking, the commander brought us a real Bible, the first any of us had seen in prison. He said we could keep it for one hour. We made the best of it. One of us read aloud the favorite passages called out by the others. We also checked some of our handwritten Scripture. Amazingly, we weren't far off.

We didn't see that King James version again for several months. Finally, after continual requests, one of us was allowed to go out and copy from it for "one hour" each week.

But when we'd start to copy, the interrogator would plant his elbow on the Bible for 15 minutes. Then, after he'd let us start, he'd ask mundane questions to distract us. I'd just ignore him and write as fast as I could. The next week, we'd have to return the previous week's copy work. They seemed to be afraid for us to keep the Scriptures, as if they sensed the spiritual help kept us from breaking.

From that, we learned a most important lesson. Bible verses on paper aren't one iota as useful as Scriptures burned into your mind where you can draw on them for comfort.

After five weeks, we didn't see the Bible again. But that had been enough time for us to memorize collectively the Sermon on the Mount, Romans 12, First Corinthians 13, and many of the psalms. Now we had our own "living Bible," walking around the room. By this time, too, we held Sunday worship services and Sunday school classes. Some of the "eat, drink and be merry" type fighter pilots took part; some of them contributing as much to the services as the guys who had always professed to be Christians.

We learned to rise above our surroundings, to overcome the material with the spiritual. In constantly exercising our minds, we developed teaching seminars in which we studied special subjects led by men experienced in various fields. These included learning Spanish, French, German, Russian. I particularly enjoy music and will never forget the music course.

Bill Butler, the leader of this program, drew a giant-sized piano keyboard on the floor with brick dust. Then, standing on a "key," one assistant would hum its note. Other assistants, up the keyboard, hummed each note of the chord which was being demonstrated, while Bill explained how chord progression works.

Two years passed this way at Heartbreak Hotel, years of continuing degradation, sickness, endless hunger and never knowing whether we'd see home again. But instead of going mad or becoming animals, we continued to grow as a community of men, sustaining one another in compassion and understanding.

For as one of the verses I heard thumped out on the wall one night said: "Man does not live by bread alone, but by every word that proceeds out of the mouth of the Lord." (Deuteronomy 8:3)

His Word became our rock.

When Major General Jerry Curry learned that a battalion was trapped by Viet Cong, fellow officers said the soldiers were beyond saving (Guideposts 1981). But Curry called for a horseshoe barrage, a screen of artillery fire to permit escape through the horseshoe's open end. The battalion officer asked by radio where the opening would be. The enemy was eavesdropping so Curry said, "Remember when Jesus was born? And a star came up?" That's the direction to run." Shared faith pointed the way to safety.

APRIL 1980

The Cross That Came Back *by Jeremiah Denton*

When our nation has a confrontation with another nation and our citizens are maltreated or abused, it's very easy to despise our adversaries and condemn them all, without exception. And yet, whenever I'm tempted to do that, I remember something that happened years ago when I was a prisoner of war in North Vietnam.

In the fortress-prison where I was confined, the most reliable way we prisoners could communicate with one another was by tapping in code (like Morse code) to neighboring cells. Each covert "conversation" ended with a tapped "GBU" (God Bless You). But our requests for church services were denied, and every sign of religion was ruthlessly destroyed.

I had a small cross that meant a lot to me. It had been made by a fellow prisoner of war—out of bamboo strands from the pallet he used for a bed. Making it had been a great risk for him; getting it to me surreptitiously was a great risk for both of us.

I knew the North Vietnamese guards would never let me keep the cross, so I hid it in a propaganda pamphlet they had given me, along with a list of other prisoners in the camp. By day, the pamphlet was under my pallet. By night, I took it out and held the cross in my hand as I prayed. There was great spiritual comfort in it for me.

I'd had the cross several months when one day I was told that a North Vietnamese work crew was making its way through the camp, cutting down the ventilation openings in each cell by adding bricks. When my turn came, I was ordered outside while a guard made a search of my cell. In a few minutes, I heard his grunt of triumph. He had found the cross.

Coming out, he stood glaring at me as he broke the cross into bits and threw the pieces into an open sewer. I was furious. And helpless.

The work crew had been standing by, watching, five or six very old Vietnamese men and women, too old for any other kind of work. They were ordered into my cell to do their job. A half hour passed before they came out and I was allowed to return.

Immediately, I reached under the pallet and found the propaganda pamphlet. The list of prisoners was gone. Still angry, I began tearing the pamphlet apart. Then I felt a bulge among the pages.

There was a cross. A new one, carefully and beautifully woven from the straw strands of a broom. Obviously the work crew had made it. There was no other explanation. I shuddered at the thought of the punishment they would have suffered had they been caught.

Then I realized something, something that gave me even more spiritual comfort and hope for the future as I prayed with the new cross. Despite the deeds of men that can make enemies out of strangers, the love of God can still reach down and make men brothers.

Headline—April 4, 1974:

THE XENIA DAILY GAZETTE

93rd Year, No. 115   ★   *Xenia, Ohio, Thursday, April 4, 1974*   ★   *8 Pages—15 Cents*

Xenia digging out from day of horror

APRIL 1975

The City That Came Back *by Jack Jordan, newspaper editor*

An uneasiness nagged at me as I checked over proofs for the next day's paper. It was Wednesday, April 3, 1974, about four o'clock on a gray afternoon. The weather had been strange, ominous. The radio beside my desk announced tornado warnings. More than 100 twisters had been sighted to the southwest.

We had had such warnings before, but the twisters had always missed Xenia, a city of 27,000 people in southwestern Ohio. Born there, I knew every bit of Xenia, from its busy downtown to its residential areas where beautiful old trees had shaded early settlers almost two centuries ago. I delivered *The Daily Gazette* as a schoolboy, later became its sports writer, then returned to be editor and general manager after serving as a naval aviator in World War II.

Suddenly the radio crackled: "Tornado!... Southwest of town...expected in six minutes!"

I leaped from my desk and hurried out into our office, which faces the main downtown street. Police shouted, "Take cover!" through bullhorns. Already, white-faced shoppers and business people were streaming into our new annex building for the protection of its steel-beam and thick-concrete construction.

Suddenly an ominous green darkened the street. A rumbling roar like a thousand freight trains crossing the ceiling filled the building with a grinding thunder. Our street doors flew open. I rushed to close them and found myself looking up into a black, swirling sea of debris

and giant trees. I fought my way back and threw myself down on the stairs among other praying and sobbing people.

Then an eerie stillness filled the air; the monster had passed. I got to my feet, made sure everyone was all right, then dashed into the street. Shocked, I stood rooted. The sidewalks were full of rubble; buildings gaped with cavernous holes. I looked to the intersection two blocks away where the three-story Xenia Hotel had stood. It looked as if it had been hit by artillery fire.

My family! Home was two miles away. I ran behind our building to my convertible. Its side windows had been sucked out, but it started. Sitting in broken glass, I drove into the street. But it was impossible. There were no more streets—only mountains of debris—and people, wandering, dazed people.

I pressed on, stumbling, climbing over wreckage, gagging at the sickening stench of gas spewing from ruptured pipes. Rounding a corner, I saw our new high school, now just a mound of rubble bristling with twisted steel beams.

Finally I got to Morningside Drive. My house was still standing; my wife, daughter and son-in-law were just emerging from the basement. Breathing thanks, I looked down the block to Greene Memorial Hospital. Thank God, it had been spared. Ambulance lights were flashing, sirens wailed.

After making sure my family was all right, I turned and ran back to the newspaper office.

tornado striking Xenia, Ohio, 1974

In the meantime, city manager Bob Stewart had crawled out from under shattered glass and brick dust in city hall and was out in the street with other city officials. Armed with maps and radios, they began mobilizing rescue operations right then and there.

Icy rain now slashed our city and as dusk fell, families shivered in a city without electricity, gas or water. At one a.m., distraught Xenians were still searching for missing family members. Stark desolation was everywhere, even in the sounds of the night: the whimpering of a homeless dog, the anguished cry of a mother calling for her lost child, a man weeping beside the sheet-covered form of his wife in the improvised morgue.

In the battered *Gazette* building, we waded in water as candles sputtered on the desks. I had felt that keeping Xenians informed through their paper would be vital to the community. But in the cold gray Thursday dawn, I wondered if there was enough left to make a community.

The tornado had bulldozed a seven-mile path half a mile wide, right through Xenia. Thirty-three men, women and children were dead. Almost half of Xenia's buildings were destroyed.

Nearly 10,000 people were homeless. Six of our nine schools were smashed, along with nine churches and 180 stores and industries, including Xenia's largest employer, the Kroehler Furniture factory. More than half of Xenia's jobs had been wiped out.

As I stood that morning in what had once been the center of town, I felt overwhelmed.

Over in city hall, broken glass crackling under their feet, sat Xenia's seven overcoated city commissioners huddling with city manager Bob Stewart in the icy city chamber. As the wind whipped the contents of overturned files around them, they bowed their heads in prayer for the guidance and strength to face the tremendous tasks awaiting them.

The question on everyone's mind that morning was, "Where do we start?" Judge Herman Weber gave the answer in these words: "A stick at a time."

The first sticks to be lifted were from the leveled homes. How many people still survived in them? Fire chief John Troeger organized 180 men into a giant search party.

"The eeriest aspect of the search was the telephones," one of the men told me later. "Sometimes we could hear them ringing under the rubble.

"When we could reach them, the caller would often be a worried relative from as far off as California asking, 'Are you all right?'

"We had to tell them we didn't know," he added soberly.

Air Force and National Guard trucks rumbled up to the *Gazette* building during the night, taking cover in the basement shelter as tornado warnings continued. Concerned people came from as far as Seattle, Dallas and New York and immediately pitched in, helping in any way they could, from scrubbing floors to cooking meals.

Emergency supplies streamed in from many firms. Xenia clergymen and lay people joined

tornado's aftermath…
National Guardsman in Xenia, Ohio

together to form the Inter-Faith Council, headed by Methodist minister Dick Pope and Presbyterian minister Bob Huck, to coordinate relief and provide facilities for volunteers.

As I saw such generosity, and watched Xenians respond to it, my heart began to rise—Xenia might just make it after all. Ads began to appear in the *Gazette:*

"Steve Vagnor family at 946 Shoshone Terrace can house a family of four, also has extra car available for someone."

"Mr. Everett Zambaren of 112 Hillcrest Drive has a camper."

"Dayton Economy Drugs has free disposable diapers and other baby needs."

Even some of the youngest Xenians could see a bright side. One father told us that on the day after the storm, his toddler walked outside and returned to report, "House all broke; toys all broke; but birds all working."

But it was chiefly in Xenia's churches that the keynote of that victorious spirit sounded. Easter came a week and a half after the tornado. And for his church's service, Steve Adams, music director of the First Church of the Nazarene, wrote this litany, which he said came to him as he emerged from a destroyed building:

"We rejoice because we can see.

"We rejoice because we can breathe.

"We rejoice because we can reach out and embrace our wives, our husbands, our sons and our daughters.

"We rejoice because at this very moment we can feel the pulse of life running through

our veins and the throb of tomorrow's potential coursing through our minds."

Soon everyone began discussing plans to build a new and better Xenia. The federal government promised $5 million in loans and grants if the city could draft an acceptable rebuilding plan in 60 days. Engineers and planners worked around the clock to meet the deadline.

To get all possible suggestions and support from Xenians, a Spirit of '74 committee was formed—19 people representing a cross section of residents, linking townspeople and their officials.

Meanwhile, day after day rubble-filled trucks rolled out to a giant quarry eight miles outside Xenia. The wreckage amounted to 285,000 truckloads—half the city, including the remains of 2,000 homes. Familiar sights, things I'd seen every day of my life had vanished as though they had never existed.

The new desolation affected everyone. The brave spirit of the early days following the tornado seemed to fade.

Adding to the new sense of depression were the reports that many of Xenia's damaged industries were finding it difficult to stay in business now. Some businessmen picked up their insurance money and left town.

Then the crushing word came that the Kroehler Furniture plant, the city's biggest employer, wasn't going to stay in Xenia. To rebuild, they would need more space; their old site was too confining.

In a Guideposts series called "The Day America Prayed," there was an article about locusts. Ever since the beginning of time, there have been locusts. In the 1870's, plagues of locusts attacked the crops in Minnesota. When things seemed hopeless, the governor declared April 26, 1877, a day of prayer. At dawn the next morning, a deep freeze set in and for several days the earth was frozen, killing the larvae underground. Thus when summer came, the fields were lush with wheat, bringing a rich harvest.

On one hot July evening, I attended a Spirit of '74 meeting that seemed under a pall of negative feelings, disagreement and discouragement. I heatedly lectured the group and when it was over I went out to my car, put the top down and drove aimlessly through the city. The "For Sale" signs in front of empty lots deepened my mood of defeat.

Then I passed one lot with a neat pile of bricks standing at the front of it. Suddenly I was reminded of a photo the *Gazette* had carried about Mr. and Mrs. Ernest Dietrich, whose house had been completely demolished. Mrs. Dietrich's arms had been badly bruised. However, within a few days she and her husband began collecting and cleaning the bricks from the ruins of their house. "We're going to rebuild," they promised, "brick by brick."

I also thought about Clyde Hyatt, the Penn Central telegrapher who had seen the awful black cloud approaching and sped toward home to warn his wife. On the way, he had spotted some small children rooted to the curb in fright. He had stopped his car, hustled the children to safely, then emerged, only to be swallowed by the tornado. In the Penn Central tower where he worked, his co-workers had found a box filled with his writings. One asked: "Can I truly tell myself that I have paid the price to my fellow partners in humanity? Have I expressed my appreciation personally to each and every one of those people? If so, I shall rest this night."

Reassured, I turned my car around and headed toward the *Gazette* office.

A couple of weeks later, the silver lining began to show through. Our long-awaited urban renewal plan had been approved. Government grants and loans were also okayed for the rebuilding of Xenia's downtown section. People began to talk excitedly about rebuilding the area into an attractive shopping mall.

Many of Xenia's homeowners found that they didn't have to wait for the government to begin putting their homes and their lives back together again. Private insurance adjusters were working rapidly.

Homes began to spring up all over Xenia, many better than the old ones.

Then businesses began to reopen downtown. Tuffy Snider used the *Gazette*'s pages to announce the opening of his new Corner Pharmacy. The Ponderosa Steak House, rebuilt, donated its first day's profits to the Xenia Tornado Relief Fund.

And then came the most exciting business news—Kroehler Furniture was staying in Xenia. They had purchased 94 acres of land, enough not only to rebuild a larger plant, but to make Xenia's first industrial park.

The biggest test of Xenia's survival, though, was yet to come. School was scheduled to reopen in September. We'd know best how many families had moved permanently by the number of children starting school in newly acquired modular classrooms and the surviving schools. By holding classes in shifts, there would be enough room for every child to attend; but would they come back?

*Why "disaster" stories in Guideposts? Because God's power is so
often revealed in dire situations. High on a Scottish sea cliff, a young
girl slipped and fell to the bottom far below. "Save her, dear God,"
her frantic father prayed. And when he reached the beach, he found
his daughter unharmed. If you should go to Tobermory Bay today,
you will find painted on the rock wall the truth that overwhelmed
him, a sign that says, "God is Love."*

I'll never forget the day that school superintendent Carl Adkins got the fateful figure. We shifted uneasily on our chairs as we waited for his announcement. "Enrollment this year," he said, "will be only a hundred and fifty less than last year."

Big smiles filled the room. People *were* coming back!

Perhaps the high point of Xenia's return came later in September when Hurricane Fifi ravaged Honduras, a little country most Xenians had never seen and knew little about. But with hearts swelling in compassion, they reached into thin wallets and in donations of $5 and $10 came up with $24,000. They gave it to relief workers heading for Honduras, saying, "Go in the name of the One who brought you to us."

In October, seven months after the tornado, I was walking down Main Street when deep, melodious *bongs* suddenly filled the air. At the sound, people stopped, looked up, then smiled at one another. The great clock in the courthouse had been restored and was running again. Another part of Xenia had returned.

I stood there thinking amid the bustle of the traffic, staring into the streets crowded with cars carrying bumper stickers proclaiming, "Xenia lives!"

Yes, Xenia lives, I thought. It lives even though we still have differences of opinion as rebuilding continues. Our people still look anxiously over their shoulders when storm clouds gather, and our children sometimes still wake up crying at night. And faraway strangers are still mailing us back bits of Xenia in the form of snapshots, personal papers and other items that were carried by the wind to places as distant as Windsor, Ontario, in Canada.

Then I looked to the southwest, from whence the tornado had come, and I thought of the questions that Xenians had asked after the storm, questions that many survivors had spray-painted in anguish across the fronts of their ruined homes: "Oh God! Why us?" and "Only God knows why."

I remembered what Dick Pope had said when he tried to give his congregation an answer to those questions on that Easter of 1974, just eleven days after the disaster had hit.

"For the first time, many people are really going to understand what resurrection means," he said. "You have to realize that Christ was even more effective after His resurrection than before. And this storm can be a turning point for this town.

"The Christian faith does not promise that we will not have suffering," he went on, "but it does create the character in us that can face it and know how to use it."

Now, as I looked around me at the city that had come back from disaster with a new, stronger character and deeper faith, I could see what Dick Pope had meant—especially when he concluded, "I have seen the hand of God, not in the tornado, but in the people after the storm went by."

Mount St. Helens erupting, 1980

JANUARY 1981

The Day the Mountain Exploded *by David Crockett, photographer*

A strong foreboding suddenly awakened me during the night. The impression given me was unmistakable: *The mountain will erupt today.*

I peered at the clock; its luminescent face showed 3:00 a.m. Even so, I crawled out of bed, donned my climbing clothes, grabbed my camera gear and slipped out into the cool darkness to my TV news car. It was Sunday morning, May 18, 1980.

Like a sixth sense, strong and urgent, such prophetic nudges have come to me before during my 28 years. They have always turned out to be true; that's why I felt there was no time to waste. I'm a photographer for KOMO-TV News in Seattle. And my home on Puget Sound is 150 miles from Mount St. Helens. I wanted to be there when it happened.

For me, the volcano was a welcome change from the usual disaster stories I chased, such as shoot-outs, riots, exploding tank cars and burning buildings.

Part of my coverage of the possible eruption meant reporting on the seismologists' warnings of mud slides, ash fallout and almost-odorless toxic gases that would result. One of the gases mentioned was carbon dioxide. Heavier than air, it could, they warned, settle into lungs, forcing out oxygen and causing suffocation.

Once, as we newsmen stood on the mountain's north slope, a volcanologist said: "If she erupted right now, we'd all be dead within seconds." He pointed to an area on the side of the mountain where sophisticated tilt-meters indicated it was bulging like a weak spot on an inner tube.

Even so, few people expected the mountain to erupt. For the past several days she'd been so quiet we newsmen had had little to report.

But what would happen today? I wondered, as I raced down Interstate 5. I swung off the freeway onto picturesque 504, the Mount St. Helens highway that parallels the winding Toutle River.

I decided the South Fork of the Toutle would provide the best view of the summit. So I turned onto a smaller road and slowed about a mile from the peak in a peaceful valley, a bit below and slightly to the west of the ominous bulge that had been pointed out by the volcanologist.

I was searching for the ideal spot from which to shoot pictures when another instantaneous, unmistakable impression suddenly came: *Stop here.*

It turned out to be a perfect vantage point. I got out of the car, stretched and glanced at my wristwatch. It was 8:30 a.m. What a glorious morning!

Fresh. Clear. Clean. Quiet. Peaceful.

I drank deeply of the fresh, evergreen-scented air and stretched my arms to the luxuriant forest around me and the mountain

*Why "disaster" stories in Guideposts? Because we learn that God
is a very present help in trouble. Nobody knows this better than
David Crockett who very nearly lost his life witnessing St. Helens'
eruption. A short time after his terrifying experience, he read Psalm
46. It brought such comfort to him that he put a copy of the following
portion in the corner of a large photograph of Mount St. Helens
erupting, which now hangs on his wall:*

looming above. This was where it was all
at. This was the eternal where I could really
sense God.

Taking my 35mm camera, I aimed it at the
mountain to take a few shots.

My breath caught.

An awesome, immense black plume suddenly rocketed from the peak! More angry-
looking plumes joined it. As they billowed
larger and larger they mushroomed together
into furiously boiling clouds, roiling black,
blue and yellow-rimmed, like an exploding
atomic bomb.

I clicked off four shots of the awesomely
beautiful and incredible sequence.

But I wasn't ready for what happened next.

The side of the mountain *moved.* It was the
bulging part the volcanologist had
pointed out as dangerous. Slowly and majestically at first, like a slow-motion film, billions of
tons of rock and earth began descending, then
a portion of it cascaded faster and faster, heading… *straight into the valley where I was!*

I leaped into the car, whipped it around and
raced back down the mountain road. Through
the rearview mirror I saw a horrifying sight.
Instead of a lazy mud slide, an immense 20-
foot-high wall of what looked like steaming,
wet cement was overtaking me like a speeding
tidal wave!

Obviously I was to be its next victim!

I floored the accelerator and my car careened and bounced down the mountain road
reaching 60, 70 miles per hour. Even so, the
tidal wave of molten mud loomed higher and

higher in my rearview mirror. It was traveling nearly 150 miles per hour, and was 100 city
blocks in size!

I had to find higher ground! Frantically I
searched for a turnoff road. Oh! A logging
road just ahead. I wrenched the wheel, careen-
ing onto it, and had reached a slight rise when
the steaming, roaring wall caught up.

I slammed to a stop, shifted into reverse and
screeched backward. But the road behind me
was gone.

I was caught on a tiny island surrounded by
a raging torrent of hot ooze.

I knew I was dead. The road was gone, the
mountain was coming down on top of me!

I shot out of the car, grabbing my still camera and the TV sound camera, all 42 pounds of
it, probably as a reflex action from my years as
a newsman. I knew I *had* to get to higher
ground!

But to reach higher ground meant crossing
200 feet of still-flowing mud that followed the
main slide wall.

I had no other choice. Tentatively, I stepped
into it. It was like quicksand, but my foot found
bottom. Holding my cameras high above my
head, I waded into the mire. Surprisingly, it
was merely warm; it had to have been boiling
when it started traveling down the snow-
covered terrain.

Fighting my way through the sludge, I finally reached the other side and started up a
hill. But when I'd walked only a few feet, I was
completely exhausted, and staggered, gasping
for breath.

What's the matter with me? I thought. *I'm not*

"God is our refuge and strength, a very present help in trouble.

"Therefore will not we fear, though the earth be removed, and though the mountains be carried into the midst of the sea.

"Though the waters thereof roar and be troubled, though the mountains shake with the swelling thereof.

"Be still, and know that I am God ... I will be exalted in the earth."

Psalm 46:1–3, 10

this winded after my daily four-mile jogging or even when climbing a mountain.

Carbon dioxide must be settling in my lungs, forcing oxygen out!

The thought kept me from slumping down to rest.

Only five or ten minutes had passed since the mountain first began erupting. Now it started getting dark. Heavy, dense clouds of volcanic ash blackened the sky, leaving only one light spot on the horizon. It was what remained of the sun, burning through the murk.

Well, I've had it, I thought. *So I might as well shoot it.*

Turning on the sound camera, I tried to describe what was going on because I thought these would be my last words, and perhaps someone would find the camera.

"Dear God! Whoever finds this...I can't see—it's too dark. I've left the car behind... I'm walking toward the only light I can see—on top a ridge. I can hear the mountain behind me rumbling....I honest to God believe I'm dead....

"The ash is in my eyes...It's getting very hard to breathe...It hurts to talk...it hurt, hurts to breathe...It burns my eyes."

Gritty, sandy ash pelted down on me. Roiling, volcanic clouds above were creating their own weather. Hot winds raged. Lightning flashed and cracked. Fires shot up where the bolts struck. Thunder cannonaded, and the ground heaved and shook.

It was like words I had heard from the Bible: "He opened the shaft of the bottomless pit, and from the shaft rose smoke like the smoke of a great furnace, and the sun and the air were darkened with the smoke from the shaft." (Revelation 9:2, RSV)

I'd jogged every day. I'd scuba dived. I'd climbed mountains. I'd considered myself in excellent physical condition. But breathing gas and ash was beyond my endurance. Death was closing in.

"One step at a time—if I can just keep walking. God, if I can just breathe...It's now totally pitch-black—I can't see to keep on walking... I'll just have to sit down here and wait it out."

From scuba diving, I had learned to conserve air by staying motionless. So I spent the next hours in complete darkness, slumped still. But my mind wouldn't stay still.

No one knew where I was! Naturally I hadn't phoned anyone that early in the morning to tell them I was leaving. I thought about my mother and dad and sister at our family home near Seattle, and about my friends.

I thought of those with whom I'd worked, and attended church. I recalled that I sometimes hadn't been too patient with what they said, did or believed. If I got uptight, I simply took off into the mountains and forests.

Now I wouldn't come away from it alive....

And yet, I felt God was somehow watching over me in spite of my circumstances. That thought was comforting, and soon I began to feel strangely relaxed sitting there. I thought to myself, *I'll just stay here.*

Then that instantaneous, unmistakable impression came again: *Get up and keep going!*

*Why "disaster" stories in Guideposts? Because in desperate
moments, we find God-given strength we never knew before. One
summer day, Mildred Shell watched her husband's tractor pitch over,
its 3,000 pounds setting on Howard Shell's chest, suffocating him.
Mildred lifted the tractor off his chest, and though Howard's leg was
still pinned, he was able to breathe. Mildred held the tractor for an
hour until help came. "A few months later," she said, "I tried to lift it
again and couldn't budge it. God lifted."*

How could I? I'd reached the end. I'd eaten nothing since the night before. It was late afternoon now—eight or nine hours on a mountain that was still rumbling.

But I got up and walked some more.

Eventually the sky lightened somewhat so I was able to see some of my surroundings. And I couldn't believe my eyes!

It had been such a beautiful green valley. Meadows, elk, deer, wildlife of all kinds. Now it was gone. Instead I faced a bleak, ghastly landscape of bone-gray ash as far as I could see. Several inches of ash covered everything, stumps, trees, rocks.

In the silence, everything looked, felt and smelled like death. I was the only living thing in sight.

If by some miracle I was going to make it out of here at all, I knew that help had to come from outside of myself. From above. I knew I had reached the end.

My prayer wasn't formal; it was pleading:

"God...It's very, very hard to breathe in this ...if only I could keep walking. If only I could do something. If only I could do *something.* You know...instead of just sitting here."

Many hours passed, then as I sat there in the deathly silence, staring at the ashen desolation, a distant sound startled me, a faint *thump-thump-thump.* As it grew louder, I looked up with a pounding heart.

Helicopters! I watched them fly over, one by one.

But one by one they passed on by.

Naturally they couldn't see me; I was covered with gray ash the same color as everything else. But wait! A fire would help them spot me.

Maybe there was a flare in my TV news car! In all my wanderings I had tried to stay close to it, although climbing higher.

From within, came a reserve of strength—and hope—to help me clamber back down the slope and wade through the muck again to the car. After scratching around inside, sure enough, I found a flare! I was thankful for the co-worker who'd put it there.

I recrossed the mire and climbed the hill again, setting up the flare just as another aircraft *thump-thumped* overhead.

It'd be so great to be rescued at last! Rescued! *Rescued!*

But that chopper, too, passed by. No one saw the flare.

And that was also understandable. The whole hillside as far as I could see was already dotted with fires—ignited by lightning bolts. My hope fizzled even faster than the flare.

Dear God...Oh, please! Please...

Just as the flare began to burn down, another instantaneous, unmistakable impression came: *Use it to light three fires.*

Of course; three fires, three shots, three anything is an international sign of distress.

So when the next *thump-thump-thump* came overhead, someone saw me—all because of my three fires.

A Coast Guard helicopter descended, and never had I seen such a welcome sight. As it neared the ground, however, the rotor blades

Fern Mann survived a car crash (Guideposts 1981) only to find herself, her bones shattered, immobilized in an isolated spot hidden from the road, at the bottom of a snow-covered cliff. Screaming would do no good. For 36 hours, in near-zero temperatures, Fern strengthened her will to live by talking constantly with God. When she was rescued, her doctor was amazed that she was conscious and rational. As Fern said, "Whatever the ordeal—physical, mental or spiritual—God will keep you company in it."

whipped up such thick clouds of powdery ash that the pilot and crew could see neither me nor where to land.

So it rose up a ways and lowered a basket for me to get in. I tried to grab hold of the swinging basket. But the ash was suffocating and blinding. I couldn't see the basket. The crew couldn't see the ground, the basket or me.

The pilot made more passes. A smaller Army helicopter tried. Each result was the same. Failure.

I was totally frustrated. I'd been climbing and fighting the mountain all day, breathing gas and ash. There was just no strength left. I was absolutely exhausted. I'd never make it off the mountain after all.

But through my hazy mind, yet another instantaneous, unmistakable impression came: *Go up the road a ways.*

Sure enough—the road was a little wider ahead. It also was inundated by ash, of course, but it allowed the chopper to maneuver. I again found enough strength to struggle toward it.

To avoid as much as possible stirring up the talcum-powder ash, the crew let out 150 feet of steel cable with the basket dangling from it.

The basket bounced and bumped along the ground, disappearing in billows of dust. I held my breath and leaped into the thick, suffocating clouds, desperately groping for my only hope.

Then a miracle happened.

I grabbed the basket.

It lay on its side. I snatched hold of it with one hand, heaved the camera gear in with the other and was diving in when the chopper jerked up, slamming the heavy basket rim against my head.

Everything went black.

I regained consciousness to find myself swinging in the basket. And when I was finally pulled up inside the aircraft, I was treated for exposure, exhaustion and gas inhalation. I remember how fresh the oxygen smelled.

It was during my overnight stay in the hospital for observation that I learned Mount St. Helens was 1,300 feet lower in elevation as a result of her blowing a cubic mile of earth off her top. The avalanche of mud that had charged by me had swept on down the Toutle River—clear into the mighty Columbia River where it filled the channel and blocked ship traffic.

I thought back over my experience. As my car careened down that mountain road, had I been a few feet ahead or a few feet behind, a little faster or a little slower, my life would've been gone.

I'd always thought of the outdoors as being safe and secure. But during those ten hours, I saw a mountain fall apart. I saw a forest disappear. It wiped away many of my set beliefs.

I saw that God is the only One Who is unmovable, unshakable, infallible. As the Bible says, He is our refuge and strength. And He was there with me in that desolation. I feel somehow that I'm being allowed to start over.

In fact, because of the eruption of Mount St. Helens, it seems God's given me not only ten minutes more but many minutes more—whatever is in His master plan for me.

Headline—December 18, 1981:

Red Brigades Kidnap American General in Verona

JANUARY 1983

A Story of Answered Prayer *by Brig. Gen. and Mrs. James L. Dozier*

General James L. Dozier: My wife and I glance at each other.

Our apartment doorbell just rang; someone is in the hall. This is strange; visitors usually first ring the building bell downstairs.

As deputy chief of staff for logistics in a headquarters in the North Atlantic Treaty Organization's Southern Region, I have just returned from work to our apartment here in Verona, Italy. It is 5:30 p.m., December 17, 1981, and Judy is preparing dinner.

She touches my arm as I step toward the door. "I don't like it when the doorbell rings on our level," she says.

"I'm sure it's all right," I say, "probably one of the building people."

As I open the door it appears I'm right. Two bearded men in dark clothing politely explain they are plumbers. The smaller one carries a tool bag. Water, they say, is dripping into the apartment below and they need to find out if any of our fixtures is leaking.

I take them down the hall to the utility room where they seem to find everything in order. The bigger man uses an Italian word I don't understand so I go back to the kitchen and pick up my Italian-English dictionary. I'm suddenly jumped from the rear by one of the men.

Judy gasps as the other grabs her and we look into the muzzles of two pistols.

"We are the Red Brigades!" barks one of the men. The Red Brigades, the infamous terrorist group in Italy who have kidnapped and murdered numerous government and business leaders.

The smaller man pushes Judy to the floor while the large one and I continue to struggle. I fight, but pain explodes in my head from a blow and I crumple. I see Judy with a pistol pointed at her head and I stop fighting.

My arms are jerked behind me, steel handcuffs clamp my wrists; a gag is jammed into my jaws, and a cloth blinds me. Helpless, I hear the men let others into the apartment. Desk and bureau drawers clatter open and papers rustle as they ransack. I know they won't find anything confidential. But I worry about Judy and pray she won't be harmed.

Something sounding hollow and heavy is dragged up to me. Hands grasp me and I am stuffed into a large trunk.

I remember Aldo Moro, Italy's former prime minister, who was found dead in a car trunk 54 days after his kidnapping by the Red Brigades. The box lurches as I'm carried downstairs, and then it is slid onto a hard surface. A truck engine roars and we bounce over streets.

My chest begins to pound and I take small breaths to conserve oxygen. From time to time the lid flies back and fresh air pours in. Hands check my pulse; then the lid slams shut. They want to keep me alive, for the moment anyway. We rumble on and the trunk is transferred to what seems to be a car. Finally, we stop, and my trunk is lugged into a building. An elevator

Brig. Gen. James L. Dozier upon his release, 1982

motor whines; controls click as we rise, drop and ascend. They are trying to disorient me. The door clangs open, I'm carried a short distance. The lid lifts; I am pulled out and lugged through what seems to be an opening and dropped onto a cot. The gag and blindfold are removed and I sit blinking.

I'm inside a blue canvas cubicle about six feet square; it seems to be part of a tent erected inside an apartment. Three masked men chain my right wrist and left ankle to the metal cot. There is just enough slack in the shackles to reach a chemical toilet in a corner. This is my prison. For how long?

Mrs. James L. Dozier: I lie facedown on the floor, ankles chained to wrists. I feel strangely calm. God must give this inner strength when we need it most. Just before the big man blindfolds me, I see a trunk by our kitchen door. I sense it is for Jim. Will I ever see him again? I pray for guidance to know when it will be safe to call for help.

A terrorist drags me down the hall to a room. I remain motionless while praying for Jim. Finally, the men leave. I dislodge the blindfold and look up into the blue flame of the water heater in our bathroom. Still chained wrist to ankle, I hunch along the tiles to the washing machine. I bang its metal side with my knees and call for help. But I do not know that our neighbors in the apartment below sit in the other end of their flat watching television. No one hears me.

Three hours have passed since Jim was taken. My knee is numb from thumping the washer, and my voice is dwindling to a croak. The doorbell rings; I call out again. Minutes later, the glass crashes in a terrace window and the man who lives below rushes in crying, *"O mio Dio!"* His wife has already phoned the police. Our neighbor's daughter had heard my calls when she had gone to the bathroom, which lies just below ours.

Gen. D.: Is Judy safe? It's all I can think of. My captors assure me that she is, and I sink back on the cot breathing thanks. I am not afraid of death; it has been a close companion for years, especially during combat. I know that death is only a transition into another life, a much better one promised by our Lord. But I am concerned for my family; we have a grown son and daughter and I don't want them to worry. I pray for them and everyone involved in this, that we maintain our proper perspective and be sensitive to God's guidance.

I survey my cell. In the outer section of the tent a masked guard sits, a call button taped to his chair arm. Another guard steps in and slips a stereo headset on my head. It is to prevent me from overhearing conversations. I am stunned by the volume of hard-rock music.

The din of exploding drums is excruciating. I have never cared for rock and roll and slump back onto the cot; the steel chains numb my wrist and ankle. How much longer can I stand this? I reach for the earphones but my guard is half out of his chair, shaking his head no. Finally my mind turns off the noise.

The net. I gotta stay in the net.

Staying in the net is Army parlance for

Conrad Hilton (1887–1979), the famous hotelier, believed in prayer and if it had helped him in his life, couldn't it make a difference in the life of our nation? Musing while on a train to Chicago, Hilton had a vision of Uncle Sam at worship—strong, with the work-toughened hands of a laborer clasped in prayer. In 1953, he commissioned a portrait of this vision (see next page) and wrote a prayer to carry his message: not that God be on our side, but that we be on His.

keeping in radio communication with your commander and fellow troops while out in the field. It is vital during battle; once you are out of the net, you are in trouble. My net with my Commander is maintained through prayer. Now, more than ever, I must keep in communication with my Commander. I learned this, long before my Army days, back in Arcadia, Florida. Dad died when I was 14, and Mom supported my sister and me there by teaching school. Only five feet tall, she was a spiritual powerhouse, continuing her teaching Sundays at the Methodist church. It was she who taught me to stay in the net. "God created you for a purpose, Jim," she said, "and the way to fulfill it is to keep in close touch with Him."

Keep in touch with Him. I set my mind on this. I see no human faces, only black masks. No matter what happens, I know He will guide me. His will shall be done. A deep peace floods me and I fall asleep.

I awaken. They bring me toast and milk for breakfast. Now my inquisition begins. A terrorist squatting on the floor fires questions about NATO, my political beliefs.

I feel vulnerable. I do not want to discredit my country, Italy or NATO, and I pray for guidance. Then I feel a strange calm, as if I am in the company of others, praying for me, guiding me. *I'm trying hard to stay in the net.*

I answer the questions with harmless information. When we finish, they return my earphones. I ask for different music. One brings George Gershwin's *Rhapsody in Blue.* I sigh

gratefully, but the volume is still high and my hearing is deteriorating.

I cannot tell time, either, as they took my watch. However, I find that when my guard is reading a magazine or talking with someone I can sneak the headset away from my ears an inch or so and hear sounds outside the building.

There are street noises, and I soon make out the typical traffic pattern of an Italian city. First, the morning rush hour, then the early afternoon *reposo*, with traffic picking up about 5:00 p.m., until the stores close at eight or so, and everything dropping off at midnight.

Now I can track passing days, and I attempt to follow a daily regimen, beginning and ending each day with push-ups, sit-ups and other exercises. I ask for a Bible and other books; they bring me only novels and news magazines. Perhaps they don't have an English Bible handy. I am grateful that I have read it through and remember some of it.

Mrs. D.: The Red Brigades have issued their first communiqué. It had been deposited in a trash container in Rome. They call Jim a "NATO hangman" and say that he has been taken to a "people's prison and will be submitted to proletarian justice." They say they have declared war on the entire NATO alliance as a "structure of military occupation."

Their fuzzy snapshot shows a bruise under Jim's left eye. The police assure me that a search is on. All that can be done is being done.

Even in my sleep, I think of Jim. My dream last night was so vivid. It was as if we were talk-

Uncle Sam as envisioned by Conrad Hilton

ing. The strange thing about it was Jim's hair; instead of his usual crew cut, it was long and wavy. I know God sometimes speaks to us through dreams. Is there some meaning in this? I don't know and continue to pray for him.

Gen. D.: I feel a closeness with Judy as if she were with me. I *know* she is praying for me; I sense it. After 26 years of marriage there is a special relationship that distance and prisons cannot touch.

A week has passed since our separation and my face itches from beard growth. The earphones' volume has been lowered, but I'm tired of Gershwin. I have yet to see a human face, only photos in old copies of *Time* and *Newsweek* that my masked captors bring. They clip out the stories they don't want me to see, but they did give me a news photo of Judy; it becomes my pinup picture.

I pray for her peace of mind, for she knows my captors' reputation for cold-blooded murder. In spite of my predicament, I remain optimistic about the outcome. I am helped by something quite strong, a force supporting me like the lift one feels from an ocean wave, a powerful buoyancy.

I had the first feeling of this wave several days ago while I was doing push-ups; a vivid impression came to me of my executive officer. He is a deep-thinking friend. I've always felt confident about bouncing my thoughts off of him. At first I wondered why I felt his presence so closely; then I knew. He was praying for me. I felt invigorated.

A few days later while I was playing solitaire, I sensed the closeness of another friend. He teaches in the American school in Verona and is a gentle man who truly lives his faith.

And this morning while reading, I found myself chuckling; it wasn't the book but a graphic impression of the feisty wife of a fellow general officer. She is an outspoken woman, and I can just imagine her calling Judy and saying, "Golly, as soon as I leave, things go to h--- in a hand-basket." She had left Europe shortly before I was kidnapped.

Now I know that not only Judy but all our friends—and other people—are praying for me. I know that all the resources of my country and Italy are at work endeavoring to free me. But nothing is more powerful than prayer. I long to thank these people who are praying for me, and I do so, in prayer.

Mrs. D.: Here in Verona, where my daughter and son have come to spend Christmas, the postmen bring packets of mail from Italians who write that they are praying for Jim. We also pick up more mail from Americans at our post office. They write of prayer chains and groups meeting on Jim's behalf.

It seems that prayers are rising for Jim around the clock everywhere. And friends are so supportive. The American and Italian communities have been such a help, and prayer groups are being organized worldwide.

The momentum appears to be building. I find myself smiling for the first time in weeks. What would we do without caring friends? I

Conrad Hilton's Prayer

Our Father in heaven:
We pray that You save us from ourselves. The world that You have
made for us, to live in peace, we have made into an armed camp.
We live in fear of war to come. We are afraid of "the terror that flies
by night, and the arrow that flies by day, the pestilence that walks
in darkness and the destruction that wastes at noon-day." We
have turned from You to go our selfish way. We have broken Your
commandments and denied Your truth. We have left Your altars to
serve the false gods of money and pleasure and power. Forgive us.

am also deeply touched by the many Italians who bashfully come to our door with flowers and gifts. So many say they are praying to Saint Anthony. "He is the one who finds anything missing," an elderly woman assures me. "I pray for him to find your husband. He will; you wait, you see."

It is Christmas Eve, 1981. As we return from chapel, I see the little candle in our window. It burns every night. It was a gift from a local mother whose little boy insisted that she buy it for "the general." As I light it, I am reminded of the prayers and love of people everywhere.

Gen. D.: From my reckoning, I believe Christmas has passed. But my guards, who seem to know everything, told me about our son's and daughter's and my sister's arrival in Verona. I'm grateful for that, but these chains are a nuisance. My unwashed body smells.

Mrs. D.: Jim has been reported dead. An anonymous caller told the police that he had been killed and hinted where his body could be found. The authorities are dragging a lake in the mountains. Can I keep my thoughts on God with such horrible news? But isn't this what Jim used to call "staying in the net"?

Gen. D.: The hoaxes I read about in news magazines regarding my death disturb me and I complain to my captors. They snort and say they "do not do tricks like that." I believe them. They play for keeps. But the waiting is tedious. A month has gone by; my beard is full

and my hair long and wavy. But the chains are a nuisance. Wasn't there something in the Bible about Peter being in chains? I can't exactly remember. If Mom were here she'd know. Even after I graduated from West Point in 1956 and married Judy, Mom continued to send us copies of her weekly Sunday-school lessons.

I smile in memory. When she was nearly 60, she gave God what she called "an extra mile" by spending a year in India as a missionary. I lean back on the cot, my eyes moistening. Mom died just a year and a half ago but I can sense her presence. If she could do what she did, then I should be able to do whatever God expects of me right here, chains and all.

Mrs. D.: Six weeks have passed and the news isn't good. The authorities assure me that thousands of investigators are searching for Jim. Yet to the press they express total frustration. "Dozier," said one official, "could be in the hands of the Martians, for all we know." Worse, the Red Brigades won't discuss Jim's release. "Negotiate? For what?" demands their latest communiqué. "The proletariat has nothing to negotiate with the bourgeoisie."

I have left Verona, first to visit friends in Naples and then on to Germany to stay with other close friends. I awaken this January morning feeling very optimistic. Why? I walk into the bathroom and look into the mirror wondering. All I know is that this is the day that the Lord has made and I should rejoice and be glad in it. But even when your husband has been a prisoner for 42 days?

Now, darkness gathers around us and we are confused in all our counsels. Losing faith in You, we lose faith in ourselves. Inspire us with wisdom, all of us, of every color, race and creed, to use our wealth, our strength, to help our brother, instead of destroying him. Help us to do Your will as it is done in Heaven and to be worthy of Your promise of peace on earth. Fill us with new faith, new strength and new courage, that we may win the battle for peace. Be swift to save us, dear God, before the darkness falls.

Gen. D.: I am starting to read the novel *1984* by George Orwell. It is not the most enjoyable story to read when a captive. "Big Brother" is all-pervasive. Yet I only have to remember the most powerful force of all, the love of our Father against Whom the principalities and evils of this world are nothing.

My calculations tell me that I'm somewhere around my 40th day of captivity. Jesus spent 40 days alone in the desert. I guess we all have to wander through our own wilderness at some time. Yet, something strange has been happening. Lately, I have found myself playing a scenario in my mind of what I will face on my release or rescue: the press conferences, debriefings. From where do such thoughts come?

There is a crash of splintering wood outside my tent, scuffling and shouts. My guard leaps to his feet and, with pistol aimed generally toward me, looks out the tent flap. A masked man bursts in and with one blow crumples him unconscious. Is it a rival gang invasion? My chains clattering, I grasp the masked invader, then feel the bulletproof vest under his black sweater. He hugs me and laughs. He is a commando from Italy's crack antiterrorist unit. The locks on my two chains are released and they fall away; and I am escorted downstairs to a waiting car. They tell me that 6,000 Italian investigators, working closely with the American and European experts, had conducted a mammoth sweep of suspects, following thousands of clues that led them to this apartment building in Padua, a town 48 miles east of Verona.

Thank God it is over.

Mrs. D.: I tell my friends how great I feel. We continue with our plans, and while preparing lunch, phone calls start to come in. Jim has been rescued! He's in good health and waiting for me in Italy. As our friends encircle me, cheering and crying, I stand in stunned silence. Our prayers have been answered— Jim is safe and coming home!

They say that Jim had been found in Padua. As with all Italian cities, it has a patron saint. The patron saint of Padua is Saint Anthony.

Gen. D.: Strange how the impressions given me in captivity have worked out in reality—the press conferences, the welcomes by the authorities and friends.

But, above all, one salient truth has been proven to me in a most amazing way. That our prayers for others, expressed in the love of God, can be our most powerful communication with them, transcending time and space.

For when I sat down with my executive officer, the American schoolteacher, the fellow general officer's wife, the American missionary and the many others whose loving, sustaining presences came to me in captivity so vividly, I learned in comparing notes with them that these happened at the very time they were earnestly praying for me.

"Who shall separate us from the love of Christ?" asks Paul. "Shall tribulation, or distress, or persecution, or famine, or nakedness, or peril, or sword?" (Romans 8:35,37)

"Nay," is his ringing answer, for "in all these things we are more than conquerors through Him that loved us!"

When Courage Is Needed

Most people think of courage as great acts of daring. They fail to see the numerous times when they themselves are called upon to be courageous during the course of an ordinary day. It takes courage for a parent to say no; it takes courage for a teenager to turn away from his drug-taking friends; courage for a businessman to take a loss by redeeming a defective product. Sometimes it takes courage just to be yourself. Roland Hayes, for one, knew about this.

Hayes was a man of many firsts. He was an American black, a member of the first generation to be born into freedom; he was the first of his family to go to college. And, in 1917, he was the first black classical singer to appear in Boston's Symphony Hall.

In 1924, Hayes was scheduled for a concert in Berlin. He had been warned not to go there. Editorials in German newspapers ranted that this black "from the cotton fields of Georgia" should not be allowed on a Berlin stage. People were incensed that he would presume to sing the great German songs of Schumann and Schubert.

When he stepped out on stage the night of the performance, the audience burst forth with a volley of boos and hisses. Hayes stood beside the piano and bowed his head. He prayed—not for himself, but for the audience before him. Two minutes, five minutes, ten minutes, he stood silently until the auditorium became still. Then he sang.

The concert was a success. Roland Hayes was praised for his interpretation of the German classics as well as the black spirituals that made up his program. But the victory was a larger one. Hayes had found the courage to face that crowd in resources outside himself. "It was God's victory," he wrote in Guideposts.

It takes courage to be the first to speak out. It takes courage to be a follower of Jesus Christ. And yet, the glorious truth is that the courage we need comes from Him.

baseball player Jackie Robinson (1919–1972) signing contract with Branch Rickey

AUGUST 1948

Trouble Ahead Needn't Bother You *by Jackie Robinson, baseball player*

I'll never forget the day Branch Rickey, president of the Brooklyn Dodgers, asked me to join his baseball organization. I would be the first black to play in organized baseball—that is, if I were good enough to make the grade.

Mr. Rickey's office was large and simply furnished. There were four framed pictures on the wall. One was a kodachrome snapshot of Leo Durocher, the field manager of the Dodgers. Another was a portrait of the late Charlie Barrett, one of the greatest scouts in the game. A third was of General Chennault. And the fourth and largest smiled down on me with calm reassurance, the portrait of the sad, trusting Abraham Lincoln who had pleaded for malice toward none....

This was the never-to-be-forgotten day when our Marines landed on the soil of Japan, August 29, 1945. It was a hot day with venetian blinds shutting out the sun, and the Brooklyn clamor of Montague Street mingled with the noisy traffic around Borough Hall.

From behind his desk, the big, powerful, bushy-browed Branch Rickey, who seemed a combination of father and boss, mapped out to me his daring strategy to break the color line in major league baseball.

I was excited at the opportunity. It was a tremendous challenge. But was I good enough?

"Mr. Rickey," I said, "it sounds like a dream come true—not only for me but for my race. For 70 years there has been racial exclusion in big league baseball. There will be trouble ahead—for you, for me, for my people and for baseball."

"Trouble ahead," Rickey rolled the phrase over his lips as though he liked the sound. "You know, Jackie, I was a small boy when I took my first train ride. On the same train was an old couple, also riding for the first time. We were going through the Rocky Mountains. The old man sitting by the window looked forward and said to his wife, 'Trouble ahead, Ma! We're high up over a precipice and we're gonna run right off.'

"To my boyish ears the noise of the wheels repeated 'Trouble-a-head-trouble-ahead...' I never hear train wheels to this day but what I think of this. But our train course bent into a tunnel right after the old man spoke, and we came out on the other side of the mountain. That's the way it is with most trouble ahead in this world, Jackie—if we use the common sense and courage God gave us. But you've got to study the hazards and build wisely."

I've never forgotten that little story. It helped me through many of the rough moments I was to face in the future. I signed my contract that day with a humble feeling of great responsibility. I prayed that I would be equal to the test.

"God is with us in this, Jackie," Mr. Rickey said quietly. "You know your Bible. It's good, simple Christianity for us to face realities

Branch Rickey (1881–1965), a longtime friend of Guideposts, deserves the credit for some of the finest innovations in professional baseball. As manager of the St. Louis Cardinals, he virtually invented the minor-league farm system. Later, when he brought Jackie Robinson on to the Brooklyn Dodgers, breaking the color barrier, he faced considerable criticism. As he said in Guideposts (1954), "I would feel unworthy if criticism…dulled the edge of my courage." Branch Rickey went to bat for his faith.

and to recognize what we're up against. We can't go out and preach and crusade and bust our heads against a wall. We've got to fight out our problems together with tact and common sense."

To give me experience and seasoning, Mr. Rickey sent me the first year to play with the Montreal Royals, a farm club for the Brooklyn organization. I was the cause of trouble from the start—but we expected it. Preseason exhibition games were cancelled because of "mixed athletes," although the official reason was always different.

Some of my teammates may have resented me. If so, I didn't blame them. They had problems enough playing ball without being a part of a racial issue. I tried hard not to develop "rabbit ears," a malady picked up by all athletes who are sensitive to abuse and criticism shouted from the fans.

One of my top thrills was my opening game for Montreal at Jersey City. The pressure was on and I was very nervous. But during that contest I slapped out four hits, including a home run. I couldn't have dreamed up a better start.

But as the season began to unroll game after game, my play grew erratic. I was trying too hard. I knew I had to keep my temper bridled at every turn. Guarding so carefully against outbursts can put a damper on one's competitive spirit.

Every athlete at some time or another likes "to blow his top." It seldom does any harm and acts like a safety valve. A hitter in a slump may

drive the ball deep to the infield, then leg it to first—sure that he has beaten the throw. The umpire calls him out. With this, the frustrated athlete jerks off his cap, slams it on the ground and thunders all his rage at the umpire. The crowd roars its approval or dislike depending on whether the player is on the home or visiting team. The umpire merely turns his back, and the ball player, after giving vent to his unhappiness, trots back to the bench feeling much better. It's all a part of the game.

But I didn't dare let loose this way. Many would have dubbed me a "hothead" and point to my outburst as a reason why blacks should not play in organized baseball. This was one of the hardest problems I had to face.

As the season rolled along, however, the players became accustomed to me. My play improved. When the season ended, Montreal had won the Junior World Series. I admit proudly to winning the batting championship of the league with an average .349.

On April 10, 1947, Branch Rickey made the announcement that gave me my greatest thrill. I was to join the Brooklyn Dodgers and become the first black to compete in the Major Leagues.

To add to my regular problems of bucking the expected publicity and criticism, I was placed at a strange position—first base. At Montreal I had played second base.

It was Montreal all over again, only this time the pressure was much greater, the competition keener and the stakes tremendous. It wasn't a question so much of a minority ath-

*Moral courage, physical courage…Corrie ten Boom (1892–1983)
had both. Corrie and her family hid Jews from the Nazis in their
home in Haarlem, Holland, during World War II. And sheer nerve
led Corrie to conceal a Bible under her prison dress after the ten
Booms were taken away to a German death camp. The source of
Corrie's courage? "A stronger power that had the final word…
even at Ravensbrück."*

lete making good as a big leaguer, but whether the whole racial question would be advanced or retarded.

I prayed as I never had before.

As a first baseman I had many fielding shortcomings. I worked hard to iron them out and both fans and players by and large were rooting for me. This encouragement was a big factor in helping me improve my game.

That year, the Dodgers won the pennant. I was thrilled to know that my efforts were considered an important factor in winning. But I also cherished another triumph. Baseball as a whole had come to accept blacks. From now on the black ball player, to make the grade, will simply have to be a good enough player. As Mr. Rickey says, a champion is a champion in America, black or white.

NOVEMBER 1956

Five Minutes Longer *by Dr. Harold W. Ruopp*

More than five years ago, ill health compelled me to resign my position as minister of a large church in a Midwestern city and move to a different part of the country. A stranger in a strange land, cut off from creative activity and the accustomed greetings of friends, I was having a none-too-easy time of it. I had to do daily battle with self-pity. Worst of all, I kept projecting the "bad" times of the past and present into the future.

"I can't take it," I found myself saying.

Then one day—quite by chance (or was it chance?)—I came upon these words: "A hero is no braver than anyone else; he is only brave five minutes longer."

Wonderful medicine—those words! Sure, the future was uncertain—intolerable indeed, if I thought of it in terms of weeks and months and years, but I could "take it" five minutes at a time.

So I found a short piece of rope, tied a knot in one end, and hung it over a picture at the foot of my bed. When the pain was great or self-pity started to take over, I would look at the rope and say to myself: "When you come to what *seems* to be the end of your rope, there is still one thing you can do—you can tie a knot and hold on."

For sometimes, just to hold on—five minutes longer—spells victory.

Corrie ten Boom (center) with Guideposts editors John and Elizabeth Sherrill

NOVEMBER 1972

I'm Still Learning to Forgive *by Corrie ten Boom, writer and lecturer*

It was in a church in Munich that I saw him, a balding heavyset man in a gray overcoat, a brown felt hat clutched between his hands. People were filing out of the basement room where I had just spoken, moving along the rows of wooden chairs to the door at the rear. It was 1947 and I had come from Holland to defeated Germany with the message that God forgives.

It was the truth they needed most to hear in that bitter, bombed-out land, and I gave them my favorite mental picture. Maybe because the sea is never far from a Hollander's mind, I liked to think that that's where forgiven sins were thrown. "When we confess our sins," I said, "God casts them into the deepest ocean, gone forever."

The solemn faces stared back at me, not quite daring to believe. There were never questions after a talk in Germany in 1947. People stood up in silence, in silence collected their wraps, in silence left the room.

And that's when I saw him, working his way forward against the others. One moment I saw the overcoat and the brown hat; the next, a blue uniform and a visored cap with its skull and crossbones. It came back with a rush: the huge room with its harsh overhead lights, the pathetic pile of dresses and shoes in the center of the floor, the shame of walking naked past this man. I could see my sister's frail form ahead of me, ribs sharp beneath the parchment skin. Betsie, how thin you were!

Betsie and I had been arrested for concealing Jews in our home during the Nazi occupation of Holland; this man had been a guard at Ravensbrück concentration camp where we were sent.

Now he was in front of me, hand thrust out: "A fine message, *fräulein*! How good it is to know that, as you say, all our sins are at the bottom of the sea!"

And I, who had spoken so glibly of forgiveness, fumbled in my pocketbook rather than take that hand. He would not remember me, of course—how could he remember one prisoner among those thousands of women?

But I remembered him and the leather crop swinging from his belt. It was the first time since my release that I had been face to face with one of my captors and my blood froze.

"You mentioned Ravensbrück in your talk," he was saying. "I was a guard in there." No, he did not remember me.

"But since that time," he went on, "I have become a Christian. I know that God has forgiven me for the cruel things I did there, but I would like to hear it from your lips as well, *Fräulein*—" again the hand came out— "will you forgive me?"

And I stood there—I whose sins had every day to be forgiven—and could not. Betsie had died in that place—could he erase her slow terrible death simply for the asking?

It could not have been many seconds that he stood there, hand held out, but to me it

In October 1941, the Nazis bombed England's Coventry cathedral, leaving behind a ruined shell. Twenty years later, within those charred walls, a group of Germans built an international center with a small chapel at its heart. They called themselves, Aktion Sühnezeichen, *a German phrase that means "atonement, reconciliation and restitution" (Guideposts 1962). For with these stones, they built proof of the reconciling power of Christ's love.*

seemed hours as I wrestled with the most difficult thing I had ever had to do.

For I had to do it—I knew that. The message that God forgives has a prior condition: that we forgive those who have injured us. "If you do not forgive men their trespasses," Jesus says, "neither will your Father in heaven forgive your trespasses."

I knew it not only as a commandment of God, but as a daily experience. Since the end of the war, I had had a home in Holland for victims of Nazi brutality. Those who were able to forgive their former enemies were also able to return to the outside world and rebuild their lives, no matter what the physical scars. Those who nursed their bitterness remained invalids. It was as simple and as horrible as that.

And still I stood there with the coldness clutching my heart. But forgiveness is not an emotion—I knew that too. Forgiveness is an act of the will, and the will can function regardless of the temperature of the heart. "Jesus, help me!" I prayed silently. "I can lift my hand. I can do that much. You supply the feeling."

And so woodenly, mechanically, I thrust my hand into the one stretched out to me. And as I did, an incredible thing took place. The current started in my shoulder, raced down my arm, sprang into our joined hands. And then this healing warmth seemed to flood my whole being, bringing tears to my eyes.

"I forgive you, brother!" I cried. "With all my heart!"

For a long moment we grasped each other's hands, the former guard and the former prisoner. I had never known God's love so intensely as I did then.

And having thus learned to forgive in this hardest of situations, I never again had difficulty in forgiving: I wish I could say it! I wish I could say that merciful and charitable thoughts just naturally flowed from me from then on. But they didn't. If there's one thing I've learned at 80 years of age, it's that I can't store up good feelings and behavior—but only draw them fresh from God each day.

Maybe I'm glad it's that way. For every time I go to Him, He teaches me something else. I recall the time, some 15 years ago, when some Christian friends whom I loved and trusted did something that hurt me. You would have thought that, having forgiven the Nazi guard, this would have been child's play. It wasn't. For weeks I seethed inside. But at last I asked God again to work His miracle in me. And again it happened: first the decision, then the flood of joy and peace. I had forgiven my friends; I was restored to my Father.

Then, why was I suddenly awake in the middle of the night, hashing over the whole affair again? *My friends!* I thought. *People I loved!* If it had been strangers, I wouldn't have minded so.

I sat up and switched on the light. "Father, I thought it was all forgiven! Please help me."

But the next night I woke up again. They'd talked so sweetly too! Never a hint of what they were planning. "Father!" I cried in alarm. "Help me!"

His help came in the form of a kindly Lutheran pastor to whom I confessed my

Coventry Cathedral, England, 1943

failure after two sleepless weeks. "Up in that church tower," he said, nodding out the window, "is a bell, which is rung by pulling on a rope. But you know what? After the sexton lets go of the rope, the bell keeps on swinging. First *ding* then *dong.* Slower and slower until there's a final *dong* and it stops.

"I believe the same thing is true of forgiveness. When we forgive someone, we take our hand off the rope. But if we've been tugging at our grievances for a long time, we mustn't be surprised if the old angry thoughts keep coming for a while. They're just the ding-dongs of the old bell slowing down."

And so it proved to be. There were a few more midnight reverberations, a couple of dings when the subject came up in my conversation. But the force—which was my willingness in the matter—had gone out of them. They came less and less often and at last stopped altogether. And so I discovered another secret of forgiveness: that we can trust God not only above our emotions, but also above our thoughts.

And still He had more to teach me, even in this single episode. Because many years later, in 1970, an American with whom I had shared the ding-dong principle came to visit me in Holland and met the people involved. "Aren't those the friends who let you down?" he asked as they left my apartment.

"Yes," I said a little smugly. "You can see it's all forgiven."

"By you, yes," he said. "But what about them? Have they accepted your forgiveness?"

"They say there's nothing to forgive! They deny it ever happened. But I can prove it!" I went eagerly to my desk. "I have it in black and white! I saved all their letters and I can show you where——"

"Corrie!" My friend slipped his arm through mine and gently closed the drawer. "Aren't you the one whose sins are at the bottom of the sea? And are the sins of your friends etched in black and white?"

For an anguishing moment I could not find my voice. "Lord Jesus," I whispered at last, "who takes all my sins away, forgive me for preserving all these years the evidence against others! Give me grace to burn all the blacks and whites as a sweet-smelling sacrifice to Your glory."

I did not go to sleep that night until I had gone through my desk and pulled out those letters—curling now with age—and fed them all into my little coal-burning grate. As the flames leaped and glowed, so did my heart. "Forgive us our trespasses," Jesus taught us to pray, "as we forgive those who trespass against us." In the ashes of those letters I was seeing yet another facet of His mercy. What more He would teach me about forgiveness in the days ahead I didn't know, but tonight's was good news enough.

When we bring our sins to Jesus, He not only forgives them, He makes them as if they had never been.

*Well into this century, women found their athletic prowess derided.
Then along came Babe Didriksen Zaharias (1914–1956). With
native strength and grace, she won two Olympic golds in 1932,
pitched in an exhibition for the St. Louis Cardinals and starred for
a barnstorming men's basketball team. Later, as a golfer, she won
every available tournament title. In 1950, she was named the half-
century's greatest woman athlete. God gave Babe great gifts and her
exuberant play surely gave Him pleasure.*

SEPTEMBER 1954

Spiritual Muscle *by Babe Didriksen Zaharias, athlete*

A little dazed, my husband and I left the doctor's office and walked through the streets of Beaumont, Texas, to the hotel where we were staying. George kept saying: "Cancer? That's impossible."

It seemed impossible, for me. I had never been ill a day in my life. Years of athletics had practically guaranteed good health. I had just won the 1953 Babe Zaharias Open in Beaumont and was packed for an early start for Phoenix where I wanted a few days' practice before the next tournament. I had been feeling unusually tired, so George and I decided on the medical examination. Now I found myself headed, not for a golf tournament, but to the hospital.

Most dreadful was the thought that I would never again participate in sports. The most important part of my life was being slammed shut. From now on, I could only look back.

I could look back on the 1932 Olympics when I won two first-places—in javelin throwing and the 80-meter hurdles. I could look back on a 20-year career that took me into 334 contests in every amateur sport, and I had won all but two. And I could look back on golf, the game I loved, in which I had won every tournament it was possible for me to enter.

It was summer of 1952 when I became aware of a strange weariness. My drives were falling short. On the green, I missed easy putts. George sensed my doubts.

"This tiredness, honey," he said. "If it worries you, maybe you ought to see a doctor."

Once we had the doctor's diagnosis, nobody made a secret of the fact that I had cancer. I've never understood why cancer should be unmentionable. In golf, you know where the sand traps and water holes are ahead and you try to guide your shots accordingly. With cancer, you know that recovery will require something more than surgical skill, so—in a sort of spiritual way—you guide your shots.

Soon the newspapers everywhere announced that I had cancer. Thousands of cancer patients and thousands of others who were afraid of the disease wrote, wired and telephoned in the few days before my operation.

Everybody promised prayers.

This was something new for me. All my life, I had looked upon prayer as something very personal between God and me. I guess I've prayed for the same blessings and with the same gratitude as everyone else, but it never occurred to me that thousands of people, separated far from each other, could effectively join in a barrage of prayers for the sake of one person—for me.

Being an athlete, I could express my feelings by saying: "Here is wonderful teamwork in faith."

Many times after a tournament, I recalled, a fan would say something like, "My heart was in my mouth when you lined up that tricky putt

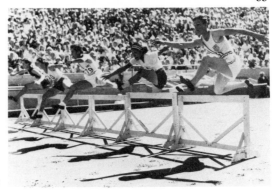

Babe Didriksen (far right) in 1932 Olympics

on the 10th hole. I was praying all the time." Yet, I didn't think anybody was really praying. Now, lying in the hospital, waiting for surgery, I felt differently. If I was going to be all right again, I'd need more than my own prayers: I'd need the prayers of everyone who had promised them.

Suddenly I looked upon prayers as muscles, and I realized that the strongest people in the world must be those who pray for each other. There was strength in this sharing, but I soon realized that I had to give to others as well as accept for myself. It would help us all move closer to God, "from Whom all blessings flow." Praying for each other struck me as a spiritual training that kept everyone spiritually fit to deserve those blessings.

After the operation, the doctor came to me. "All right, Babe," he said, "I want to see you up and out of here real soon, and before the season's over I want to read on the sports pages that you've won another tournament."

The doctor had performed a colostomy— surgery that meant vital changes in my entire way of life. People I had known with colostomies were virtual invalids. For a fleeting moment, I was terrified—until I remembered that I hadn't gone into this thing alone.

Many letters had come from people with cancer, people who seemed more concerned about my recovery than their own. One kind man wrote:

"You must return to your game, Babe. Knowing you're back at golf will be a victory for us, too. Cancer kills more than a human body; it kills the human spirit because we feel we who have it are incurable. Your physical recovery, Babe, will provide a spiritual steadiness for all the rest of us. That's why our prayers are always with you."

Suddenly I realized that golf now for me was more than a sport. Because of what it would symbolize to thousands of cancer patients—a victory through spiritual strength—my game would become, in a way, a symbol of faith.

A few months after the operation, I stepped up to a tee for the first time. Despite my confidence, I couldn't suppress a small uncertainty. I was anxious for the first shot, yet a little afraid of it.

I swung. When I looked up, I saw the ball arching far down the fairway. I glanced at my husband. He was smiling.

Now there was a job to do. First, the doctor's prescription: Play Golf. And there were the cancer patients, many of them with colostomies, who were looking to me for the same sort of help I had received from them. Knowing now that God answered prayers, I wanted to return to golf to demonstrate this—and also to show others that they, too, could resume their normal lives.

In August, 1953, just four months after my operation, I entered Chicago's Tam O'Shanter Tournament. Back among the best players in golf, I was keenly aware of the competition. Tenseness tired me quickly. I began missing easy shots.

*As a young girl, Althea Gibson first played tennis in Harlem streets.
She soon grew expert, but until 1950 she was limited to all-black
tournaments. When she was free to play with all women, she did not
enjoy instant success. For seven years she struggled, relying on hard
work and faith, at last winning Wimbledon in 1957. The struggle
made her wise. Faith, Althea said in Guideposts (1960), is believing
steadily; persisting is doing steadily. You need both to succeed,
because faith gives you the strength to persist.*

We were on the fifth green when an important putt stopped just short of the cup. Shattered, I stretched out my hands, still gripping the club, and buried my face in my arms and cried. This was my blackest moment, even worse than learning I had cancer. The tournament had taken on a special meaning, and there were thousands of others, I felt, who would be on the losing side with me.

Standing there, so terribly alone, I heard George approach me, and Betty Dodd, my playing companion. I felt their comforting hands on my shoulder—and, in a wonderful way, the hands of the many others, I whispered a prayer.

"Please, God...You've helped me this far. Give me the strength to go on...please."

I came in third in this tournament, better than anyone expected. In quite a different way, I scored a first.

Somewhere between the fifth hole and the last, I made up my mind that there would be no more tears. Perhaps, for the first time, I really flexed my spiritual muscles.

A few months later, I won the Serbin Invitational; then the Sarasota Open and last spring the National Capitol Women's Open.

And this past July, I came out on top in the United States Women's Open, the most important tournament of the year.

Actually *we* won it.

We are the thousands of people whose faith helped make me strong. United through our prayers, we share our separate victories.

José Rivero, 1961

FEBRUARY 1961

The Night Our Paper Died *by José I. Rivero, newspaper editor*

Havana was filled with an excitement that you could see in the brightness of men's eyes and hear in the pitch of their voices. The hated dictator Batista had fled. Rumors flew from lip to lip that Fidel Castro was on his way to Havana, coming from the mountains where he had fought Batista for five years. Already the city was filled with Barbudos, the bearded, war-dirty Revolutionaries, carrying carbines, waving to the crowds that lined the Prado.

And then Castro himself did come, bearded, smiling; yet if you looked closely you'd see that his eyes did not pick up the smile on his lips.

At first I was happy to throw the support of our newspaper behind this man. I am sure that Castro was happy, too, about that support. *Diario de la Marina* was the oldest and most influential paper in Cuba, with a reputation for speaking out against tyranny. My grandfather had been stoned because of his editorials. My own earliest memories are of exiles: my three brothers and I were taken often to the United States "to visit relatives" while my father stayed on to fight the dictator Machado.

When it was my turn, I, too, printed the truth as I knew it about Batista, and rejoiced to see his regime topple. None of us was aware that the biggest fight was still ahead.

I was full of hope as Fidel Castro came into Havana. Within a week, however, I began to suspect that something was wrong. For Castro was bringing Cuba not freedom, but hatred.

He spent long hours before the TV, spitting out promises of revenge. He showed us how he dealt with his enemies: he executed them before TV cameras. On home sets, children were watching the death throes of men who were shot before the *paredon*—the firing wall.

Castro's reforms? He seemed bent on coupling them with vengeance. New schools were rising, but with this went a harsh proclamation: any academic degree earned during Batista's regime was invalid.

Economic aid? He had promised cheaper housing: arbitrarily he cut all rents in half, whether the landlord was a millionaire speculator or a widow whose only income was the rental of a spare room. Under another law, hundreds of farms were seized. Farm workers had their wages cut almost in half. Of this, only 50 cents a day was paid in cash, the rest in script usable only in "People's Stores."

A suspicion was growing that Fidel Castro was a Communist. In my mind, I began to review: his use of hate to gain support; his People's Courts; his division of society into two classes, one the hero, the other the villain.

What should I do about it, I asked myself? I had watched Castro handling his enemies before the paredon. There was no doubt in my mind that if I crossed him, mobs would appear outside our windows shouting *"Paredon! Paredon!..."*

What should I do? I was proud of the new

When Dagoberto Jorge worked as a designer in a Havana advertising agency, he often brought printing plates to José Rivero's newspaper office. Castro closed both the agency and the paper in 1960. Dagoberto arrived in New York on a Thursday in 1965, with only his God-given talents and courage. He began work as a dishwasher on Friday, using his first wages to pay for English lessons. He came to Guideposts in 1967 as a one-week temporary. He is still here today, serving as the magazine's assistant art director, and our most exuberant staffer.

buildings that housed *Diario* now: the roto-gravures, gleaming behind glass doors; the thump and whir of our new presses. Here was a powerful, ready-made medium, but it could speak only if I told it to.

Then one day, early in January 1960, I sat down at my desk, and suddenly, I was aware of the crucifix. It was a simple ivory crucifix that my mother had given me. I had mounted it on velvet and hung it over my desk to remind me to always use the power of the paper in a Christian manner. Now, it seemed almost as if Jesus were looking down at me with sadness in His eyes, saying:

"You will lose the paper. You may lose your life. But do you have any choice?"

I knew in that moment that I did *not* have any choice. From that day on, I began to write editorials about the things I did not think cor- rect in Fidel Castro's regime.

Castro reacted as I knew he would. After my first editorial, he berated me on TV, shouting that I was the newest "enemy of the people."

But I did not stop the editorials.

A month passed. And another. Castro broadened his barrage: not only on TV but also on radio and through the controlled newspapers, he urged the public not to buy *Diario*. When our circulation doubled under his attack, he turned to the brute strength of the mob.

"I cannot take responsibility for the actions of fired-up Fidelista," he shouted over TV.

And the Fidelistas took the hint. They burned bundles of *Diario* on the street. Crowds of hundreds appeared outside my office. I began to hear the cry I had been awaiting: *"Paredon! Paredon!"*

And they began to harass my family. One evening, my home was surrounded by 62 secret police. The next day I sent my wife and part of our family to Miami "to visit relatives." I never went back to our home. From then on, I spent each night in the house of a different friend, and drove to the office in a different car. I felt the end was near.

I cleared the office of all valuables. Almost all, that is. I didn't know what to do about the crucifix. I didn't want to lose it when the paper was seized; yet I didn't want to be without it. I do not mean, of course, that an ivory crucifix had any power of its own. But it did remind me of my need to be especially close to Him. I left the crucifix on the wall. It gave me the sense of Christ's participation in our paper's martyr-dom, and this gave me the strength to carry through the next few days.

It happened just as I had expected. A group of Fidelistas arrived at the paper, walked through the plant, urged our employees to strike. After the Fidelistas left, however, our men passed a petition supporting the paper. I wrote an editorial about that petition and sent it to press. Later that day, while I was away from the paper, the Fidelistas came again— this time with machine guns. They broke through the glass doors into the rotogravure room and smashed the plates. Then they left.

No one could say that George Smith didn't have courage. A daring jet test pilot in the 1950s, back when the sound barrier was first being broken, he could face anything—until he had to bail out of a jet going 805 miles per hour (Guideposts 1958). Though he survived, he was afraid of ever flying again. Then, during his hospital stay, a nurse gave him an antidote to fear. He took her words to heart: "Courage," she said, "is knowing the worst—and discovering that, in God's world, the very worst can't really hurt you."

I returned as quickly as possible and my three brothers and I went through the roto-gravure section picking up fragments of the plates. As we stood there amid the debris, I heard a stir from the employees behind us.

I turned around. There stood Mother! She was supposed to be in Miami, safe. "If my sons are going to die," she said, "I am going to die with them."

"Now, Mother," we answered, "no one is going to die. But you can't stay here in Havana."

Mother stood firm. "The *paper* is going to die," she said. "I am not going to watch it happen from Miami. I fought beside your father and I'll fight beside you."

We literally had to pick her up and carry her from the building.

Mother's visit had stirred us with still greater determination.

We prepared another engraving of the petition, then started the presses. I waited at the plant until nearly 11 o'clock, then went to the home of friends for dinner. We had barely seated ourselves when the telephone rang.

"They have stopped the presses. Do not come down, José. They are after you now…"

That night, as the button was pushed and the presses stopped, the *Diario* died, the last independent journalistic voice in Cuba.

That night, I was hidden in a friend's house. I cannot identify the person who later took me to asylum in the Peruvian Embassy, but this much I can say: it was not easy to arrange. The Fidelistas had guessed my plan. Before dawn they lined up at the embassy, carrying their machine guns. I hid beneath a shroud-like sheet in the back of an automobile and was driven up to the embassy door. Minutes later, I slipped into a private entrance.

I was safe. A few hours later I escaped by plane to Peru.

Looking at it one way, I have lost my fight. Our home is gone. I sneaked out of my own country. Our newspaper is dead there.

But I wonder if the battle is really lost? A few days after I reached Peru, I boarded a plane for the United States. We landed at Miami where, to my amazement, a crowd was waiting, shouting and waving placards saying, "Hurrah for *Diario de la Marina!* Viva Rivero!"

It wasn't really "Viva Rivero!" that they were shouting. It was "Viva!"—that power which each of us is given to stand for what he believes. It was "Viva!"—the spirit in each of us which can stand up to injustice. As long as this spirit lives, is the battle lost?

I am sure, quite sure, that it is not.

In a comfortable middle-class neighborhood in Queens, N. Y., on March 13, 1964, 3:00 a.m., Catherine Genovese was stabbed to death ... and 37 people witnessed the crime without reporting it. That incident of public apathy caused America to recognize its moral values. We did much soul-searching at Guideposts too, and, whenever we could, we carried the stories of brave and caring people who did more than stand and watch. Meet one on the opposite page.

MARCH 1966

One Who Cared *by John Sherrill, editor*

Most of the boys had been drinking. Arms locked, they marched in threes and fours—a dozen or more of them— through the streets of downtown Philadelphia. They had a plan in mind; they were going to crash the Saturday night dance at a local hotel because they lacked ticket money. They were dressed for the occasion. Beneath topcoats they wore neatly pressed suits and ties, their shoes were shined, and even in the sharp March wind their hair showed signs of having been combed. The oldest of the boys was 18, the youngest 13.

The ticket taker at the dance remembers them. She recalls that they used vulgar language when she told them that they could not come in. The boys withdrew to a corner of the hotel lobby, huddled, then advanced toward the ballroom door. There they were stopped again, this time by a man who was big enough to scare them. They left, swearing revenge. In the all-but-deserted street outside, they met four boys coming to the dance. They jumped the newcomers and knocked them to the sidewalk. Then arm-in-arm the gang marched away laughing.

Another person who remembers them is the cashier at the change window in the Vine and Race Street subway station. She heard the boys run down the stairs behind her, and she saw them jump the turnstile and scurry down the flight of stairs to the subway platform.

Below, on the passenger platform, six men carrying bowling balls were waiting for a train. The boys looked them over.

"Hey, Dad! What time is it?"

"Ten o'clock."

The gang moved down the platform, out of sight of the men behind the wide green-and-white tiled pillars that support the subway ceiling. A short while later there was a sound of a bottle crashing against the tracks.

Fifteen minutes earlier and two blocks away, a young girl, Debbie,* pocketed her baby-sitting money and stepped out into the street.

Debbie was 16 years old. She was not from Philadelphia and the city streets at night made her nervous. The cousin she was visiting had got a date for that evening, and Debbie had taken her baby-sitting job. Now the dark empty sidewalk frightened her. She was glad when she reached the lighted stairway.

She dropped a coin in the turnstile, pushed her way through and went down the second flight of steps onto the subway platform. A group of men stood chatting at the north end. Instinctively she edged away from them and wandered south down the platform until they were out of sight behind the pillars.

A noise came from the tracks: it sounded like a bottle breaking.

Debbie stopped. From behind a pillar a heavyset young man appeared, moving toward her. Debbie backed away.

*Name has been changed.

On July 6, 1981, Jack Brignoli, the father of an autistic boy, was watching the TV news when he heard about another autistic boy missing on Black Mountain (Guideposts 1984). Without hesitating, he drove 100 miles to help. All night, he hiked through the woods, asking God to guide him. Just as he was about to quit, he heard a sound, a very particular sound. It's a good thing Jack Brignoli was willing to get involved, for among scores of rescuers combing the mountain, only he recognized the cry of an autistic boy.

Now she could see a whole gang of boys behind him. The first one said something but a rush of air whistled up the subway tracks and she could not hear. If only the train would come. And then suddenly the boy grabbed her arm and pulled her to him. Debbie could smell alcohol. She screamed and his hand went over her mouth. Now another boy grabbed at her. She heard her dress tear. She bit the hand at her mouth and screamed again. The men at the other end of the platform! They would hear her!

Perhaps half an hour before Debbie entered the subway station, a 23-year-old college student from Chamblee, Georgia, James R. George, bought a second cup of coffee at the cafeteria where he'd just finished dinner. A Naval Air Reservist, "Bud" George was spending his spring vacation at a training session in antisubmarine warfare at Willow Grove Naval Air Station outside Philadelphia. It was his first trip north and he'd spent his afternoon visiting historic sites.

"Kind of funny," he mused. "Here I am with an overnight pass in my pocket, and what do I do? I go to Independence Hall."

Bud's parents had had one simple method of bringing up children. They raised them on the Bible. Every evening, Mrs. George assembled the children and methodically, a chapter a night, read straight through the Bible. She was not reading to entertain; she was reading to train. The children were sometimes bored, but often their eyes glistened at the stories of Daniel, Joseph, David—stories of men responding heroically to the situations that God presented to them.

Bud finished his coffee and left. He passed the Vine and Race Street subway station. It was 10 past 10: getting late. He thought he'd go back to Willow Grove and save a hotel bill.

Bud did not come into the station by the main entrance but by a secondary entrance at the south end, where there is an automatic turnstile. He put his money in the slot, pushed through and went down to the platform.

At the other end, a group of men carrying bowling balls were peering curiously down the track in his direction. Nearby, he could hear scuffles and laughter.

"Teenagers cutting up," he thought.

And then he heard a scream.

"Let me alone!"

Bud ran toward the sound. Suddenly, around the column, he came upon a scene so unbelievable that for a minute he could only mistrust his eyes. There, out on the open subway platform—with several men standing within earshot and a train rumbling down on them—a group of boys were holding a screaming and nearly naked girl on her back.

Several of the boys saw him and jumped up. "Get that guy!"

Bud swung and hit the first one in the mouth. He felt a blow in his stomach and missed his next punch.

A headlight appeared down the track. Four of the boys were dragging the girl out of sight beneath the stairway. A fist hit Bud in the nose

At the end of World War II, people wanted God's peace to rule all nations. To further this hope, the United Bible Societies —an international union of Bible missionaries—came into being in 1946. Much progress has been made in their effort to spread God's Word worldwide. The Bible is now available in 1,600 languages. Each year, UBS distributes nearly 300,000 copies of Scripture. All told, more people now read the Bible than at any previous time in the world's history.

and blood spurted out. The train screamed into the station. The group of men who had been waiting quietly stepped aboard.

Another fist hit Bud in the eye. He felt his own slam into bone. Then he got a rabbit punch in the back of the neck. Someone was kicking him with sharp-toed dancing shoes. He does not remember climbing the stairs, only crawling up the last one, shouting to the cashier in the subway change booth.

"Call the police! They're attacking a girl down there!"

The cashier picked up her telephone and dialed the number. Bud went back down the stairs, steadying himself on the railing. Far down the tunnel, the red taillights of the train receded into the distance. The boys jumped onto the tracks and started running in the opposite direction. In what seemed like seconds the station swarmed with police; one ran down the tracks looking for the boys, one gave Bud first aid, another went to help the girl.

An officer came down the platform, his coat around the girl. "Let's get you two to a hospital." Above, a row of police cars waited, red lights whirling. The police put the girl in one, Bud into another, and, with sirens blasting the night, the cars sped away.

When the doctors had treated Bud's cuts and bruises, they let Bud inquire about the girl. She had been badly beaten and one of her teeth knocked out, but Bud had reached her in time. Within 24 hours, all of the boys involved had been arrested. Bud testified at the trial. The boys were sentenced to a long term in a correctional institution.

And Bud found to his amazement that he was a celebrity. Newspapers, radio, TV, everyone wanted to interview him.

"Where did you get the guts?" one reporter asked him. "From the things we read today, people don't want to get involved."

Bud thought a minute. He thought of his parents' living room in Georgia, to the Book always open....

"It depends," said Bud, "on what you read."

*Russian tank in Prague, Czechoslovakia,
August 1968*

AUGUST 1969

Appointment in Prague *by Brother Andrew, evangelist*

It was hot that August morning in our crowded attic rooms. This space above the family living quarters is headquarters in Holland for our work of bringing Bibles and encouragement to Christians in Communist countries.

I was glad when 12 o'clock came and I could go downstairs to catch the noon news on television and join my wife, Corrie, and the kids for lunch.

Corrie handed me a cup of coffee as I waited for the TV set to warm up. Then I saw, coming into focus on the TV screen, a column of troops moving slowly down a street.

Now they were marching across a broad open place. I recognized it: Wenceslas Square, Prague. It was not a movie, not an old war film, but events taking place in Czechoslovakia that very day.

Now, what did it mean—those Soviet tanks that the TV screen showed rolling up a tree-lined Prague avenue? Was God saying something in that column of marching soldiers? What was His plan in Czechoslovakia? I knew I must go and find out.

That was noon on Wednesday. It took us the rest of that day and part of the next to load our Citroën sedan with Czech and Slovak Bibles, and Russian Bibles for the occupying troops. At noon Thursday, I said good-bye to Corrie and the children.

At 3 p.m. on Friday, August 23, I pulled up to the Czech border station east of Nuremberg, Germany. The customs officials were preoccupied with the endless line of cars waiting to leave the country. After a long while, one of the customs officers spotted me.

"You want to go *in?*" he asked in German.

"Yes, sir. Very much."

"But—do you not know the trouble that is in our country?"

"Yes. That's why I want to go in."

He studied me. "You are the first through here since Wednesday," he said. Then abruptly, with not so much as a glance at my luggage, he stamped my papers and lifted the gate. And so I and my precious cargo rolled into Czechoslovakia.

I was wondering if I would make Prague by daylight—and if not, whether I could find the apartment house where I was headed—when up ahead I saw two enormous tanks drawn up on either side of the highway, guns trained on the road. As I slammed on my brakes, a soldier in a green Russian uniform stepped into the road and signaled me to pull over.

He stared at me curiously for a moment. Then he pointed to the trunk of the car and the suitcases in the back seat. One by one I opened things, avoiding even a glance at the spots where Bibles were hidden. At last he told me with a gesture to close the bags, and held out his hand for my papers. I am sure he could not read a word of Dutch, but he made a brave show of examining each one in great detail. Then with a little salute he returned them to me and waved me on.

The Russian author Boris Pasternak (1890–1960) defied the Soviet authorities to publish his novel, Doctor Zhivago. *He spoke out. And for it, he paid a price by having his book banned. Never retracting a word, he stood behind what he had written. It was the truth. He was quoted in* Guideposts *(1961) as follows, "What has for centuries raised man above the beast is not the cudgel, but the irresistible power of unarmed truth."*

Twice more, between the border and Pilsen, I was stopped at Russian roadblocks. I longed to give Bibles to these men and to speak my few Russian words about God's love for them; but until the bulk of my cargo was safely delivered in Prague, I dared not.

At Pilsen, I overtook part of the advancing occupation force. Before I realized what was happening, I was wedged into a column of tanks, mounted guns and transport trucks, all moving toward Prague. In each village, the Czech people lined the roads to watch this foreign army take possession of their land; some weeping, some scowling, all deathly silent.

And then they would spot me, a small gray car with blue Dutch license plates in the endless convoy of military green. Here was a Westerner who was not *leaving* Czechoslovakia, he was coming *in*. A shout would go up, a roar of welcome and approval. Grown-ups waved and children raced to keep abreast of me. Whenever the column halted, someone would dash into the street, lean through the window and pin to my jacket one of the tiny red-white-and-blue Czech flags they all were wearing—until my chest bristled with them. And I, who had wanted to attract as little attention as possible, found myself the most conspicuous thing on the highway.

Whenever I could, I darted forward six or seven places before squeezing back into line again. At last, weaving my way in and out of the column, I passed the lead vehicle and quickly put as much distance as I could between myself and it.

My destination was the small Moravian church I had visited on my very first trip to Czechoslovakia in 1955. The church had no building, just a few rooms in an apartment house, and I knew it would take me a while to find it again in that ancient and bewildering treasure chest of a city.

By the time I topped the hill that overlooks Prague, a rain had started. In the fast-growing dusk, I drove into the city.

Down one avenue after another I went, peering through the strokes of the windshield wiper in mounting confusion, searching vainly for a street sign. It wasn't just the rain and the twilight. There *weren't* any street signs!

I gazed at blocks of storefronts downtown. There wasn't a name anywhere. The signs in front of churches were gone. Numbers on residences had disappeared. Gradually I realized that I was seeing a city gone anonymous, a city attempting to gain precious hours for those who had to hide.

At last I spotted a hitchhiker and stopped to ask him, in German, if he knew how to get to the address I was looking for. He hopped into the seat beside me and guided me there. The painting of an open Bible that usually stood in front of the building was gone, along with the street number; but I recognized the place, thanked my guide and ran up the steps to the second floor.

The pastor's face when he saw me standing in his doorway made me forget the sleepless hours behind the wheel. It is always a joy for Christians to meet, but never more so than when one of them is in special need.

Russian writer Boris Pasternak, 1890–1960

Inside the apartment, I noticed that the window shades were drawn. But it was not until I opened a window, at bedtime, that I saw that the rainy street outside was pitch black. Not a street lamp, not a glimmer of light from a window anywhere.

"They've ordered a blackout?" I said.

In the dark, my host chuckled. "We have," he said. "There's still a lot to do. Signs we couldn't get down last night, people to get away —lots to do."

And again I had a glimpse of what the day had already shown me, a nation traditionally so divided, between Czech and Slovak, Protestant and Catholic, political liberal and political conservative, discovering in this crisis their essential oneness.

Early Saturday morning we were out on the sidewalks, my pastor friend, a dozen other Christians and myself, armed with the tracts I had brought. We had to plead, not to get people to take them, but to leave us some for the next block. Never before had I stood in a public place and had Christian literature literally snatched from my hands. Of course, I could not fool myself that they were all potential converts; probably anyone who wasn't Russian and a soldier could have gathered a following that day.

I found myself wondering if God allows trouble in the world because it's the only time He can attract our attention.

At any rate, it was again a time of trouble in Czechoslovakia. And as I traveled about the country during the next week, speaking through a translator in churches, in homes, on street corners, I knew with a certainty that it was also God's time.

I knew that I would go back to Holland only long enough to fill the car once more and find others to come too. And the day I knew it best was the day I met Dr. Jan Benes.*

This Princeton University graduate has spent years in a forced labor camp for his Christian beliefs. He has the most radiant face I have ever seen. At his home, I asked him the question I had asked all over Czechoslovakia. "Why the invasion?"

I had heard political answers, military answers, angry answers and despairing ones. He offered none of those. Eyes glowing with trust, he said, "God took away our idol."

"Idol?" I asked.

"Why, yes. Every country—every man— has an idol. With us, it was Russia. We admired her so. And rightly. Her advances in literacy, science, living standards—how God must love those things!

"But you see, we had begun to think she was infallible—and this is something God wants us to believe only of Him. He had to show us what people—even idealistic people—do when we place them where He belongs.

"He had to show us that even noble goals, when they are short of Him, must be corrupted along the way. He had to take our eyes off men and put them on Jesus."

*Name has been changed.

baseball star Johnny Bench

MAY 1978

Thank You, Philip *by Johnny Bench, baseball player*

If you had told me five years ago that a little boy was going to come into my life, steal my heart and turn me into a person capable of giving and receiving deep love, I'd have scoffed at the idea. I was a 25-year-old major-league baseball player for the Cincinnati Reds with only one goal—to become the best catcher in the history of baseball.

That was before I met Philip. He was a sad-looking kid, I remember thinking, when he showed up at an autographing session I was doing in 1973 as part of a product-promotion tour at a Dayton, Ohio, department store. It was November, so there weren't many suntans in that group that stood waiting for me to write my name on shopping bags, sweat shirts, ball gloves, even sales receipts, but Philip's complexion was as white as a flour bag. Also, he was skinnier than a stray dog and he seemed to have no hair. Sue Lilly, an employee of the department store, who was helping me work the crowd, whispered that his name was Philip Buckingham, that he had leukemia and that chemotherapy treatment had left him bald.

"Come 'ere, Pardner," I said with an enthusiasm I didn't feel. It took little encouragement. Running as fast as his four-year-old legs would go, Philip jumped onto my lap and threw his arms around my neck. For an instant I started to pull back, then caught myself.

"I love the Reds, and Johnny Bench best of all," he announced with a beaming smile.

"Attaboy!" I answered, pulling his oversized Cincinnati baseball cap over his eyes. Then I gave him my autograph and sent him on his way. "Good luck to you, Philip."

"You better win a pennant next year," he called back. I wondered if he would even be around the next year. Regardless, I was glad that was over. It made me nervous to be around sick people, and I'd had enough talk about cancer to last a lifetime. Late in the 1972 baseball season, I had developed some pain in my back. Doctors diagnosed it as a lung lesion, a tumor that would have to be removed. Could it be malignant? Not likely, I was told. Even so, I was enormously troubled, and I let few people know about the operation. Fortunately for me, the growth was benign, but the emotional shock waves were still vibrating when this four-year-old leukemia sufferer came along. I was happy to get him out of sight as quickly as possible. The trouble was, I couldn't get him out of my mind.

Later, I commented to Sue Lilly about "that poor kid." She told me how poor. The hospital expenses had been so astronomical that the Buckinghams were afraid of losing their home. Furthermore, they were without a car and Philip had to be taken by bus to the hospital for treatments. On the long bus ride, he would often become sick from the chemotherapy and the public ordeal had further embarrassed and upset his parents.

Johnny's young friend, Philip Buckingham

For the month following our meeting, Philip's exuberant hug and brave grin had haunted me. It was such a heart-rending case. I wanted to do something, knew instinctively that I *should* do something, yet I was scared of getting involved.

Still, this feeling that I was obligated to do something for Philip gnawed at me, and after a month of vacillation I called the department store in mid-December and asked for Sue Lilly. Under the guise of business, I eventually got to the point. "By the way, Sue," I asked, "what do you hear about that little kid…what's his name…Philip…the one with leukemia?"

Sue told me that she had talked with Philip's mother and that he seemed to be doing fairly well. But the best news was that through a local newspaper story, money had been raised to help the family. "Some of us from the store are going to visit the Buckinghams the day before Christmas to take them a few things. Would you like to come along?"

I groped for an excuse. "Well, I've got this trip…I really can't because…I…I…I'd love to," I finally heard myself saying.

On the afternoon of December 24, Sue, myself and some friends knocked on the door of the Buckinghams' modest frame home. Philip's greeting nearly bowled me over. "Johnny! Johnny! Johnny!" he yelled, jumping onto my back.

Out came the toys we'd brought along for Philip and his older brother and sister. There were stuffed beanbags, a model airport, wooden building blocks, and a sack of groceries my mother had provided.

While Philip was overjoyed with the gifts, he paid more attention to me personally. Grabbing my hand, he pulled me down on the floor and together we began building a fort out of blocks.

Suddenly Philip looked up at me and asked point-blank, "Did you *really* want to come, Johnny?"

"Sure I did," I said, but his question startled me. Had he sensed a hesitancy about my coming, somehow knowing that I'd almost chickened out? I was ashamed to think I'd had reservations about reaching out to this little boy. Me, a guy who has so much.

Just as we were about to go, someone asked Philip, "Don't you think Santa Claus should give your mommy and daddy something?"

"Santa"—a friend of Sue Lilly's—pulled out a set of keys to a used car Sue had arranged to buy for the Buckinghams, and an envelope containing a check to keep them from being evicted. Tears of gratitude filled their eyes.

I don't think I've ever had a better Christmas. I was glad I could brighten Philip's day, but more than that, I sensed that I, too, had received something. Just what it was, I didn't know then, but something significant had happened to me.

When it was time to go to Florida with the Reds for spring training in February, I called to tell Philip good-bye. "Don't forget to win the pennant," he reminded me. "We'll sure try," I told him.

When Tommy John's son Travis lay in coma after a fall, the Johns
tried to keep their anguish to themselves. But because of Tommy's
fame as a Yankee pitcher, the whole country soon offered prayers
and sympathy, freeing the Johns from much pain. In an Open Letter
to Guideposts readers (1982), Sally John said: "You shouldn't hug
your grief to your heart. Don't fear that pain makes you awkward. If
you want God to ease it, just accept the love of people who offer to
share your pain. God's love flows through them."

Philip, I discovered while in Florida, could talk all day on the phone, and while he was surely feeling pain, he refused to let on. He was a very brave boy, and I found myself rooting for him as much as he was rooting for me. I didn't hit too well during spring training, but when I'd call from time to time, he'd tell me to keep trying. "You, too," I'd answer.

Just before the '74 season began, I asked Philip, "How'd you like me to dedicate my first home run to you?"

"Wouldja?" he shouted so loudly through the receiver that he nearly popped my eardrum.

In April, Sue Lilly helped arrange Philip's first visit to Riverfront Stadium, home of the Reds. It was a dream-come-true for the little guy because the only baseball games he'd seen had been on TV. Even though we were beaten by the Dodgers that night, you'd never have known it from the way Philip carried on. When I met him in the locker room afterward, his eyes were full of excitement and his smile was as wide as home plate.

"Hey, Phil," I asked when we left the ball park, "would you like to take a ride in my car?" He war-whooped his answer. After the ride, he gave me a big hug. This time I squeezed back. "Thank you, Johnny," he said. "Thank you, Philip, for being my buddy." A relationship that had begun on pity had blossomed into one held together by love. That was the truth. I really loved the gutsy little guy.

As the year went by, the news from Dayton became more and more important to me. "Treatments are continuing..." his mother Melissa would report. "Philip is holding his own ...

he asks about you every day." One morning on the telephone, Melissa told me something Philip had said to her that startled me.

"Mommy," he had said, "Baby Jesus came to visit me last night and soon I'm going to live in Heaven with Him." That's a pretty big thought for a boy not yet five, but Philip had experienced a lot in his brief life, so maybe it wasn't so surprising. Philip's childlike faith was impressive and it started rubbing off on me. Never big on prayer before, I found myself praying for him—in airplanes, during batting practice, in the shower —everywhere.

When another Christmas came around — 1974—again I was drawn to Dayton. Though Philip looked better—golden hair had grown back on his head—I knew the doctors had increased his drug dosage. For the second year in a row, Sue Lilly and the gang rounded up presents for the Buckingham family, including a Bible that we all signed and gave to Melissa and her husband Carl.

When we got ready to leave, Philip followed me outside to my car. Reaching into the glove compartment, I pulled out one last present for him—a little china Cincinnati Reds doll, emblazoned with No. 5, my uniform number.

"Can you use this, Phil?" I asked.

"You bet," he said, grabbing it from me and running back to the house.

Several weeks later, I received a telephone call from Melissa Buckingham.

"I knew you'd want to know right away, Johnny," she said. "Philip died just a few hours ago."

Prayer for Courage

Dare to be a Daniel!
Dare to stand alone!
Dare to have a purpose firm!
Dare to make it known!

by Philip Paul Bliss

"Thank you," I said, struggling for something to say while fighting back tears.

"Johnny," Melissa went on, "when Philip went into the hospital for the final time, he was clutching that little china doll you gave him. He wouldn't let go of it....We want to bury it with him."

As she spoke, Philip's words, "Soon I'll be living in Heaven with Baby Jesus," flashed through my mind and now the tears really started running down my face. Words couldn't express the deep loss I felt, and even today it's hard to explain what Philip meant to me. How could a skinny little kid with big blue eyes and a half-nelson hug turn me into such a softy?

But Philip showed me something very important: that we should be open to everyone we meet, no matter who they are. Because I was open to Philip, his love flowed through me, making me vulnerable and more caring and breaking down my fear of letting real feelings come out.

Thank God for that little boy who truly opened my eyes as well as my heart.

AUGUST 1978

A Sound of Humming *by Drue Duke*

My mother-in-law kept bees at her home, the hives placed on a wooded hill. I would watch in fascination as she strolled calmly up the hill, wearing no protective covering. As she went, she clucked softly, much as one does to chickens, and she spoke endearments to the bees that flew down to meet her. When she came down again with the treasure of golden honey, her head and arms would be covered with bees, all humming accompaniment to her sweet words.

"How do you do it?" I demanded in awe. "I would be scared to death."

"And you would be stung!" she replied. "But they know I love them, that I won't hurt them and that I don't expect them to hurt me. And they don't."

I'd still be scared to do it, but perhaps I could, if my faith were stronger. For after all, it's not courage that's required, it's trust. And trust, I've found, has a beautiful way of inspiring more trust.

In Finding God's Guidance

Guideposts readers have always kept us Guideposts editors on our toes. From your letters, we've learned that you won't settle for pat answers or simplistic advice. In this light, we've found that you won't accept stories that simply say, "In times of trouble, seek God's guidance." You've insisted on knowing more: *How* do I find God's guidance? *Where* do I find it? *When* will it come?

Over the years, many Guideposts authors have written about these questions out of their own life experience, and none more effectively than Catherine Marshall. In fact, the very first of her 44 stories for the magazine was called "How You Can Find God's Guidance." It was a quest that Catherine pursued constantly.

Catherine's first clue to God's guidance had come years earlier when, as the young wife of the Reverend Peter Marshall, she suffered through a long illness. Repeatedly she asked in prayer that God heal her. When no healing came, she at last saw that she must ask God to do *His* will. She must relinquish to God her pride, her fears, her strong-willed ambitions.

"I gave God a blank check with my life," Catherine wrote. "This amounted to the willingness to take my marching orders from God for the rest of my life." And in doing so she evoked Christ's words in Gethsemane: "Father, if thou be willing, remove this cup from me; nevertheless not my will, but Thine, be done" (Luke 22:42). Only then did Catherine begin to get well.

Later, this spiritual adventurer found other clues to God's guidance through Bible study and people and prayer, and through being alert to the unfolding of each event in her life. Each hard-won discovery was described for the reader in her clear, meticulous style.

The goal for Guideposts stories has always been to provide practical advice that is steeped in Scripture, rooted in real-life experience, and meant to be used. In keeping with this goal, our writers are people, like Catherine Marshall, who *work* at their faith. And that's why this chapter isn't titled "Waiting for God's Guidance." It is called "Finding God's Guidance."

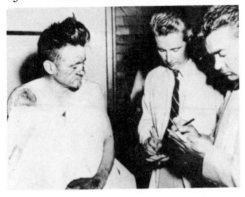

Jack Sullivan interviewed by reporters after accident

NOVEMBER 1955

God, Send Someone! *by Dick Sullivan, journalist*

At four p.m. June 14, my brother Jack was just crawling down into a ten-foot-deep trench, which ran down the center of Washington Street, a main thoroughfare in West Roxbury, Massachusetts.

It was near quitting time. Jack is a welder, and he wanted to finish one particular part of his job before he left. He said good-bye to the other men as they quit, took his welding lead in his right hand and lowered himself and his electric power cable into the trench. His head was well below the surface of the street.

It was Jack's job to weld the joints of a new water main, both inside and out. First he crawled into the 36-inch-diameter pipe, lowered his mask to protect his eyes against the bright welding arc, then went to work. After completing the inside of the joint, he crawled out of the pipe. It was 4:30 p.m. He began to weld the outside. Halfway through the job he stood up to get the kinks out of his legs. Jack stretched, turned toward the pipe and pulled down the shield again.

Suddenly the bank caved in. Tons of dirt came crushing down on him from all sides.

Jack was rammed against the pipe with the force of a sledgehammer. He went down, buried in a kneeling position, his shield slammed against the pipe, his nose flattened against the inside of the shield.

He felt his shoulder burning against the red-hot section of pipe he had been welding. He tried to move it back from the pipe. But he

couldn't. Then his nose began to pain him. It was bleeding. And he couldn't move his head.

Jack tried calling. Three times he shouted. The sound of his voice died in his shield. He tried to breathe slowly to preserve oxygen.

It crossed Jack's mind that he might die.

Slowly he began to pray. Going to mass at St. Patrick's once a week suddenly seemed quite inadequate. My brother continued to pray. He had his eyes open, but everything was black.

Something cool crossed his right hand. He wiggled his fingers and found they moved freely. His right hand had not been buried. He moved the hand again. He tried to scratch around with his hand to open up an air passage down his arm. But the weight of the earth was too great; it didn't do any good.

Then it occurred to him that he'd been holding the welding lead in that hand. So he fished around with his fingers. He found the rod, still in the holder. He grasped it tightly and moved it, hoping it would strike the pipe. Suddenly his wrist jerked and he knew he had struck an arc—the electric current would be making its bright orange flash. So he kept on tapping the pipe, making an arc, hoping it would draw attention.

That must look like something! Jack thought. *A hand reaching out of the ground striking an arc against the pipe. That must really look like something!*

He began to figure out how long he'd been buried, since there was no way of telling time.

Deep inside a closed compartment of the cruiser Topeka, *shipfitter Roland Allen had finished welding ... when he lost the wrench needed to loosen the hatch bolts (Guideposts 1957). He was trapped. He panicked, screaming, clawing at the bolts. Then he stopped, knowing he himself could do nothing. Quickly, he put his trust in God. An inner voice told him, "Take out the pin in the hinge ..." He was saved when he remembered to stop, trust—and listen.*

He wondered how much gasoline was left in the engine-driven welder on top of the trench—whether it would last until dark when the arc might draw attention. Then he remembered that it was almost the longest day in the year; darkness wouldn't fall until nine o'clock. Still, if he had enough oxygen in his little tomb and if the gasoline held out, maybe...

He thought of all the hundreds of people passing within feet of him up above.

He thought of his family and wondered if he'd ever see his little grandson again.

He thought of Tommy Whittaker, his assistant, out on another job on Route 128.

He figured there wasn't anything to do but lie there and wait and keep tapping flashes, and hope that enough air would filter into the mask. There wasn't anything to do but lie there and pray, "God, send someone..."

In another part of Boston, out on Route 128, Jack's assistant, Tommy Whittaker, had quit his work for the day. Whittaker was 47 years old, Jack, 41. They had known each other for over 15 years and were close friends, so close that within the next few moments one of the strangest prayer phenomena in modern times took place.

Tommy Whittaker did not know that Jack was on the Washington Street job. Whittaker got in his truck and started off down Route 128 with the full intention of driving directly home. Route 128 is a main artery, a superhighway that could take him home within minutes.

But as Whittaker drove, he began to have the feeling something wasn't right.

He tried to shake the feeling off. He kept driving. The strange and unexplainable sensation grew. He thought that he ought to drive up to the Washington Street job and check it, then dismissed the idea. It meant driving six miles out of his way at the peak of the rush hour. Whittaker approached the intersection of Washington and Route 128.

Suddenly he turned.

He did not try to explain it to himself. He just turned.

Meanwhile, Jack continued to pray. It was the same simple prayer, "God, send someone." The bleeding in his nose hadn't stopped; the blood ran down his throat and began to clot. "God, send someone." He spat the blood out, but it was getting more difficult. All the while he listened to the sound of his welding motor outside. He wondered if it was dark yet. It seemed forever. Things were getting hazy....

Tommy Whittaker drove along Washington Street. The job was divided into two sections. He stopped his truck at a spot several blocks away from the cave-in and got out. He chatted with an engineer for the Metropolitan District Commission for 15 minutes. Whittaker did not mention the gnawing sensation that still would not leave him alone. The time was 5:45. It was still broad daylight.

Back in the trench, Jack struck some more arcs. He thought it might be dark now. He listened to the welder popping. He hoped someone would come—soon. The clot of blood in his throat was getting harder to bring up. He was a little surprised that he wasn't in a state of panic. Jack just kept praying, "God, send..."

In 1955, Dr. Sam Shoemaker told in Guideposts of the Pittsburgh Experiment, a challenging new program of prayer for businessmen. Inspired by the Pittsburgh story, Herb Hilmer started a Cincinnati Experiment… and his Guideposts story (1980) was read by Bob Miller, who started a New Jersey Experiment… and Bob's story (1982) was read by a housewife in Erie, Pennsylvania, who started…. Guideposts doesn't take credit for the success of these Experiments. We simply provide a forum for a message people are eager to hear: Prayer works!

Up above, a little way down Washington Street, Tommy Whittaker got into his truck and started up again. The gnawing sensation grew stronger. He reached a stoplight. It was his turnoff to get back to Route 128. If he stayed on Washington Street, he'd have to go out of his way. Tommy Whittaker braked his truck for a brief instant, then continued on up Washington.

Underground, Jack finally gave up striking the arc. It was making him breathe too hard. He didn't think he could last much longer. He couldn't get the blood clot out of his throat. He was gagging.…

A t that moment, up above on Washington Street, Tommy Whittaker arrived at the spot where his friend was dying. Nothing seemed unusual. He noticed the stake-body truck. But it was a truck that Sullivan never used. Whittaker thought another man from the shop was down in the trench. Whittaker pulled up. He got out of his truck and noticed the welder was running. He thought someone was inside the pipe, welding. Nothing, still, struck him as unusual.

Then Tommy Whittaker saw the hand— and saw it move.

"Oh, God!" he whispered.

Whittaker jumped down into the trench and dug like a chipmunk with his hands. The earth was too packed. He scrambled out of the trench, looked back at the hand and shuddered. He shut off the welder and raced through the traffic across the street to a garage.

Underground, Jack heard the *pop-pop* of the welder stop. It was then that he began to prepare to die. He knew it was over. He was gagging and trying to throw off the mist that had come over him.

Tommy Whittaker, just feet away, shouted to the men in the garage. "There's a man buried alive over there! Get a shovel."

Back across the street Whittaker raced, carrying a snow shovel. He ran to the place where the hand stuck up, still not knowing it was his friend.

My brother, below, felt an extra pressure on top of his head. He knew someone was above him. He fought to keep from fainting.

The garagemen hurried over.

"Send for the police. There's a firebox down the street," Whittaker called.

Tommy Whittaker began to dig. He uncovered a wrist watch. He thought he recognized the watchband. He kept digging, until he uncovered the man's side. He saw the man was still breathing, but his respiration was weak.

Then Whittaker recognized my brother. Jack had fainted. Whittaker dug frantically.

The rescue squad arrived. They applied an oxygen mask to Jack while they were still digging him out. From busy Washington Street, a crowd gathered.

Jack revived slightly when they put him on a stretcher. He spied Tommy Whittaker.

"Who found me?" he asked.

"I did," said Whittaker.

With his lips, Jack formed one word: "Thanks." There was no more powerful word.

The gnawing sensation that had been bothering Tommy Whittaker went away.

Those Monday night meetings—they often didn't end until Tuesday. We'd sit around an old scarred table, some of us editor-writers in from daytime jobs elsewhere; we'd say a prayer, dig into cold cuts from the deli and then start talking stories and projects. That's how Guideposts grew, in substance and spirit. We were always ready for new ideas, such as the night Ruth Peale said, "I met a man today named Dave Wilkerson," and John Sherrill was listening...

NOVEMBER 1961

Too Strange To Be Coincidence, Part I *by John Sherrill, editor*

One winter morning in 1958, Dave Wilkerson, a skinny country preacher, was sitting in his living room, reading *Life* magazine. He turned a page and saw a picture of seven boys. That picture was to change his life.

Dave was the pastor of the small Assemblies of God Church in Philipsburg, Pennsylvania. He was at home in the slow-paced rural community; life for him, his wife and three small children was comfortably routine and it probably would have remained that way except for one thing. Dave Wilkerson had turned over his life to God. He had simply handed over his feet and his hands and his heart and asked the Holy Spirit to use them.

For Dave, the Holy Spirit was no vague theological term; He was the Spirit of Christ, a living personality to be listened to and obeyed. On that particular morning, looking at the picture in the magazine, Dave Wilkerson began to weep.

It showed seven teenage defendants on trial in New York City for the death of Michael Farmer, the young polio victim, who was brutally beaten by members of a teenage gang. But it wasn't the story of the murder itself that especially gripped Dave. It was the faces of the defendants. In their eyes he saw an anger and loneliness he had never known existed. All that day he was drawn to the picture. And during the next week he felt the conviction growing that he himself—David Wilkerson—should take a toothbrush, get into his car, drive to New York where he had never been in his life, and try to help these boys.

At last Dave told his wife. "I don't understand why," he said, "but I must go." It was the boldest step of obedience to the Holy Spirit that he had yet taken. Almost before he knew how it happened, Dave and Miles Hoover, the youth director of his small church, were driving across the George Washington Bridge. It was the afternoon of February 28, 1958.

In New York, he parked in front of a drugstore and telephoned the office of the District Attorney named in the article.

"If you want to see the defendants," he was told, "the judge himself will have to give you permission." So Dave tried to telephone the judge. He was unsuccessful. But he was not discouraged.

The next day David and Miles went to the trial. All morning they sat quietly watching the seven young defendants. Toward the end of the court session, Dave popped to his feet, ran down the aisle and stood before the bench. He knew that if he were going to see the judge at all he would have to do it then and there.

"Your honor? Would you do me the courtesy of talking with me for a few s...."

"Get him out of here," the judge interrupted brusquely.

Two guards swept down on Dave, picked him up by his elbows and rushed him toward the rear. Reporters and photographers jumped to their feet. Flashbulbs popped.

David Wilkerson (back to camera) talking to street youths

Later it was learned that the judge had been threatened by gang members and had thought the skinny preacher was one of them.

That evening the newspapers carried stories about the Reverend David Wilkerson being ejected bodily from the courtroom. As Dave and his youth director drove home, they were both depressed and confused. What kind of guidance had this been? David remembered biblical accounts of men who were guided by the Holy Spirit. He'd started his own grand experiment assuming that Christ's Spirit would guide people today, just as it did in New Testament times. Why, then, was he in trouble?

At home, he and Miles faced a disgruntled congregation, annoyed that their minister had made a public spectacle of himself. And as the days passed, Dave's confusion increased. Not only was it difficult to explain why he had gotten into such a mess; it was still more difficult to explain why, as soon as possible, he was going back to New York.

But that's where he was, the next week. When he telephoned the District Attorney's office a second time he was told that if he wanted to see the boys he needed written permission from each of the parents.

"Fine," said Dave. "Could you give me their names?"

The line went dead. Dave stepped out of the phone booth. He smoothed out the now crumpled page from *Life* and scanned the caption. The leader of the boys was named Luis Alvarez. He began to call all the Alvarezes in the telephone book.

In each case, the answer was indignant. No, of course they didn't have a son Luis who was a defendant in the Farmer trial!

Dave was running out of dimes and there were still more than 150 Alvarezes to go. He gave up and stepped outside, praying, "All right, Lord. I just don't know what to do next. If this is Your business I'm on, then Your Spirit will have to show me the way."

Dave got into his car and began to drive aimlessly through the strange streets. Eventually he found himself in the heart of Spanish Harlem. Tired of driving, he parked in the first empty space he found. He got out and asked a boy if he knew where a Luis Alvarez lived.

"Luis Alvarez?" said the boy. "You parked in front of his house." He pointed to a brownstone building. "Fourth floor."

"Thank you, Lord," said Dave.

"What you say?"

Dave put his hands on the boy's shoulder. "Thank you. Thank you *very* much."

Dave climbed to the fourth floor, found the Alvarez' apartment and knocked on the door.

"Come in."

He pushed the door open and saw a tired-looking man sitting on an overstuffed chair. Señor Alvarez barely looked up. "Ah, here you are, Preacher. I been expecting you. I see your picture in the paper. I say my prayers that you will come." At last Dave seemed to be getting his go-ahead sign.

Early the next morning he was back at the city jail with seven written permissions to visit the seven boys on trial.

Wilkerson holding a rally in New York

Again he failed.

The jail chaplain, feeling that the boys were in his own spiritual care, refused to allow him entrance. David was crushed. "What are you trying to say to me, Lord?" Dave asked. "Show me where my vision is too small." He had no way of knowing that this door had to be closed in order for another—much larger—to be opened.

Suddenly a jolting idea occurred to him. Perhaps his vision *was* too small. Perhaps the Holy Spirit didn't intend him to work just for the seven defendants in the Michael Farmer trial *but for all the lonely, angry kids on the New York streets.*

Two weeks later Dave Wilkerson was back in New York. On this trip he brought with him no preconceived ideas of whom he was to help or how. He simply walked the streets, and everywhere he walked he made the same discovery: the picture of him in a New York tabloid that had seemed to Dave like a mockery of his guidance—was his entree to the street gangs of New York. Wherever he went he was recognized, "Hi ya, Preach!" from a cluster of kids on a street corner. "You're one of us, Davey!" from a tenement stoop.

Soon the churches were asking questions about this man who was "in" where they'd never even had a toehold. Fifty parishes got together and asked him to conduct a two-week youth revival in St. Nicholas Arena. Five thousand teenagers flocked to hear him. A few months later Dave had a weekly television show where teenage dope addicts, adolescent alcoholics and 14-year-old prostitutes told the stories of their conversions. Eventually, Dave moved his family to New York so that he could minister full time to these young people. Today he directs Teen Challenge Center in Brooklyn, a home where boys and girls in trouble can come for a new start—and where the fresh paint and the new flower beds are largely the work of the kids themselves.

As for the seven defendants in the Michael Farmer trial, three were acquitted; four sent to prison. When Dave visits them at the penitentiary it is no longer as an unknown country preacher begging admission. It is as the man whose results among teenage hoodlums have people in New York shaking their heads in wonder.

As they say, it's amazing what can happen when the average man—any average man—lets the Holy Spirit be his guide.

David Wilkerson with Nicky (on left) and Israel

DECEMBER 1961

Too Strange To Be Coincidence, Part II   *by David Wilkerson, preacher*

Whenever I talk about two strange events, someone usually comments, "That's very hard to believe."

They are hard to believe. Yet I myself saw them take place, one on a street corner, the other in a prizefight hall: two rather unlikely places for conversion. But maybe that's the very point of these stories: that when the Holy Spirit begins to work on your heart, something pretty nearly unbelievable takes place.

Almost five years ago, after a series of strange "coincidences" brought me to New York City to work with teenage street gangs, I was invited to lead a citywide revival aimed at teenagers. Fifty churches raised over $4,000 and rented a prizefight hall, St. Nicholas Arena, for two weeks. The funds were supplied by the churches; all I had to do was supply the teenagers.

Now I have always been a little suspicious of poeple who are "guided" into positions where they attract attention to themselves; and I was suspicious of myself. "Lord," I said, "I don't want to stay in New York five minutes unless it's Your idea, not mine. I'm going to contact the leaders of the roughest gang in the roughest section of all New York. If they respond, I'll know it's You at work and not me."

Talking to police, I found that two gangs qualified as toughest, the "Chaplains" and the "Mau Maus," both in the Fort Green section of the city. The Chaplains had recently de-

clared war on the police department: one method of fighting was to drop sandbags on passing officers from a rooftop. The leader of the Chaplains, I learned, was a boy called Buckboard. Buckboard had a vice-president named Stagecoach. The name of the Mau Maus' leader was Israel; his vice-president, Nicky.

I set out for Fort Green looking for Israel and Buckboard. My only weapon was a trumpet—blown by a friend. We parked in front of P.S. #27 where members of the Chaplains and Mau Maus went to school. I began my ministry that afternoon by the simple technique of telling my friend the bugler to blow *Onward Christian Soldiers.*

Two hundred teenagers swarmed to the corner where we stood. They yelled, whistled, threw obscenities and catcalls. How was I going to get them quiet long enough to talk to them? I tried the most direct technique I knew: prayer. I climbed up on a box so that everyone could see me, lowered my head, closed my eyes and prayed. My heart ached for these boys and I could not stop the tears from rolling down my face. Soon there was silence and I began to talk.

I preached a simple sermon that afternoon, using as my text, *For God so loved the world…* (John 3:16). When I finished I stepped down from the box, wondering what to do next.

No one in the crowd moved. "I would like to meet some of your leaders," I said.

God has His hand on our lives, often without our knowing it. Young Blood Johnson, a onetime heroin dealer and addict, can testify to this (Guideposts 1971). One day, a stranger carrying a Bible came up to him saying, "I've been watching you. God wants to change you." Days later, Johnson did change—going cold turkey, kicking his heroin habit, without a single withdrawal pain. Amazed, he turned his life around and became a minister, directing a drug prevention clinic, serving the God Whose hand had guided him.

Silence.

I waited a moment and then went on: "What's the matter? Are you afraid to shake hands with a skinny preacher?"

From the edge of the crowd, someone shouted: "Yeah. What's the matter Buckboard, you chicken?"

Two figures separated themselves from the group. They wore dark glasses, long hair with duck-tail cuts, tapered trousers, continental shoes. They carried canes.

"I'm Buckboard," one of them said. "I'm president of the Chaplains and this is my vice-president, Stagecoach. Slip a skin, Preacher."

I had never heard this expression. When I held out my hand, he didn't grasp it, but slid his palm along mine. Then I slipped a skin with Stagecoach. After that, I spoke to them quietly for perhaps five minutes. To this day I do not know exactly what I said. It was as if I, Dave Wilkerson, were not speaking at all, but were being spoken through.

And then, this nearly incredible thing happened. While I talked, Buckboard became emotionally distressed. Tears welled into his eyes. He dropped to his knees in front of the bystanders. Stagecoach looked at him in amazement and then he became distraught also.

"You're coming through, Preacher," Buckboard said, oblivious to the snickers around him. "Keep talking."

I did keep talking. I talked about the power of Christ to end hatred.

Then I said, "Now I'd like to meet the president of the Mau Maus."

Buckboard raised his head long enough to point out a boy standing on the edge of the crowd. "That's him—Israel."

"Slip a skin, Israel," I said.

Israel hesitated but the crowd egged him on. Slowly he and his vice-president, Nicky, moved forward. We separated the four boys from the crowd, walking them over to our car for more privacy. There, all but Nicky began to cry openly, and as the teenagers looked on from a distance in openmouthed disbelief three of the four boys dropped to their knees and asked for prayer. I blinked hard, wondering if it could be real.

Then I turned to Nicky. The boy only stared at me sullenly. Then he spat on my shoes. "Keep away from me, Preacher, you're not going to make me cry."

God did not reach Nicky—not then. I did, however, get a promise from Buckboard and Israel to bring their gangs to the St. Nicholas Arena for the revival the following week.

They came with their thumbs hooked in their pockets, cigarettes hanging from the corners of their mouths, some swinging switchblades. Just as I stood up to speak, Nicky walked down the aisle and took a seat with his gang in the forward rows. He slouched low in the chair and blew a smoke ring into the air. I looked down into his face and saw nothing but hostility. When I started to speak, my words sounded hollow. Catcalls interrupted me and cries of: "Let's have action!"

After several attempts at speaking, I stopped.

Why have celebrities like Carol Burnett always told their stories in Guideposts? Because beyond the glitter and glamour in their lives, these celebrities want it known that faith—not fame—is what helps them overcome problems and make decisions. In fact, one famous family is represented in Guideposts by two generations. In 1957, Pat Boone wrote about The Question That Lights Up My Life—*two decades later, his daughters Debby and Cherry told how faith illuminated—and eliminated—their fears.*

I folded my hands in front of me, as I had on the street corner, and I simply stood still and prayed. I prayed silently for five minutes, a long time in front of restless teenagers. But as I prayed the calls for "Action!" died away and St. Nicholas Arena became unimaginably quiet. When I finally spoke again, all I said was a simple, "Come." Not in a loud voice—just "Come forward now."

And then, Israel was rising from his seat. He turned to his companions. "All right, you guys," he was saying, "on your feet."

His friends rose. "You followed me everywhere before, didn't you?" Israel said. Nods. "Then follow me now. I'm going up there."

Without waiting, Israel turned and walked to where I stood. "Preach, I want to know this Christ you talk about."

If it hadn't been for the tears in Israel's eyes, I would have thought it was a joke. One by one, every boy in Israel's gang rose and walked forward—including Nicky.

That night I gave each of these new fledgling Christians a Bible. I tried to give them pocket-size New Testaments but they wanted big Bibles, the kind you carried in your hand and everyone saw.

This was the beginning of a new life for these boys and a new ministry for me. A few days after the revival, a group of ministers invited me to come to the city as their full-time gang preacher. I accepted, and today I am director of "Teen Challenge," the organization formed to back this work.

The hardest part of my ministry now, as at the beginning, is to believe what I see with my own eyes. Could they be real—these lightning conversions? Will they last? These are not easy questions to answer.

When a boy is converted, we take him to his local church where the never-ending process of Christian growth really begins. Eighteen months after their conversions, I met Buckboard and Stagecoach and Israel again in Fort Green. They were each wearing a freshly pressed Army uniform. Very proud. Very straight.

And Nicky—the boy who had spat on my shoes when I talked to him?

This week, his schooling over, Nicky Cruz is coming back to New York with a license to preach, and a new bride. It's hard to tell which he is more excited about. He's joining me, full time, in this evangelistic work with troubled or simply lonesome kids at our Teen Challenge Center in Brooklyn. He will be working with the same tools I used: a trumpet and a willingness. A trumpet to get someone to listen, and a willingness to let the Holy Spirit do the talking.

Carol Burnett (center) on her television show with guest star Dick van Dyke and regular Vicki Lawrence

OCTOBER 1977

The Secret I Had To Share *by Carol Burnett, actress*

My career—TV, stage, movies, all of it—was founded on a strange event that was to be a deep mystery to me for years. Only after my life had changed drastically did I begin to solve the puzzle I was confronted with one long-ago June evening in California.

In those days, I was one of a group of stage-struck drama-school students at UCLA, living on hopes and dreams and not much else. As school ended, one of our professors was leaving for a vacation in Europe. He had a house near San Diego, and a *bon voyage* party was planned. It was suggested that some of us entertain his supper guests with scenes from musical comedies.

Nine of us agreed to go. One of the boys and I had rehearsed a scene from *Annie Get Your Gun*, I remember, and that was our part of the program. Everything went well. The guests seemed to enjoy our singing, and we enjoyed it, too.

After our performance, supper was announced. I was standing at the buffet when a man I had never seen before spoke to me pleasantly. He said he had admired our performance. Then he asked me what I intended to do with my life.

I told him that I hoped to go to New York someday and make a career for myself on the stage. When he asked what was stopping me, I told him truthfully that I barely had enough money to get back to Los Angeles, let alone

New York. I might have added, but didn't, that at times my grandmother, my mother, my sister and I had been on welfare. The man smiled and said that he would be happy to lend me the money to go to New York. A thousand dollars, he added, should be enough to get me started.

Well, in those days I was pretty innocent, but not *that* innocent. So I refused his offer politely. He went away, but in a few moments he was back with a pleasant-faced lady whom he introduced as his wife. Then he made his offer all over again. He was quite serious, he said. There were only three conditions. First, if I did meet with success, I was to repay the loan without interest in five years. Next, I was never to reveal his identity to anyone. Finally, if I accepted his offer, I was eventually to pass the kindness along, to help some other person in similar circumstances when I was able to do so.

He told me to think it over and telephone him when I got back to Los Angeles. He added that he was prepared to make a similar offer to my partner in the scene from *Annie Get Your Gun*, and he gave me his telephone number.

The next day, half convinced I had dreamed the whole thing, I called the number. I was told that if I had decided to accept the conditions, I could drive down on Monday morning and pick up my check. Still unbelieving, I told my mother and grandmother. Their reaction, not surprisingly, was to urge me not to have anything to do with my mysterious benefactor.

A Place to Pray…Facing major surgery, Faye Field felt afraid, distant from God (Guideposts 1984). At last, she consulted the staunchest person she knew, her Aunt Theodocia. "Find an undisturbed place in your home," the older woman advised. "Go to this place even when you feel bad or least like praying. Don't let company interfere. Sincerely ask the Lord to take away your fear." After faithful daily visits to her prayer place, Faye began to feel confident and close to God again.

But somehow I was convinced that the man was sincere, and I believed that the good Lord was giving me, Carol Burnett, a strong and unmistakable push. I was *supposed* to accept the offer. I was being *guided*. And if I didn't go, I would regret it for the rest of my life.

At sunup on Monday morning my partner and I were on the road. We drove for three hours. At nine o'clock, we were at the man's office. We had to wait perhaps half an hour—and believe me, that was the longest half hour of my life! But finally we were ushered in. Our friend was crisp, serious, businesslike. He reminded us of the conditions, especially the one about not revealing his identity. Then he had his secretary bring in the checks. I watched as he signed them. I had never seen so many beautiful zeros in my life.

We tried to thank him, but he just smiled and ushered us out. When we came to the car, still dazed, we realized we didn't have enough gasoline to get back to Los Angeles—and not enough cash to buy any. We had to go to a bank, present one of the $1,000 checks, then wait while the astonished bank officials telephoned our friend's office to make sure that we weren't a pair of international forgers. But finally they did cash it for us.

Back in Los Angeles, I wasted no time. I spent a little of the money on a visit to the dentist where I had two teeth filled and one extracted—I hadn't been able to afford a dentist for years. Then, with my family's anxious admonitions ringing in my ears, I headed for New York.

In all of that vast city I knew just one soul, a girl named Eleanore Ebe. I called her up and found that she was staying at the Rehearsal Club, where in those days young theatrical hopefuls could find room and board for $18 a week. So I moved in with Ellie, and settled down to the long grind of finding work on the New York stage.

It was the old story. No experience? Then no work. But how can you get experience if you can't get work? My funds got lower and lower. I went to work as a hatcheck girl in a restaurant. Unfortunately, it catered mostly to ladies who had no desire or reason to check their hats. Still, I managed to make about $30 a week from tips—enough to get by.

My grandmother wrote me sternly that if I hadn't found a job on the stage by Christmas I had better come home. So I redoubled my visits to theatrical agencies. Finally one agent said wearily, "Why don't you put on your own show? Maybe then you'd stop bothering us!"

That sparked an idea. Back at the Rehearsal Club I talked to all my jobless friends. If we were really bursting with talent, as we were sure we were, why not hire a hall, send out invitations to all the agents and critics in town, and put on our own revue?

Everyone agreed that it was a great idea. We started chipping in 50 cents apiece each night for a fund to hire the hall. Talented youngsters took on the task of creating scenery, writing music and lyrics, doing the choreography. When our first act was ready, we performed it

A Time to Pray... In 1959, Catherine Marshall was newly remarried and trying to raise three stepchildren. With much to pray about, she and husband Len LeSourd, nonetheless, couldn't find time to pray. So they began The Coffeepot Experiment (Guideposts 1980), in which an automatically timed percolator would aromatically wake them every morning at six. Feeling sleepily peaceful, they gave themselves fully to God in prayer. His peace then stayed with them all day. The best time for prayer, Catherine concluded, isn't found. It's made.

for the board of directors of the Club who then gave us some additional help. When the "Rehearsal Club Revue" finally opened and ran for three nights, it seemed to us that everyone in New York show business was in the audience. The day after it closed, three agents called me with offers of jobs. From that point on, the magic doors swung open and I was on my way.

I reported all my progress to my benefactor back on the West Coast, but I heard very little from him. He continued to insist upon his anonymity. He showed no desire to share any spotlights, take any credit.

Five years to the day after I accepted his loan, I paid him back, and since then I've kept my pledge never to reveal his identity. He never told me his reasons for helping me in the manner he did, but as the years have gone by I've been able to unravel the mystery of this man, at least to my own satisfaction, and in the process I've discovered a powerful spiritual principle to use in my own life.

I stumbled upon the key clue one day when I was glancing through a copy of the recently published Living Bible. I had turned to the sixth chapter of Matthew because I wanted to see how the Lord's Prayer had been translated.

Suddenly, some verses seemed to leap out of the page: "When you give a gift to a beggar, don't shout about it as the hypocrites do... When you do a kindness to someone, do it secretly...And your Father Who knows all secrets will reward you..." (Matthew 6:2–4)

Do it secretly, the passage read, and at once I thought of my secretive friend. From that moment, what he had done and how he had done it began to make sense.

I began to see that when he made his offer to me, my benefactor had employed the spiritual principle of giving-in-secret-without-seeking-credit. He had done it partly to be kind, of course, but also because he knew that great dividends flow back to anyone who is wise enough to practice this kind of giving.

I believe that, as the Bible says, there is a great liberating force in not trying to take credit for one's good deeds. It tames the ego. It moves us away from petty vanity—and I'm convinced that the further we move away from ourselves, the closer we come to God.

So that's the story of how my career began. I shall always be grateful to my anonymous friend. With pride I repaid his loan, and with pride I have kept his name secret. As for his stipulation about passing the kindness along to others—well, that's *my* secret!

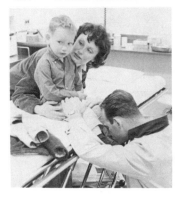

Wessie with his parents after being rescued

AUGUST 1969
The Search for Little Wessie *by Ernest M. Snyder, National Guardsman*

The news came over the car radio that April Sunday afternoon as my wife, Martha, our three-year-old daughter, Robin, and I were driving to my mother's house. A three-year-old boy was lost somewhere in Cunningham Falls State Park in western Maryland. He had wandered away from his family during a picnic.

"Just Robin's age!" I said to Martha. I thought of that rugged mountain terrain. "Hope they find him quick."

But hours later, driving home after dinner at Mother's, there was another bulletin. That little boy was still missing.

I looked at our own three-year-old sitting between us on the front seat. Then I wondered how many men of my National Guard unit I could locate on a Sunday evening. "Let's drive by the park," I said to Martha.

It was 6:15 when we reached the parking lot from which the search was being directed. The mountain slope seemed alive with searchers. I stopped a state trooper and asked if they could use some National Guardsmen.

"What can you give us?" he said.

"Mostly men and communications," I said, "and probably a jeep or two."

From a radio car, he phoned police headquarters and in a moment had the necessary official request. I drove Martha and Robin home, called three local radio stations and asked them to broadcast an appeal for Guard volunteers. I also contacted Staff Sgt. Charles Lockard, the unit's full-time employee, and asked him to open the armory.

By the time I had changed into my uniform and driven the ten miles to the armory in Frederick, men were already gathering. I went through a mental list of items needed—radios, compasses, flashlights, a radio vehicle, batteries, maps. Twenty minutes later, I was enroute to the park in the radio jeep with the first contingent.

As we reached the park, our eyes fell on the sight everyone dreads in a search operation. Firemen with grappling hooks were dragging a small pond just south of the picnic area where the young boy had been playing. After setting up a command post for the Guard activity, I questioned the police about the details of the disappearance.

The boy, Wesley Eans, three-year-old son of Mr. and Mrs. Claude Eans of Laurel, Maryland, had been playing with his six-year-old brother and four older children a short distance from where his mother was setting out their picnic lunch. At 2 p.m. when she called them to eat, little Wesley—or "Wessie" as he was called—failed to appear. His parents started hunting at once, joined by other picnicking families, and then, as anxiety mounted, by park rangers and the state police.

I went to talk to Wessie's parents now, where they waited in their white station wagon, assuring them that the Guard would stay until

A Search for Little Wessie tells of a boy lost in Maryland wilderness. In That Night on Black Mountain *(1983), Jack Brignoli told of searching all night for a young boy lost in New Hampshire. Don Bell, in 1976, recalled the blinding blizzard that trapped him in Wyoming woods for three days. In each story, an Inner Voice helped the rescuer or survivor. And that's why Guideposts so often carries "lost sheep" stories. Whether it's a child lost in the wild or an adult lost in doubt, God is determined that no one among us will be lost to Him.*

Wessie was found. Night was closing in fast; I could see in the couple's eyes that hope would be hard to maintain in the dark. The only consolation was that the dragging operation in the pool so far had turned up nothing.

Returning to the jeep, I reviewed the patrols that would go out as soon as enough men arrived. We planned a fan operation based on compass azimuths, continuing until all of the park within one and a half miles in all directions from the base point had been covered. Soon the first patrol of six men started up the mountain. Throughout the night and into the early morning, as more of my company arrived, they were dispatched into the surrounding areas.

It grew cold. The temperature fell to near freezing, and as I shivered in the open jeep I thought of a small child in a thin cotton jacket somewhere on that mountain. At approximately 2:15, our last group went out on a three-quarter-ton truck with a generator and floodlights. They were to travel the small trails west of the park, an area dotted with open cisterns.

And meanwhile, the earlier patrols were returning. We began sending men home as they came in, because there seemed no place left to search. A bloodhound pack had just come back with no results either. The dogs had picked up a trail that led up into the rugged, rocky area to the northwest. After struggling after the hounds for more than a mile over terrain difficult even for adults, the search party decided the dogs had crossed scents. Doubtless the men were right: One of our Guardsmen, Staff Sgt. John Wilcox, had injured an ankle trying to get into that same area earlier. It was generally agreed that a three-year-old could not have made such a climb, daylight or dark.

About 2:30 a.m., I walked through the floodlights illuminating the parking lot to the white station wagon. I leaned down to the window and was murmuring the conventional reassurances to Mr. and Mrs. Eans when all at once my voice just stopped functioning. My throat choked up, my eyes burned. Astonished at myself, I whirled away and walked back toward my command post.

I kept walking, into the cover of the woods, and there they began, great racking sobs that I thought would tear me apart. And along with them, a sense of helplessness that I had never known before. Then, perhaps because the whole experience was so strange, I did something else completely out of character for me. I looked up through the branches to the stars shining cold and brilliant, and I said a prayer.

"Dear God," I said, "please help these people! Don't let this suffering continue. You know where Wessie is. You see him right now. Show us, dear God. Show us." It must have been ten minutes before I went back to the jeep.

About 3:30, our last group came in, and with them the expected bad news: no sign of Wessie. The police had checked into the family's history and financial status and found no motive for kidnaping. But there is always the

*As a youngster, Gladys Aylward, who grew up to be one of the great
20th–century missionaries, had no firm purpose in life…until
she just "happened" into a church revival. That was when God
spoke to her. "It was the guidance of a call," she wrote in
Guideposts (1960), "and it is just as available today to ordinary
people, as it was to Saul on the road to Damascus."*

deranged individual, and opinion was growing
that Wessie was not in the park at all. Nevertheless, it was announced that the search
would resume as soon as it was light.

I went home to catch a little sleep. Before
turning in, I stepped into Robin's room and
stood there for a minute looking down at this
three-year-old snug in her own bed. Martha
was awake. "I've looked at her a dozen times
tonight," she said.

By 6:30, Martha was fixing eggs and coffee.
I looked out the kitchen window to the mountains west of the park and realized what I had
somehow known ever since that prayer was
wrenched from me under the stars—that I was
committed to this search until the child was
found, no matter how long it would take.

When I reached the park, between 600 and
700 people were gathering in the pale
dawn light. Sergeant Wilcox was there, hurt
ankle and all. He said he could still work the
radio in the jeep. With me at the wheel and two
state troopers in the back seat, we started the
jeep up a trail northwest into the mountains.

The going was rough, and soon I had to
shift into the lowest gear in four-wheel drive.
Occasionally the two troopers would call out
the boy's name. Then I'd have to stop and shut
off the engine so we could listen. We passed
the place where Wilcox had twisted his ankle
in the dark. Now we were approaching the
ruggedest part of the park, an area known as
Cat Rock. Two miles from the base, the four of
us reached the same conclusion earlier search

parties had—a three-year-old could not have
made it up here.

We had made about half a mile on the
return leg and were descending a downgrade
with the engine roaring and the squelch on the
radio going, when somewhere off to my left
I heard the sound I can still hear today. It
was a voice, a deep male voice, saying the
word, "Here."

I slammed on the brakes. The others turned
to stare at me. Not a sound came from the
woods around us. I switched off the engine.
Silence.

"What's the matter?" Trooper Mills said.

"Nothing," I said.

And yet there had been something. I was so
sure of it that I climbed out of the jeep and
walked 150 feet back up the trail. The three
others were getting restless. "What are we
waiting for?" one of them called.

I knew it sounded ridiculous, but I said it
anyway: "I heard something."

At that, Trooper Mills stood up and shouted
Wessie's name. Immediately I heard another
voice, but this time it was a child's. The others
still had heard nothing. When it came the second time, I determined the direction and
plunged into the woods toward it, the two
troopers right behind me. Over rocks and logs
we scrambled, branches lashing our faces.

I reached him first, sitting behind a log, not
at all surprised at seeing us. I scooped him up
and crushed him to me. "Where's Mommy
and Daddy?" he asked me. "I couldn't find
them. I bet they went home."

Iloree Wilson told how at a family reunion in a small Michigan town,
her family decided to pray each day for a brother who had been a
missing person for decades (Guideposts 1967). A year later, a man
on a cross-country trip stopped at a local grocery. "You got a brother
named Joe?" the clerk asked, gesturing to an old family portrait. And
there in the picture, the traveler, who was suffering from amnesia,
saw himself as a young man—part of a family he didn't know he had.
The family's prayers had brought him home.

We assured him that they had not. And then we looked around for the direction we'd come in. We were 250 to 300 yards from the jeep and had got turned around. I remember that we yelled for Wilcox several times before he heard us, and when he shouted back, we could barely hear him.

As he caught sight of us, Wilcox radioed back that we were bringing Wessie in safe and sound. We found a cheese sandwich, which the little fellow finished in no time. As we started the return trip down the mountain, Trooper Mills looked at me. "You could not possibly have heard that boy," he said.

"I know," I said.

Before the jeep had completely stopped, Wessie was in the arms of his parents. Then all three were whisked away in a police car to the hospital in Frederick. The doctors' examination there confirmed what our eyes had shown us: Wessie was fine.

Wessie now is probably well on the way to forgetting what many will remember for years to come. I know that I for one have returned to that spot in the mountains where we found him. I have sought an explanation from all points of view, and I know that the only answer is the one that came to me on that day.

Wessie was miles from anyone in a cold, lonely, dark mountain. Yet he was not alone. And, for that matter, from the moment I cried out to God for help, neither was I.

APRIL 1978

Roles—and How We Play Them *by Marie Curling*

Whenever I'm disappointed with my lot in life, I stop and think about little Jamie Scott. Jamie was trying out for a part in his school play. His mother told me that he'd set his heart on being in it, though she feared he would not be chosen.

On the day the parts were awarded, I went with her to collect him after school. Jamie rushed up to her, eyes shining with pride and excitement. "Guess what, Mum," he shouted, and then said those words that remain a lesson to me: "I've been chosen to clap and cheer."

Legson Kayira, 1964

APRIL 1964

Barefoot to America *by Legson Kayira, student*

My mother did not know where America was. I said to her, "Mother, I want to go to America to go to college. Will you give me your permission?"

"Very well," she said. "You may go. When will you leave?"

I did not want to give her time to discover from others in our village how far away America was, for fear that she would change her mind. "Tomorrow," I said.

"Very well," she said. "I will prepare some maize for you to eat along the way."

Next day, October 14, 1958, I left my home in the village of Mpale, in northern Nyasaland, East Africa. I had only the clothes I wore, a khaki shirt and shorts. I carried the two treasures I owned: a Bible and a copy of *Pilgrim's Progress*. I carried, too, the maize my mother had given me, wrapped in banana leaves, and a small ax for protection.

My goal was a continent and an ocean away, but I did not doubt that I would reach it.

I had no idea how old I was. Such things mean little in a land where time is always the same. I suppose I was 16 or 18.

My father died when I was very young. In 1952, my mother listened to the words of the missionaries of the Church of Scotland (Presbyterian), with the result that our family became Christian. From the missionaries, I learned not only to love God but also that if I was ever to be of value to my village, my people,

my country, it would be necessary for me to have an education.

At Wenya, eight miles away, was a mission primary school. One day when I felt I was ready to study, I walked there.

I learned many things. I learned I was not, as most Africans believed, the victim of my circumstances but the master of them. I learned that, as a Christian, I had an obligation to use the talents God had given me to make life better for others.

Later, in high school, I learned about America. I read the life of Abraham Lincoln and grew to love this man who suffered so much to help the enslaved Africans in his country. I read, too, the autobiography of Booker T. Washington, himself born in slavery in America, and who had risen in dignity and honor to become a benefactor of his people and his country.

I gradually realized that it would be only in America that I would receive the training and opportunities to prepare myself to emulate these men in my own land; to be, like them, a leader, perhaps even the president of my country.

My intention was to make my way to Cairo, where I hoped to get passage on a ship to America. Cairo was over 3,000 miles away, a distance I could not comprehend, and I foolishly thought I could walk it in four or five days. In four or five days I was about 25 miles

*The famed Dr. Samuel Shoemaker outlined four essential steps
for finding God's guidance (Guideposts 1955): 1) Right what you
know is wrong. Get rid of resentment, anger, pride, envy; 2) practice
daily devotions of Bible reading and prayer; 3) enjoy fellowship with
other Christians through church and smaller groups; 4) witness.
Make Christ live for other people.*

from home, my food was gone, I had no money, and I did not know what to do, except that I must keep going.

I developed a pattern of travel that became my life for more than a year. Villages were usually five or six miles apart, on forest paths. I would arrive at one in the afternoon and ask if I could work to earn food, water and a place to sleep. When this was possible, I would spend the night there, then move on to the next village in the morning.

It was not always possible. Tribal languages change every few miles in Africa; often I was among people with whom I could not communicate. This clearly made me a stranger to them, perhaps an enemy; they would not let me into the villages, and I had to sleep in the forests, eating herbs or wild fruit.

I soon discovered that my ax sometimes gave people the impression I had come to fight or to steal, so I bartered the ax for a knife I could carry unseen. I was actually defenseless against the forest animals I dreaded, but although I heard them at night none of them approached me. Malaria mosquitoes, however, were constant companions, and I often was sick.

But two comforts sustained me: my Bible and my *Pilgrim's Progress*. Over and over again I read my Bible, particularly finding confidence in the promise "Trust in the Lord with all thine heart, and lean not unto thine own understanding.... Then shalt thou walk in thy way safely, and thy foot shall not stumble." (Proverbs 3:5,23)

By the end of 1959, I had walked 1,000 miles

to Uganda, where a family took me in and I found a job making bricks for government buildings. I remained there six months and I sent most of my earnings to my mother.

In *Pilgrim's Progress*, I read many times of the tribulations of the Christian who wandered through the wilderness seeking God, and I compared this to my own wanderings toward the goal I believed God had put into my heart. I could not give up, any more than the Christian had given up.

One afternoon at the USIS library in Kampala, I came upon a directory of American colleges. Opening it at random, I saw the name of Skagit Valley College, Mount Vernon, Washington. I had heard that American colleges sometimes gave scholarships to deserving Africans, so I wrote Dean George Hodson and applied for one. I realized that I might be refused but I was not discouraged: I would write to one school after another in the directory until I found one that would help me.

Three weeks later, Dean Hodson replied; I was granted a scholarship and the school would help me find a job. Overjoyed, I went to the American authorities, only to be told that this was not enough. I would need a passport and the round-trip fare in order to obtain a visa.

I wrote to the Nyasaland government for a passport but it was refused because I could not tell them when I was born. I wrote to the missionaries who had taught me in my childhood, and it was through their efforts that I was granted a passport. But I still could not get the

During the Depression, the young Gene Autry was working as a telegraph operator in Chelsea, Oklahoma. When business got slow, he'd take out his guitar and sing. One night, a stranger came by. "Say," he said, "you don't sing so bad. You should go into show business." That encouragement propelled Autry into a career he hadn't dared hope for. For sometimes, through others, God can guide us. PS: The helpful customer? Will Rogers.

visa at Kampala because I did not have the fare.

Still determined, I left Kampala and resumed my trip northward. So strong was my faith that I used my last money to buy my first pair of shoes: I knew I could not walk into Skagit Valley College in my bare feet. I carried the shoes to save them.

Across Uganda and into the Sudan, the villages were farther apart and the people were less friendly. Sometimes I had to walk 30 miles in a day to find a place to sleep or to work to earn some food. At last I reached Khartoum, where I learned that there was an American consulate and I went there to try my luck.

Once again I heard about the entrance requirements, this time from Vice-Consul Emmett M. Coxson; but Mr. Coxson wrote the college about my plight. Back came a cable.

The students, hearing about me and my problems, had raised the fare of $1,700 through benefit parties.

I was thrilled and deeply grateful; overjoyed by this example of friendship and brother-hood. I was thankful to God for His guidance and I pledged my future to His service.

In December 1960, carrying my only two books and wearing my first suit, I arrived at Skagit Valley College.

In my speech of gratitude to the student body, I disclosed my desire to become prime minister or president of my country, and I noticed some smiles. I wondered if I had said something naïve. I do not think so.

When God has put an impossible dream in your heart, He means to help you fulfill it. I believed this to be true when, as an African bush boy, I felt compelled to become an American college graduate. This is to become true in June when I will graduate from the University of Washington. And if God has given me the dream of becoming president of Nyasaland, this too, will become true.

It is when we resist God that we remain nothing. When we submit to Him, whatever the sacrifice or hardship, we can become far more than we dare dream.

Lester Plowman was a humble boilermaker in Baltimore, when he accepted Christ, and started studying biblical archaeology (Guideposts 1950). Gradually, while still working his trade, he became an expert in archaeology and a scholar. Ultimately, he was instrumental in bringing the Dead Sea Scrolls—one of the greatest finds of the century—to America for study. By opening himself to God, Lester Plowman opened himself to a whole new world.

MAY 1982

The Voice Out of Nowhere *by Robert Meeler, preacher*

I was 38 when the Lord spoke to me—and told me to do the strangest thing.

We had a little farm in the mountains of north Georgia then—me, my wife Nell and our six children. I'd never been to school a day in my life and I couldn't read a word, but I did know how to farm. I'd learned that from my father. The day I heard God speak was a beautiful one, the kind where the sun blazes down and warms your bones. I was bending over, picking a mess of peas for supper, when out of the blue a Voice boomed: "I WANT YOU TO GO PREACH!"

I jerked up and looked around. *Some rascals are playing a trick on me,* I thought. I ran to the big rock on top of the hill, where I could see for miles. But when I got there, not a soul was in sight—and not a sound could be heard except the birds' chirping and the soft swish of the wind. I was sure then that God Himself had given me an order, and I began to shiver. Why would He want me, an ignorant farmer?

"No, Lord!" I cried into the sky. "I can't preach. Not a man like me with no learning. Why, I can't read Your Word. Besides, I'm too new a Christian."

A couple of weeks before, Nell had taken me to a prayer meeting, and that night I'd accepted Christ. But how could a brand new Christian preach to others?

"Don't *ask* me, God," I mumbled, looking down at my cracked, dusty old brogans. Then I started to run down the hill, away from that Voice.

As it turned out, I kept right on running for five years, because during that time I didn't go to church much. I didn't have time for it. A farmer leads a busy life. Or so I told myself.

Those were lean, hard years for our family. Everything seemed to go wrong. My crops failed, I was in a bad accident with my pickup truck, and—worst of all—my sweet little daughter Betty died with infantile paralysis. I walked around half-dazed most of the time and that got me into more trouble.

Where I lived, getting ready for planting meant burning off the fields before plowing. I knew perfectly well how to burn safely, but the spring that Betty died I wasn't paying full mind to the job. I raked brush into a pile to start the fire, and when I bent down and struck the match, I didn't notice the wind had picked up.

All at once the wind whooshed across the field and whipped my fire out of control. I *had* to keep it away from the sprouting fields my neighbor had recently planted! I panicked—raced into the fire and tried to beat it out. Instantly, I was completely surrounded by flames. They roared higher than my head, and right then and there I thought about the gates of hell. "Lord, save me!" I yelled. "I don't want to die. Save me, and I'll do what You want!" The last thing I remember is covering my eyes with my arm and dashing through a wall of fire.

Born in 1862, Amos Alonzo Stagg wanted desperately to become a minister. But when he reached seminary, he found he just wasn't good at public speaking. Instead, he made sports his ministry. To this day, he is revered as a founding father of modern sports. Until recently passed by Bear Bryant, he was the winningest college football coach in the history of the game. Stagg told his story in Guideposts (1959), at the age of ninety-seven.

I was badly burned and spent a long time in the hospital, but God answered my prayer. Now I had a promise to keep—somehow. I had to find a way to do what He wanted.

Shortly after I was on my feet again, I sold my hard-luck farm and moved my family to what I hoped was a better one near Lyerly, Georgia. Now every Sunday, without fail, I went with my family to the Belmont Baptist Church. I had a lot of catching up to do.

Several years passed and I did my best to honor God and learn about His teachings. Just by listening hard, I memorized a good amount of Scripture. I wasn't preaching, but I was never shy about testifying for the Lord. Then one day the church deacons called me aside.

"Bob," they said, "we'd like you to teach the adult Sunday school class."

"I can't," I told them. "I don't know how to read."

But those people were a good bunch of friends. "That doesn't matter, Bob," they said. "You'll make a good teacher anyhow." They wouldn't let up urging and encouraging me.

I was still ashamed about my ignorance, but I remembered my promise to God. *Maybe this is what God meant when He told me "go preach,"* I thought. *Teaching is almost like preaching. Maybe this is what He had in mind all along.*

I accepted the job.

Before each class, my wife—bless her—read the lessons to me. I couldn't have done the job without her. But Nell didn't have much

formal schooling and there were many words she couldn't make out herself. After two years, I began to feel frustrated. I needed to learn to read for myself. Even with a lot of back-patting from the folks in my Sunday school class, I felt they deserved a lot more than they were getting from me.

If only I could get some schooling…but we were still poor. And even if I could afford to take time away from my farm work, how could a codger in his 50s fit into a classroom with little kiddies? Impossible! The blues began to gather around me like clouds around a mountaintop.

One day, fed up with the daily torment, I decided to *will* myself to read. I grabbed my Bible and stomped into the woods behind our house. I sank down under a pine tree and opened the Good Book. The mass of black letters all seemed to jumble. None of those little marks printed on the page had any meaning to me. I tried so hard to make them out that my head began to hurt and my stomach knotted up. Tears welled up in my eyes, and I slammed the book shut and let them come. Inside me there was a deep ache, and it came out in great moans.

"Lord," I sobbed, "You know my misery. You *know* I'm trying to serve You. I want to do what You want me to do, but I don't know how. I need to read Your Word, but I can't. Dear God, help me!"

For hours I sat there, crying and begging for help from above. At last a peaceful feeling settled over me. I didn't know what it meant, but I

A Prayer of Relinquishment   by Helen Inwood

If I can't give You all my heart,   *Please work through me in little ways*
Lord, please accept a little part   *And let a fragment of Your light*
And let Your love transform it till   *Illuminate my mortal night*
It yields entirely to Your will.   *Until I gladly give the whole—*
If I can't give You all my days,   *All my life and all my soul.*

felt better, as if Someone had put a hand on my shoulder and said, "It'll be all right now."

That night, I was listening as Nell read the Bible to me. She stumbled on a word, and without thinking I leaned over to look at the page. "That's 'impoverished,' " I said.

She picked up reading where she'd left off until another word stopped her. Again I looked at the page. "That's 'inhabitants.' "

The third time it happened, Nell got a funny expression on her face. "You know this Book better than I do," she said.

And all of a sudden it hit me. *She was reading verses I hadn't memorized!*

Almost fearfully, I took the Bible from her and ran my eyes over the page. "I can read, Nell," I cried. "I CAN READ!"

I flipped page after page and every sentence made sense. I even picked up a magazine and read the words on the cover. "It's got to be God's work," I whispered. "Only God could do this for me."

How long had He been planting His words in me so that now, this night, they had sprouted and bloomed? Without another word, we got down on our knees and gave thanks to Him.

I stayed up late that night, searching the Scriptures with my own eyes. What a joy to read for the first time the words in Job 32:8, "It is the spirit in a man, the breath of the Almighty, that makes him understand." (RSV)

To me, those words will always have a special meaning. They say that we all have a secret Teacher Who lives within us. If you ask His help—and trust in His wisdom— you'll be given whatever knowledge you need to have.

How else could an ignorant old farmer learn to read without ever setting foot in a schoolhouse?

In Mending Relationships

"The sad thing about hate is what it can do to the hater."

Dr. Alan Loy McGinnis (Guideposts 1981)

Mending relationships, it's one of our hardest tasks—and for believers, one of the most essential. Not only does Jesus command us to love our enemies, but again and again, authorities in medicine and psychology affirm that hatred, anger and resentment can actually do us physical harm. The patient who nurses a bitter grievance beneath a real physical ailment is a common phenomenon.

Why is forgiveness so hard? Why do some of the worst fallings-out occur between those who are closest—between husbands and wives, brothers and sisters, inseparable friends?

Let's look at a simple example. Hazel Zieman and her next-door neighbor Barbara were the best of friends for years…until an old bureau at an antique sale came between them (Guideposts 1971). Hazel coveted it and Barbara, unaware, bought it. Hazel flew into a rage, Barbara stormed off; and by the time Hazel tried to apologize, Barbara would hear none of it.

Who was in the wrong? It's hard to say. Who was in the right? That's also hard to say. A just solution might be the sort Solomon suggested to the two women fighting over one child: divide the baby in half (I Kings 3:25).

But that's just it, justice is *not* the solution. Perhaps the reason mending relationships is so difficult is that we are required to go deeper than justice and fairness. The rational solution is in irrational love, the sort of love Paul had in mind when he wrote, "It is not rude, it is not self-seeking, it is not easily angered, it keeps no records of wrongs" (I Cor 13:5 NIV). To do something so extraordinary, we need His help.

Hazel and Barbara were finally reconciled when they drew on His love and put their differences behind them. We can all tap the same power, but two things are required of us. As we turn to Him for help, we also must turn to our neighbor.

We can start right next door.

Kris Welland, 1975

MAY 1975

Mother, I'm Here *by Kris Welland, Youth Contest winner*

My mother's alcoholism became apparent to me when I was about nine years old. For seven years, I watched as her illness made a grayish, skeletonlike animal out of the intelligent, charming beauty I loved. Liquor tore her apart and tore us apart too, my brother and sister and father and me, and all the other people who loved her, which included anyone who knew her.

As for me, I changed as much in those seven years as I thought my mother did. I began to hate her because hating hurt less than loving her and watching her destroy herself. Later, I felt her drinking was directed purposely at the family, and I steeled myself even more against the sympathy that made me vulnerable to soul-ache. I like to think now that had I known what she was suffering, I would have helped her. But I didn't.

I was 15 when my father carried her limp, gray, emaciated form out to the car and drove her away, and I remember distinctly the overwhelming relief I felt that hot June day. She was going away for good, far away to a rehabilitation center in Minneapolis, Minnesota, and my father was divorcing her. I would never have to see her again. I didn't, either, for almost two years.

During that time, I thought about my mother as little as possible; I was happier than I had ever been before, ignorantly happy. To appease my conscience, I read the letters she sent us; full of a love that disgusted me; but I never wondered at her struggle to regain her sobriety, her sanity and self-respect.

She won the struggle without my help. When I was 16, she wrote to say that she was leaving the rehabilitation center for an apartment and a position as a secretary in an insurance company.

I could not believe she was really well at last. Secretly I resented her licking it without us when she couldn't with us, and cynically I expected her to start drinking again within a week. But her letters kept coming; she wrote of her activities at work, of decorating her apartment, of skiing weekends.

My mother seemingly ignored the fact that we never answered her letters and she kept writing until we finally did answer them. Courtesy, I told myself. But the truth was, I had to admire her spunk. Finally, I accepted one of her invitations to visit; and two days after my 17th Christmas I boarded a plane for Minneapolis.

I have never felt so frightened as I did when I stepped off the plane that wintry evening. My mother must have been frightened too, but as I glimpsed that face in the crowded waiting room, she hurried to me and hugged and kissed me and kept her arm around me as we walked away. I wanted to shrug off that arm—one of my principles of my hate had been that I never allowed her to touch me—but she kept it there, and in my confusion I talked furiously.

We picked up my luggage and stepped out into the shocking cold and the cobalt night. As

In the early '60s at Guideposts, we noticed we were hearing from everyone—except young people. In an effort to encourage teenagers to speak out, we started our annual Youth Writing Contest. Since then, we've heard from thousands of high-school juniors and seniors, representing all 50 states, and we've given out thousands of dollars in college scholarships. But Guideposts has received so much more—their honesty, insights and faith.

we drove noisily through the dark and snow, fast along the flat highway, my ego and I began to recover from our fright, and my hauteur and hate came back. I answered reticently, even curtly, her eager questions about my sister and brother, about my friends, about school.

Sometimes with deliberate cruelty I spoke of things to remind her of her losses—of my brother's new tallness, the beauty of our Christmas tree, the family jokes around the dinner table at home—a hundred things that could only grieve and sadden her. Never did I speak encouragingly of her amazing return to health; never was I enthusiastic about the details of her new life in Minnesota; not once did I display a particle of affection.

Yet my mother kept her composure and retained in our conversation both untiring interest and, more remarkably, love. By the time we got to her home I was a little ashamed of myself, which only served to make me nastier toward her.

We walked into the warmth of her apartment and I held my breath. My mother adored daintiness and airiness and how beautiful she had made that room! Gauzy white curtains floated at the windows. The floor was blanketed richly in pale yellow, the light blue furniture was gay with sprays of tiny white flowers and around the room she had scattered great bunches of daisies in crystal bowls.

For Christmas, tables were adorned with graceful candles and delicate silver angels. The little gilt bell that had tinkled *Silent Night* for us so many years at home was now on her desk, and next to the large window stood a dainty little fir tree, bearing bugles and Santas my mother had made by hand. It was all so lovely and homelike that it caught at my heart.

I stood looking at that room while my mother bustled around putting finishing touches on everything. When she was done she led me to her room, which was as delightful as the other, and I got ready for bed. My mother was to sleep on the living-room sofa while I was there, and she too prepared for bed, all the while chattering lightly. I allowed her to kiss me good night before she left the room, and then I climbed into bed and lay watching the snow swirl against the window. My door was open, and for a long time there was no sound but the *swish* of the icy flakes against the glass. I lay awake for a long time, and inside I was as cold as that snow.

When I finally began to get drowsy, a frighteningly familiar sound started me awake. It was a soft sound, a sound I had heard often in the night, and I got up quietly and padded out into the living room. The fir tree's lights twinkled gently, and in their soft light I saw my mother huddled on the couch, her face in her hands. She was weeping as she had wept many times, alone and in the dark. I stood silently for a moment and watched her, and then my heart couldn't stand it anymore. I went to her and put my arms around her, and from that moment have never ceased to love her.

How do you mend a broken relationship? Christ said, "A new commandment I give unto you, That ye love one another" (John 13:34). The word new is important, for Christ brought a new faith that required us to do more than obey Old Testament law. We should love one another. This statement is absolute. Christ doesn't say that you should love another person if he is fair and lawful. Love one another—no ifs or buts about it. And so when a relationship needs mending, above all, keep loving.

JUNE 1983

If You Only Knew My Father *by Leilani Appleyard, Writers Workshop winner 1982*

He was an old man who seemed alone in the world. I was a young woman who was no longer in touch with her father. It's not surprising that we were drawn to each other.

We met the day I started volunteer training at a local convalescent center. Coming up the steps, I saw a big man with thick, gray hair sitting in a wheelchair on the porch. As I approached the glass doors, he rolled his chair over and, still sitting, struggled forward to grasp the door handle. Then, gallantly holding the door open, he smiled at me. "Name's Ray,*" he told me in a soft Southern drawl.

"I'm Lani—I'm a new volunteer."

"Well, you'll be 'Bubba' to me," he said. "Down where I come from that's a love-name folks give to the little one in the family."

"I like that," I said, meaning it. His way with me was so warm and open, so unlike the gruff indifference my father had always shown me.

Every Wednesday, when I came for training, Ray was waiting at the top of the steps to open the door for me. The volunteers' classes were taught by Sharon,* an energetic woman who combined sympathy and faith with a keen understanding of the social and emotional needs of the elderly. When the training was over, the patients I was assigned to didn't include Ray. But I'd visit him on my own time.

His greeting was always an eager "Hi, Bubba!" Little by little, we stored up facts about each other. When I described my husband to Ray, he told me he was married, too.

*Name has been changed.

What he said was, "We decided not to get a divorce."

"Do you have any children?"

"Oh, sure."

"Are they able to come visit you?" I asked.

"Oh, yes, they come," he said and looked away. I had never seen anyone visit Ray. *Probably his family lives far away and they don't get here often,* I thought.

Each week we spent some time together. I gave him little gifts like a soft beige washcloth and towel. He taught me to play dominoes and saved his dessert for me. With little acts of caring and relaxed conversation, we nourished our relationship.

We drew so close that as I was leaving one day a housekeeper noticed Ray waving to me from the porch and remarked, "Your father sure loves you."

"He's not..." My throat closed before I could finish the sentence. I rushed to my car. *If you only knew my father!* There were no dominoes or desserts from my always too-busy, too-tired father. Most of the time I tried not to think about him because it hurt. But now the housekeeper's comment opened up memories. And as usual I went back to the terrible thing he'd done to me on the day of my marriage; the final, embarrassing blow at my wedding reception. The band had begun a waltz and the leader came up to the microphone. "Time for the bride and her father to dance," he announced breezily.

How do you mend relationships? Jesus spelled it out for us. "Love your enemies" (Luke 6:27). And how does one love one's enemies? Bethanne Walker willed herself to look at her hostile stepmother through God's eyes (Guideposts 1983). She focused on the woman's good qualities and came up with several of them: her housekeeping ability, her care for an invalid mother... Though her stepmother didn't change, Bethanne did. "I am learning a different kind of love," she says, "loving without expecting something in return."

Everyone watched expectantly. "No!" my father said. He turned and left the room, leaving me standing by myself on the dance floor.

When my father turned away from me that day, the bitterness I'd accumulated while I was growing up took over my feelings: all the resentment about his not being on hand for important school events, the times he'd threatened to walk away from the burdens of his work and leave my mother and me. *I* could walk away from *him* this time. And I did.

That had been five years ago. Once in a while, I thought about trying to patch things up. But it seemed too awkward and complicated. Anyway, I had Ray now.

But then one day I drove up to the center and Ray wasn't on the porch. I parked the car crookedly and ran up the steps, tripping at the top. Where was he?

I raced to his room, dodging patients. It was empty. No wheelchair, no one in the neatly made bed. "Please, God," I whispered as I backed out of the room. I ran to the nurses' station.

"Where's Ray?" I blurted.

"They took him to the hospital last night. His asthma got much worse."

"What hospital is he at?"

"I'll check," the nurse said, going through some charts. "Are you family?"

"I'm his...friend." I held my breath and bit my lip to gain control. I'd almost said "daughter."

She gave me the hospital's name.

The trip to the hospital took forever. Once there, I found Ray's room and jolted to a stop in the doorway. His pajama top was off and he had many tubes. He looked hot and uncomfortable. He turned his head and saw me. "Bubba, Bubba, I knew you'd find me!"

"Ray, you weren't there! I was so scared." I started sobbing.

"Come here, Bubba. It's okay." He held out his arms as best he could. Somehow he got an arm around me.

"It's okay, Bubba, you came," he said. He patted my back. I listened while he talked, and I grew calm.

When it was time to leave, I stood in the doorway and said, "I'll come see you tomorrow, Ray."

"Okay, Bubba," he answered.

The next morning I was eating breakfast when the phone rang. I stood to answer it. When I heard Sharon's voice, my hand tightened on the receiver and I leaned against the wall, knocking down the calendar.

"We don't usually call volunteers, but I didn't want you to read it in the paper. I know how close you and Ray were. He died yesterday," she said gently.

"That can't be! I was with him yesterday."

"I know. He died a few hours later."

After we hung up, I walked slowly outside to the curb and picked up the paper. I turned to the obituaries and read about Ray O'Brien. Suddenly I felt a surge of anger rip through the sorrow. He did indeed have a wife and children! He had 12 children—six sons and six daughters—and all but two of his family lived in the area! And yet, I had been the last person to be with him, to comfort him.

I called Sharon back. "Tell me why," I de-

To make his point about checking anger, the great preacher Harry Emerson Fosdick (1878–1969) told a story (Guideposts 1970) about his boyhood temper tantrums. When he got angry, his father would say, "Where's Harry?" "Here I am!" young Fosdick would reply. "No, you're not Harry. He's lost. Go find him," his father answered. He could only return when his temper was under control, when he'd remembered who he was. "I've found Harry," he'd then say. Do you remember to look for your best self?

manded. "Why weren't his family with him? Why was I the one to be with him?"

Sharon hesitated. "I'm going to tell you something. I think you deserve to know. Ray used to be a drunk. He beat his wife and his children. When he came to live here, they never wanted to see him again."

"No, I don't believe it," I shouted. And yet I remembered Ray's reluctance to talk about his family. The family who never visited. But this person Sharon was describing couldn't be the loving man who called me Bubba.

"It's true," Sharon said. She paused. "But other things are true, too. When he came to the center, Ray talked some things out with me. By then he'd faced the unpleasant facts about himself. He'd been abused as a child, and he realized that one of the reasons he drank was that he thought it helped him with his bad feelings about himself. But it only aggravated them and then he'd take his anger out on his own family. Over and over he asked God's forgiveness, and he wanted to ask his family to forgive him, too. But it was too late. They wanted no part of him."

"I thought of him like a father," I said shakily.

"And Ray thought of you as a daughter. He told me so. You gave him a chance to feel forgiven. It's probably the most Christlike thing that one person can do for another. I think God used you to comfort a sad, lonely old man with nothing in his life but regrets."

We said good-bye. My thoughts moved slowly, leadenly. Ray and his children were estranged, just as my father and I were. What

was it that happened between parents and children? Why were the most damaging relationships always between those who had the most intimate link—of flesh and blood?

Bending down, I picked up the calendar I'd knocked off the wall. It was open to June, to a picture of a little girl and her father going fishing. Once, long ago, my father had taken me fishing. It was a good memory, a memory I had shoved under all the bad ones. It was easier to be mad at him if I didn't think about the good things—or about the hard life he'd had.

His mother had died when he was a small boy and he'd spent his childhood working in the fields with his father. He'd never gone to high school and had supported my mother and me with jobs he hated—hauling trash, cleaning the beer coils in bars. Eventually he built his own business—often working all night and falling asleep in the afternoon. He had done that so I could go to college. "So you don't turn out like me," he often said when I asked why he had to work all the time.

And, eventually, as I wandered back in memory, I came to that final, painful incident at my wedding and then, only then, did I remember an excuse someone had made for him—one that I had been too hurt to pay attention to. That day my father was wearing his first tuxedo. The fancy clothes—the customs that went with the better life he'd slaved for—were foreign to him. And he didn't know how to dance.

Slowly, I put the calendar back on the wall. Then I picked up the phone. I needed to call my father.

What makes a family strong? In Guideposts (1983), Dr. Alan Loy McGinnis cited a University of Nebraska study that distinguishes three qualities common to all strong families. Appreciation: *Family members complimented one another.* Time together: *Family members structured their schedules to spend time together.* And a high degree of religious orientation: *Families benefited especially when nurtured by a strong church family.*

OCTOBER 1965

The Bachelor Husband *by Calvin Kinzie, garage owner*

When Jerry Cooke married Barbara Bailey* in our little town a few years back, there was plenty of remarks from the sidelines.

"She's too quiet and gentle for Jerry," some people said. "She's the religious type; he's the wild one."

"That's what happens," others said. "The wildest boys pick the most straitlaced girls to marry."

"Yes," said the cynics, "because they can't get them any other way!"

"Maybe he'll settle down," said the optimists.

I myself was one of the optimists. I knew Jerry about as well as anyone, and I thought a lot of Barbara. She was a tall, blonde girl with steady eyes that a man remembered, and honesty shone through them like light through a stained-glass window.

I liked Jerry too. He was gay and dark-haired and good-looking, and girls always were falling for him. There was one in particular named Ginger, a sultry redhead, who worked as cashier at the Sapphire Inn, the only place in town where you can get a good meal, and dance too.

If you mentioned Ginger to Jerry, he would roll his eyes and whistle through his teeth. For a while, they went everywhere together. Then one day Nan, my girl friend, and I introduced him to Barbara. That was it. Ginger faded right out of the picture. Three months later, Barbara and Jerry were married.

For a while, everything went fine. Barbara

gave up her job since Jerry was running the service department in one of the biggest automobile agencies in town. They got a little house near Barbara's church. Once or twice, Jerry even went to church. But he told me he did it only to please Barbara.

"All this stuff about faith moving mountains," he said. "I don't dig it. Faith doesn't clean a carburetor, does it? I'm a realist, I guess."

The first inkling I had of trouble came about a year after they were married. It was a Saturday night and Nan and I went dancing at the Sapphire Inn. There, at a table in a corner with their heads close together, were Ginger and Jerry. When they saw us, Jerry got up with a sheepish look, and went out.

Nan was furious. "You'd better talk to that friend of yours," she said, "and set him straight on a few things. He's got a wife at home. Or has he forgotten that?"

"Don't jump to conclusions, Nan," I said. But when I spoke to Ginger later that evening I was more worried. "So Jerry's married," she said, tossing that red hair of hers. "So what? Anyone can make a mistake. And when they have, the sooner they admit it the better!"

When I spoke to Jerry the next day I didn't get much further. "Relax, chum," he said. "Ginger's lively and fun to talk to. That's all there is to it."

But that was not all there was to it. A couple of weeks later I saw Jerry's car turning into a side

*Names throughout have been changed.

Monica Patterson wanted peace in Northern Ireland, but as an English Catholic in strife-torn Belfast, she was caught between the Irish Catholics and English-descended Protestants. Valiantly, she brought women from both sides together (Guideposts 1973). One member of her group stopped a factory riot. Two others sent 200 would-be rioters to church to pray for peace. Whether in warring factions or estranged relatives, Monica Patterson would tell us that there is an overriding force in all relationships: love.

street, and the silhouette in the front seat beside the driver wasn't Barbara's. Soon after, one of the boys in my garage brought up the subject. "Quite a guy, that Jerry," he said sardonically. "Wants to have his cake and a cookie too."

"What makes you say that?"

"Oh," he said, "this is a small town. Things get around."

Nan confirmed the fact that there *was* a lot of talk going round. "Ginger would like nothing better than to break up Jerry's marriage," she said. "And Jerry is crazy enough to let her do it. Some of us have tried to warn Barbara, but she smiles and says she trusts her husband...that heel!"

"What makes her so sure of him?" I asked uneasily.

"It's just blind faith," Nan said. "She says that she loves him, and so she doesn't have to worry. She even has a quotation from the Bible pasted on her dressing table. It says, *'There is no fear in love; but perfect love casteth out fear'* (I John 4:28). That's what she believes, and that's the way she is."

I knew I was sticking my neck out, but the next day I stopped by the service department where Jerry worked. I told him that people were talking and that in my opinion he was headed for trouble.

This time he flared up like a firecracker. "If people would just mind their own business," he snapped, "there would be a lot less trouble in the world. Why don't you try it yourself?"

"Because I like Barbara," I said. "I don't want to see either one of you get hurt."

He smiled suddenly. "Barbara and I are getting along fine," he said. "Bring Nan around for supper tonight and see for yourself."

So we did have supper with them, and to me everything seemed serene. But Nan felt differently. "Jerry's fooling you, Cal," she said as I drove her home. "He's one of those men who'll be a bachelor as long as he lives. And Barbara makes it easy for him. Why, not even the notes seem to upset her!"

"What notes?" I asked.

"Oh Barbara let it slip out that she's been getting these poison-pen letters. Just a line or two saying, 'Ask your husband where he was and what he was doing at such-and-such a place and such-and-such a time.' No signature."

"Good Lord," I said, "who'd do a thing like that?"

"Some spiteful woman," Nan said grimly.

"Does Jerry know about these notes?"

"No! Barbara tears them up. She refuses to see what everyone else sees. She just believes what she wants to believe."

"Well," I said, "things can't go on much longer like this. Something's got to give."

It all came to a head sooner than anyone expected. Every year in November our Legion Post gives a Harvest Ball, and this year Nan and Barbara had arranged for the four of us to go together. I don't know who brought Ginger. All I know is that about two in the morning, just as we were getting ready to go home, she appeared at our table, two-thirds drunk and mean as a snake. She put her fists

Monica Patterson on a street in Belfast, Northern Ireland

on the edge of the table and looked down at Barbara. "Well," she said, "you're a hard one to convince."

Not one of us said a word. Barbara was perfectly calm; Jerry looked tense and grim.

"Ask him," said Ginger, still speaking to Barbara." Ask him where he was between six and eight last Thursday night."

I stood up and put my hand on her arm. "Look, Ginger," I said, "why don't you...?"

She shook me off. "All right," she said to Barbara. "So you want proof. Well, here's the motel receipt." She flung a scrap of paper on the table. "There!" she said. "Ask him to deny it! I dare you!"

Barbara looked at Ginger for about 10 seconds. It seemed like 10 years. There was no anger in her face, just serenity and confidence.

"I think you're mistaken," she said. "My husband and I love each other. We stood up in God's house and made a promise for better or worse. For richer or poorer. In sickness and in health. To love and to cherish...."

She hesitated, and it was an incredible thing: you could *feel* the power of evil that was in Ginger shrink until it seemed insignificant and unimportant.

When Barbara spoke to her again, it was almost as if she were speaking to a child. "The man I married," she said, "is the man I love. And the man I love is the man I married. So I don't think he's the one you know. In fact, I'm

sure he isn't. You must be talking about someone else." She turned to Nan. "Let's go, Nan."

They walked away together. Ginger stood there, her face dark with fury. "That fool!" she said.

She stamped off without another word. I looked at Jerry. If ever I saw self-loathing on a man's face it was on his. "We both know who the fool is, Cal," he said. He pounded his hand against the table. "Never," he said. "So help me, never again!"

All this happened about three years ago. Not one of us has mentioned the episode since. Nan and I are married now, Jerry and Barbara are our best friends, just about the happiest couple I know. But sometimes I can't help wondering....

Did Barbara let herself believe, even for a moment, that Ginger was telling the truth? Was she making some kind of distinction between Jerry, the man she loved, and Jerry, the immature, self-centered bachelor husband? Or was her trust so strong that love was able to cast out every particle of doubt and fear?

I guess I'll never know. But I learned something that I'll never forget. Faith is so strong that when you act as if something were true, it tends to become true. And when you really believe, it can move something much more difficult than mountains. It can move and change the hearts of men.

Guideposts cover, 1959: Edith Taylor embracing Aiko

MARCH 1959

Could You Have Loved This Much? *by Bob Considine, newspaper columnist*

This is the story of a woman's love for her husband. Whether he deserved that love—and why he acted the way he did—are questions I can't answer. I'm not going to write about Karl Taylor; this story is about his wife.

The story begins in 1950 in the Taylors' small apartment in Waltham, Massachusetts. Edith Taylor was sure that she was "the luckiest woman on the block." She and Karl had been married 23 years, and her heart still skipped a beat when he walked into a room.

As for Karl, he gave every appearance of a man in love with his wife. Indeed, he seemed almost dependent on her, as if he didn't want to be too long away from her. If his job as government warehouse worker took him out of town, he'd write Edith a long letter every night and drop her postcards several times during the day. He sent small gifts from every place he visited.

Often at night, they'd sit up late in their apartment and talk about the house they'd own, someday, "when we can make the down payment...."

In February, 1950, the government sent Karl to Okinawa for a few months to work in a new warehouse. It was a long time to be away, and so far!

This time, no little gifts came. Edith understood. He was putting every cent he saved into the bank for their home. Hadn't she begged him for years not to spend so much on her, to save it for the house?

The lonesome months dragged on, and it seemed to Edith that the job over there was taking longer and longer. Each time she expected him home, he'd write that he must stay "another three weeks." "Another month." "Just two months longer."

He'd been gone a year now—and suddenly Edith had an inspiration. Why not buy their home now, before Karl got back, as a surprise for him! She was working now, in a factory in Waltham, and putting all her earnings in the bank. So she made a down payment on a cozy cottage with lots of trees and a view.

Karl's letters were coming less and less often. No gifts she understood. But a few pennies for a postage stamp?

Then, after weeks of silence, came a letter:

"Dear Edith. I wish there were a kinder way to tell you that we are no longer married...."

Edith walked to the sofa and sat down. He'd written to Mexico for a divorce. It had come in the mail. The woman lived on Okinawa. She was Japanese; Aiko, maid-of-all-work assigned to his quarters.

She was 19. Edith was 48.

Now, if I were making up this story, the rejected wife would feel first shock, then fury. She would fight that quick paper-divorce, she would hate her husband and the woman. She would want vengeance for her own shattered life.

But I am describing here simply what did happen. Edith Taylor did not hate Karl. Per-

Sgt. Jacob de Shazer was one of Jimmy Doolittle's "boys," a member of the famous mission that bombed Tokyo on April 18, 1942. Later, over China, he was forced to bail out of his plane, and was captured and taken prisoner by the Japanese. For 40 months, he suffered cruel torture and punishment. And yet, at war's end, Jacob de Shazer returned to Japan on a different mission (Guideposts 1949). Practicing Christ's law, "Love thine enemy," he witnessed for his faith—to the very guards who'd held him prisoner.

haps she had loved him so long she was unable to stop loving him.

She could picture the situation so well. A penniless girl. A lonely man who—Edith knew it—sometimes drank more than he should. Constant closeness. But even so (here Edith made an heroic effort to be proud of her husband)—even so, Karl had not done the easy, shameful thing. He had chosen the hard way of divorce, rather than take advantage of a young servant-girl.

The only thing Edith could not believe was that he had stopped loving her. That he loved Aiko, too, she made herself accept.

But the difference in their ages, in their backgrounds—this couldn't be the kind of love she and Karl had known! Someday, they would both discover this—someday, somehow, Karl would come home.

Edith now built her life around this thought. She wrote Karl, asking him to keep her in touch with the small, day-to-day things in his life. She sold the little cottage with its view and its snug insulation. Karl never knew about it.

He wrote one day that he and Aiko were expecting a baby. Marie was born in 1951, then in 1953, Helen. Edith sent gifts to the little girls. She still wrote to Karl and he wrote back, the comfortable, detailed letters of two people who knew each other very well: Helen had a tooth, Aiko's English was improving, Karl had lost weight.

Edith's life was lived now on Okinawa. She merely went through the motions of existence in Waltham. Back and forth between factory and apartment, her mind was always on Karl. Someday, he'll come back....

And then the terrible letter: Karl was dying of lung cancer.

Karl's last letters were filled with fear. Not for himself, but for Aiko, and especially for his two little girls. He had been saving to send them to school in America, but his hospital bills were taking everything. What would become of them?

Then Edith knew that her last gift to Karl could be peace of mind for these final weeks. She wrote him that, if Aiko were willing, she would take Marie and Helen and bring them up in Waltham.

For many months after Karl's death, Aiko would not let the children go. They were all she had ever known. Yet what could she offer them except a life like hers? A life of poverty, servitude and despair. In November, 1956, she sent them to her "Dear Aunt Edith."

Edith had known it would be hard to be mother at 54 to a three-year-old and a five-year-old. She hadn't known that in the time since Karl's death they would forget the little English they knew.

But Marie and Helen learned fast. The fear left their eyes, their faces grew plump. And Edith—for the first time in six years—was hurrying home from work. Even getting meals was fun again!

Sadder were the times when letters came from Aiko. "Aunt. Tell me now what they do. If Marie or Helen cry or not." In the broken English Edith read the loneliness, and she knew what loneliness was.

*How do you mend relationships? "Do good to those who hate
you." New to the village, the Hyland family made friends with their
neighbors, the Stones (Guideposts 1984). But a minor mix-up
turned the Stone family against them. The Hylands' peace offerings
were snubbed. The Stones even passed by, laughing, when the
Hylands' car skidded into a ditch. Yet when Dave Hyland found the
Stones' car stuck in snow, he pulled them free. Such kindness in
the face of unkindness eventually restored the friendship. Proving
the wisdom of Luke 6:27.*

Money was another problem. Edith hired a woman to care for the girls while she worked. Being both mother and wage-earner left her thin and tired. In February she became ill, but she kept working because she was afraid to lose a day's pay; at the factory one day she fainted. She was in the hospital two weeks with pneumonia.

There in the hospital bed, she faced the fact that she would be old before the girls were grown. She thought she had done everything that love for Karl asked of her, but now she knew there was one thing more. She must bring the girls' real mother here too.

She had made the decision, but doing it was something else. Aiko was still a Japanese citizen, and that immigration quota had a waiting list many years long.

It was then that Edith Taylor wrote to me, telling me her story and asking if I could help her. I described the situation in my newspaper column. Others did more. Petitions were started, a special bill speeded through Congress and, in August 1957, Aiko Taylor was permitted to enter the country.

As the plane came in at New York's International Airport, Edith had a moment of fear. What if she should hate this woman who had taken Karl away from her?

The last person off the plane was a girl so thin and small Edith thought at first it was a child. She did not come down the stairs, she only stood there, clutching the railing, and Edith knew that, if she had been afraid, Aiko was near panic.

She called Aiko's name and the girl rushed down the steps and into Edith's arms. In that brief moment, as they held each other, Edith had an extraordinary thought. "Help me to love this girl, as if she were part of Karl, come home. I prayed for him to come back. Now he has—in his two little daughters and in this gentle girl that he loved. Help me, God, to know that."

How do you mend a relationship? Jane Braddock found a way, even though she was in a door-slamming rage because her husband Tom had telephoned a woman she knew he'd once been interested in (Guideposts 1981). Tom admitted he was wrong to Jane—and to God. But Jane could not relinquish her urge to make Tom feel bad; she was seething with resentment. Still, she forced herself to obey Jesus' commandment, "Pray for them which despitefully use you" (Luke 6:28). It was hard, but she kept at it. And when she least expected, she found her anger had disappeared.

AUGUST 1965

The Tarnished Tea Service *by Florence Botney, interior decorator*

In my family there is a silver tea service that has been handed down to five generations of us. For years, these five gleaming Georgian vessels, each classically fluted and crowned in a simplicity of silver, presided over the dining room of my family's home.

Centered majestically on our buffet, the service sat upon its silver tray with such authority that I, as a child, dashing headlong through the dining room, was known to slow up when passing it. I held this lovely heirloom in that kind of deferential awe.

But it was more than awe. The tea service was the focus of my childhood dreams of being grownup, of being the beautiful and gracious hostess in the home I would have one day. We used the tea set only on special occasions; and on very special occasions, when I was a little older, my mother would let me pour. That it would be mine one day, I knew; the only other child in my family was my younger brother Ralph, and what use would he have for such a delicate treasure? No, it was I who would accept the responsibility of caring for this particular antiquity until it should, in time, be passed on to my own children.

Years passed. We went to separate colleges. I became an interior decorator; Ralph went into the telephone company. He married Ruth, and they had two children. World War II came. Ralph served in the Signal Corps; I was in the Waves.

Meanwhile, I never married. Something always seemed to interfere: my career, the war, Father's death and then Mother's illness.

One autumn day, just after my mother had died following two painful years in and out of the hospital, Ralph's wife drove up to our family home, loaded her car with possessions, and drove off. I didn't know about it. I wasn't home at the time. I was spending the day in Indianapolis 75 miles away.

It was late afternoon when I arrived back. On my way to the kitchen, I switched on the light in the dining room. The emptiness of that room roared at me. The tea service was gone.

I gasped. Then, trembling for fear that burglars were still in the house, I ran out and sought help next door. We called the police and then I got through to Ralph at his office only to be told that it was Ruth who had been there to collect "a few things." Suddenly the significance of what he was saying hit me and right there in front of our neighbors I said, "Ruth didn't take the tea service, did she? Please Ralph, that tea service is mine." To which he said—nothing.

Later, I drove out to Ralph's house in the new suburbs south of town. I sensed what lay ahead but I kept telling myself that if I but explained my special fondness for the tea service, if I just asked for it firmly and forthrightly, my brother and his wife would urge me to take it back.

In a speech published in Guideposts, Dag Hammarskjöld (1905–1961), then Secretary General of the United Nations, told how an altar for the U.N.'s Prayer Room was chosen. The decision was to use a solid block of crude iron, a basic element God has given us to use for good or ill. "We thought we could bless, by our thoughts, the very material out of which swords have been made." From swords to plowshares. From angry words to prayers of peace.

I was a fool. She, or he, or both of them had decided upon keeping my tea service. Though we had never argued before, we argued now, so noisily and so bitterly that my little niece and nephew had to be sent upstairs. It was a vicious battle, a stinging, personal, raw-nerved contest in which we clashed our way down the alleyways of reason and into the deadends of name calling. In my eyes, Ruth was a sneak. I fought for the principles of honesty and decency. I fought because that tea service meant more to me than anything else in the world.

Who knows—I might have won out that night if Ralph had not turned on me. He was my baby brother. He had been my dearest friend, my firmest alley for as long as I could remember. But that night, he was as cruel as she. The last thing I remember was his pronouncement about being "custodian" of the tea service for little Sally and Ralph, Jr.

"And what about me? What about the children I might have some day?" I said emotionally.

Ralph laughed at that. He really laughed. It was then that I fled from the house.

It is hard to believe, but our estrangement was born out of that fight for the silver tea service. My sister-in-law remained implacable; she would not return the service and Ralph refused to talk to me about it. Once the details of Mother's estate were settled, Ralph and I fell into silence. The situation became so awkward and embarrassing for me that, as soon as I could, I moved away to Chicago.

Twelve years passed in which I refused to go home. I got a job and cultivated a new life. I joined a church not far from my apartment and became involved in a variety of useful, time-consuming projects. It was a full life, I told myself, but there was always the feeling—I could never shake it—that I was an expatriate. You know when you have no roots, when you don't belong.

You find it out while sitting at Thanksgiving tables forcing conversations with other guests who have that stray-dog look. You sense it in the gift with your name on it under the Christmas tree, the gift that was purchased at the last minute at the drugstore. And, after a while, you tell even your kindest friends that you've been invited elsewhere; turkey in a restaurant, alone, seems better, truer.

Yes, I was lonely. And I was embittered. In my apartment I had the buffet from our dining room at home. It was a fetish of mine to keep its surface clear of objects at all times. That buffet nourished the hatred I had come to bear Ralph and his wife.

Yet, often I prayed to God for strength to live my life without rancor, to live it justly. Over and over, I would review my role in the tea-service incident. To have given in, would have been wrong: it would have been weakness, an invitation for them to take further advantage of me. Within my heart, I knew I had been wronged. I knew before God that I was justified in my course.

I never spoke to my brother again, nor did he ever speak to me.

Dag Hammerskjöld, 1905–1961

It was Ruth who called me long distance. She was confused and desperate, near collapse. Ralph was dead. A sudden heart attack.

"Come home, Florence. Please. I want you to stay here…"

"No," I shot back. "I have no intention of coming."

But I did go home. I thought it over; I prayed about it. Reason alone said that I should not be childish. He was my brother. I should do the right thing. But staying with Ruth was out of the question. I checked into a local hotel.

On the day of the funeral, quite on purpose, I arrived at the church early. Ralph's casket was there, closed. Flowers were still arriving and being arranged. I sat in a pew close to the front. I sat straight; I looked straight ahead, my mind empty. Shuffling sounds told me that the church was filling behind me as I continued to stare meaninglessly.

Then Ruth arrived. For a moment—before she entered the pew across the aisle—I had the terrible feeling that she was going to come to me. She didn't. I looked at the young woman who sat on her right. That was my niece, Sally. And the boy on her left who looked like the son of a friend of mine who played basketball and couldn't pass algebra; that was Ralph Jr.

I began to weep. At first I cried for myself. I cried for all the years I had missed with these beautiful young people. The service began, but the minister was saying words that I did not hear for I was crying at last for my dead brother. I could cry for him because a simple fact, the simplest, most unadorned fact human beings can ever know penetrated 12 unhappy years. The one true guide, I realized at last, is not who is right or who is wrong, not self-pride, not justification, not who is weak or who is strong, but that Jesus said: Love one another.

Sitting there, I saw that I had failed willingly to love. Jesus never said that loving would come without effort or trial or that forgiveness was easy; He commanded us to love. Did Jesus say, "Love one's possessions?" Did He tell me to put a silver tea service first in life before all other things? For five pieces of antique silver I had betrayed Him and myself.

In the middle of the funeral service, I stood up. I walked across the aisle and my family made room for me.

Jay Meck and his family are Mennonite, a Protestant sect that takes its name from Menno Simons, a 16th-century Dutch preacher. During the fervent years of the Reformation, Simons called believers to a renewed Christian discipleship, emphasizing evangelism and pacifism. Later, persecution throughout Europe brought many of his followers to America—where today some 300,000 Mennonites continue their walk with Christ.

OCTOBER 1975

The Peace We Found in Forgiveness *by Jay Meck, farmer*

As I finished the milking that Friday afternoon last October, I was glad it was done early, for now I would have time to do some other chores before supper and we'd be able to make the pet parade at the New Holland Fair.

I knew how the boys yearned to see that parade, expecially our youngest, little Nelson, seven, who'd be home from school any minute. I poked my head our of the barn door. No sign of Nelson yet, but I did see my wife Ruth coming out of the basement. She had been storing sweet potatoes for winter. Now she would be preparing an afternoon snack for Nelson, most likely some of that gingerbread he liked so much.

Putting away the milking pails, I thought how nice it was that as a farmer I could be at home during the day to enjoy my family. I loved it when Nelson bounded up our farm lane from school. He'd come back into the barn to tell me what happened that day, his freckled face beaming. Then he'd scurry over to the house to get a nibble from Ruth and dash back down the lane to wait for his older brother Johnny to come home. When Johnny appeared, Nelson never failed to say, "Ha-ha, I got home before you. What took you so long?"

The routine was always the same and never failed to give me pleasure. How blessed I was, with a wonderful wife and three boys to share the farm.

Just then, I heard someone running up the lane. Expecting Nelson, I came out of the barn only to be faced with his school-bus driver, Mike.

"Nelson's been hit by a car!" Mike yelled frantically. "Call an ambulance!"

My head suddenly felt light. Ruth yelled from the kitchen door that she would call one.

I tore off wildly down the lane to the road. My heart was racing like a tractor in the wrong gear. My mind was in a tailspin. *Please, Lord, not Nelson!* I thought. *Who could have done this? Who?*

When I reached the road, I pushed my way through the crowd already gathered near the school bus. There, on the blacktop of Highway 340 lay my son. I bent down and touched him softly. He didn't move. As I brushed back a fold in his hair, tears stung my eyes.

Just down the highway, a car was pulled over and I saw the license plate—the orange and blue colors of New York.

The area where we live—the Dutch country of southeastern Pennsylvania—attracts a goodly number of tourists and some of them don't have a very good reputation among us natives.

I stood up over Nelson and in a choking voice asked, "Who hit him?"

There was silence until finally a young dark-haired man and a woman who looked to be his wife stepped forward. They seemed frightened and dazed.

"He just ran out in front of us," the woman said, clutching tightly to the man's arm.

Jay and Ruth Meck

I walked over to them. I'm not a man of violence—in fact I've never so much as laid a finger on anyone. I took a deep breath, unsure of what I should do. "Jay Meck's my name," I said finally.

The man flinched, but shook hands with me. Just then the ambulance pulled up and its driver urged Ruth and me to follow. As we drove away, I looked back to see the couple holding on to each other, staring after us.

On our way to Lancaster Hospital we passed an Amish family, preserved in tranquility in a horse and buggy. The New Yorkers, I thought, had intruded upon that kind of peacefulness. They had come here where they didn't belong.

At the emergency room, Dr. Show, the man who delivered all our boys, met us immediately and said what I'd suspected all along. "Nelson's gone."

The next hours, even days, became a blur. We were besieged with cards and letters. Scores of friends and neighbors dropped by to help with the milking. They brought pies and casseroles. But even surrounded by all the sympathy, Ruth and I found we just couldn't keep little Nelson from our thoughts.

Nelson had come into our lives late, almost as if he were a special gift from God. Being the youngest, I suppose we held him precious and delighted in him more. The Sunday-school librarian called him "Sunshine" because he always had a cheerful disposition and a smile that never seemed to go away. What was most extraordinary about our son was his understanding of Christianity.

In school, for instance, he was the little guy who made friends with all the unfortunates— the cripples, the shy children, the outcasts. In the evenings when I'd go to his room to tuck him in, Nelson would be lying in bed with his hands folded. "Boy, Pop," he'd say, "there's sure a lot of people I've got to pray for tonight."

Like other small children, Nelson would squirm in church, but he would then startle Ruth and me by marching out after services and announcing, "I have Jesus in my heart."

Though older, Bob, 18, and Johnny, 15, were extremely close to their brother. Tuesday, when the funeral was over and we were sitting in our kitchen, Johnny recalled Nelson's daily vigil at the lane after school. "I'll bet Nelson's up in Heaven right now and when I get there he'll say, 'Ha-ha, Johnny, I got home before you. What took you so long?'"

Johnny's words tore into my heart. Ruth's and my grief was compounded when we discovered how senseless our son's death really was. Nelson didn't die through a car's mechanical failure or by natural causes. Nelson died because someone had not stopped his car for a school bus that was unloading children.

Much to our dismay, the man turned out to be a New York City policeman, a person we thought would know the law about stopping for buses with blinking lights. But he hadn't. Both he and his wife had been taken to the police station here where he had then been arrested. After posting bond, trial was set for January 17, 1975, three months away.

Why, Ruth and I agonized, hadn't this man been more careful? The whole thing was so

the Mecks at their farm in Pennsylvania

pointless. The more we thought about it the more it filled us with anguish. And our friends' and neighbors' feelings only seemed to add fuel to our torment.

"I sure hope that guy gets all that's coming to him," a man told me one day.

"You're going to throw the book at him, aren't you?" another asked.

Even the school authorities, hoping to make a case out of stopping for school buses urged us to press charges.

Ruth and I were beside ourselves. As Christians, we had received the Lord's reassurance that Nelson was now in eternal life. But how, we cried out, were we to deal with the man whose negligence caused so much heartache?

A few weeks after Nelson's funeral, an insurance adjustor called on us to clear up matters concerning the accident. He mentioned he'd visited the New York couple shortly before.

"They seem broken up," he added.

They're broken up? I thought. *What about all the tears we've shed?*

Yet a certain curiosity—perhaps a desire for an explanation—led Ruth and me to ask if it would be possible for us to meet with them.

The insurance man looked at us oddly. "You really want to see them?"

"Yes," I said.

He agreed to act as intermediary, and to our surprise, the couple, whose names were Frank and Rose Ann, accepted our invitation to come for dinner the Monday before Thanksgiving.

As the day drew closer, I became more dubious. *Could I really face them again? Why were we putting ourselves up to this?*

Ruth and I prayed long and hard about it. We asked the Lord to provide us with His strength and guidance.

When the day came, I looked out the kitchen window to see a car coming up our lane through a light rain. My hand trembled as I reached for the kitchen door to let them in.

We gathered in the living room and the conversation was forced. Everything we talked about seemed to be an outgrowth of the tragedy. But in talking with them, I began to notice something strange. A feeling of compassion came over me.

Frank was a policeman who'd been on the force eight years. He had a spotless record, but the accident, he said, might cost him his job. As a member of the tactical force in a high crime area, Frank put his life on the line for others every day.

And Rose Ann, like Ruth, had three children at home. She had looked forward to their vacation last October—their first away from the city since their marriage. But now she was worried. The New York papers had printed an account of the accident and because of it, they were staying with Rose Ann's parents, fearful of facing their neighbors.

"I just don't know what's going to happen," Frank said.

At dinner, we ate quietly. It was while we were having coffee that they noticed a picture, which hung on the kitchen wall, a chalk drawing of Jesus and the lost sheep.

"Nelson loved to look at that," Ruth said.

A Prayer of St. Francis

Lord, make us instruments of your peace. Where there is hatred, let us sow love; where there is injury, pardon; where there is discord, union; where there is doubt, faith; where there is despair, hope; where there is darkness, light; where there is sadness, joy. Grant that we may not so much seek to be consoled as to console; to be understood as to understand; to be loved as to love. For it is in giving that we receive; it is in pardoning that we are pardoned; and it is in dying that we are born to eternal life. Amen.

"His faith, like ours, was important." She went on to explain how she and I had grown up in a local church and how we both were long-time Sunday-school teachers at our Mennonite church.

"But it's more than a church," Ruth said. "You've really got to live out your beliefs every day."

Frank and Rose Ann nodded. After dinner we drove them around for a while, showing them a wax museum and a schoolhouse, sights they'd meant to see on their first trip here.

After they left, Ruth and I faced each other at the kitchen table. We had suffered, we knew, but surely not as much as that couple. And the strange thing was, I could now understand their suffering. Frank, like me, was human. Though he came from a different background, he was a human being, with all the faults and frailties I had. He had made a mistake that anyone could have made.

Frank and Rose Ann, I could see now, were like those lost sheep in the picture, and that's why they were brought back to our house. Only through Ruth's and my compassion— only through our employing the kind of love Jesus stood for—could we find peace and they find their way home.

Realizing that, on January 17, at the trial, I did not press charges. Except for a traffic fine, Frank was free.

Ruth and I still correspond with the couple. We hope to visit them in New York City someday soon, for we want to see the city, see them again and meet their three children.

Though Nelson is gone, even in death he continues to teach us something about life. Not long ago I found a little pencil box of his. As I emptied it, a scrap of paper fell out. On it was "Jeremiah 33:3," a verse Nelson was to memorize for a skit. "Call to Me and I will answer you and will tell you great and mighty things which you have not known."

I have to believe that Nelson, in his brief life, discovered some of those mighty things, especially the greatness of God's love.

When Ruth and I called out to God, His message was just as powerful. No matter how deep the wound of sorrow is, forgiveness and faith in God will provide the strength to "occupy till Christ returns," (Luke 19:13) and the broken pieces of our lives will be made whole in Him.

In Reaching Beyond

How much can we ever know about the world beyond? Our instincts tell us there is life after death. Our faith confirms it. And yet, whenever we read about mysterious phenomena—glimpses of His presence—we long to know more.

Since the beginning of Guideposts, people have written to us about their own experiences of dying and then returning. To this day, it's not unusual for us to hear about an "out of body" experience, nor is it uncommon to have people describe the sense of light or the feeling of serenity when their hearts have stopped.

As early as the 1960s, we put together a series of these carefully documented reports under the title, "Life After Death." It was immensely popular. A decade later, Guideposts ran a sequel series, this one called "Glimpses of His Presence"—stories of God making Himself known in inexplicable ways. Since then, the magazine has created a monthly feature called "His Mysterious Ways," with more examples of God's extraordinary intervention in our lives. Not surprisingly, it is one of our best-read columns.

We all yearn to know what lies beyond. The following stories are by people who have stood on the threshold of eternity—and have returned to tell us about the profoundly reassuring things they have seen.

Alfred Hitchcock (1899–1980), the movie director, told a parable in Guideposts (1959) about the unknown. There once was a king who was granted two wishes. His first was to see the future. But when he saw all that lay ahead—the beauty and the pain—he immediately asked for his second wish: that the future be hidden. "I thank Heaven," the master of suspense proclaimed, "that tomorrow does not belong to any man. It belongs to God."

SEPTEMBER 1947

A Glimpse Beyond Tomorrow *by Natalie Kalmus, color consultant for Technicolor*

"Don't worry, but come to me as soon as you can," my sister, Eleanor Smith, wired. At the time, I was in London working out Technicolor problems with a British motion-picture company.

I felt a deep, numbing pang. I knew Eleanor had been ill with cancer for some time. Surely this was her gentle way of telling me the end was coming.

I could not picture it—or accept it. Always radiating charm, my sister had been a wonderful inspiration to those close to her. She had that rare trait of always giving others a pat on the back, lifting their spirits and sending them off with a fresh outlook on life.

But now she needed me. I returned to the States and hurried to Eleanor, expecting to find her in bed in great pain. Instead, she was in the living room perched jauntily on the sofa, looking more like a schoolgirl of 17 than an incurably ill woman.

"Natalie," she said, holding out her arms joyously. "I'm so happy now that you're here. We have so much to talk over." To anyone listening, I might have dropped in for a casual call.

Later, after Eleanor had retired for the night, the doctor drew me aside. "Mrs. Kalmus," he said, "this will be a very trying experience for you if you stay here through to the end. I'm afraid that your sister's last hours will be an agony of pain."

I knew he was right, medically. Yet the ex-

quisite radiance I noticed in my sister's face seemed somehow to refute his statement. The strange feeling swept over me that the strength of Eleanor's spirit was more than this doctor could understand.

During the next few days, I discovered that she was doing many things that baffled the doctors. They were preparing her for some grim final moments. She was ignoring their solemn suggestions and remedies. One night she had me sit down on the side of the bed.

"Natalie, promise me that you won't let them give me any drugs. I want to be fully aware of every sensation. I am convinced that death will be a beautiful experience."

I promised. Alone later, I wept, thinking of her courage. Then, as I tossed in bed during the night, I realized that what I thought of as calamity, my sister intended to be a triumph.

One afternoon, Eleanor—in the most airy and lighthearted manner—asked several friends to a dinner party that she, on the spur of the moment, decided to hold.

On the night of the party, Eleanor dressed meticulously, concealing the pain I knew she felt. We helped her downstairs before the guests were to arrive. Sitting in a turquoise chair in her yellow evening gown, she sparkled with life and gaiety. Again I noticed the schoolgirl look on her face.

The party was a grand success; the guests were never once aware of the illness that my

In 1953 in Hollywood, Dorothea Hulse was asked to weave an authentic copy of Christ's robe for the epic film, The Robe. After months of research and experimentation, she was pleased with the outcome of her work. Then, only hours before her deadline, her three-year-old grandson cut it to shreds. That evening, with a fervent prayer on her lips, she wove a new robe—in one fourth of the time she had originally spent! "Who wove the robe?" we asked in Guideposts (1955). Dorothea Hulse knew.

sister concealed. That night, however, when she was carried to bed, her deep physical weariness appeared on the surface. Then I realized that Eleanor knew this was her final social fling. She had planned it that way.

Ten days later, the final hour drew near. I had been at her bedside for hours. We had talked about many things, and always I marveled at her quiet, sincere confidence in eternal life. Not once did the physical torture inside overcome her spiritual strength.

"Dear kind God, keep my mind clear and give me peace," she had murmured over and over again.

We had talked so long that I noticed she was drifting off to sleep. I left her quietly with the nurse and retired to get some rest. A few minutes later I heard my sister's voice calling for me. Quickly I returned to her room.

I sat on her bed and took her hand. It was on fire. Then she struggled up in bed almost to a sitting position.

"Natalie," she said, "there are so many of them. There's Fred...and Ruth—what's she doing here?"

An electric shock went through me. She had said Ruth! Ruth was her cousin who had died suddenly the week before. *But Eleanor had not been told of Ruth's sudden death!*

Chill after chill shot up and down my spine. I felt on the verge of some powerful, almost frightening knowledge. Eleanor's voice was surprisingly strong. "It's so confusing here. There are so many of them." Suddenly her arms stretched out as happily as when she had welcomed me. "I'm going up," she murmured.

Then she dropped her arms around my neck—and relaxed in my arms. The will of her spirit had turned final agony into rapture.

As I lay her head back on the pillow, there was a warm, peaceful smile on her face. Her golden brown hair lay carelessly on the pillow. I took a white flower from the vase and placed it in her hair. With her petite, trim figure, her wavy hair, the white flower and the soft smile, she looked once more—and permanently—like a schoolgirl.

Never again will death frighten me in any way. This was my sister's inheritance to me—her final, beautiful gift. I had seen for myself how thin the curtain was between life and death. I had been privileged to glimpse part of the wonderful truth about everlasting life.

George Ritchie as a young man

JUNE 1963

Return From Tomorrow *by George C. Ritchie, M.D.*

When I was sent to the base hospital at Camp Barkeley, Texas, early in December 1943, I had no idea I was seriously ill. I'd just completed basic training, and my only thought was to get on the train to Richmond, Virginia, to enter medical school as part of the Army's doctor-training program. It was an unheard of break for a private, and I wasn't going to let a chest cold cheat me out of it.

On December 19, I was moved to the recuperation wing. A jeep was to pick me up at 4 a.m. the following morning to drive me to the station to catch the train to Richmond. About nine that night, I began to run a fever. Three a.m.—I decided to get up and dress.

The next half hour is a blur. I remember a nurse coming to the room, and then a doctor, and then a bell-clanging ambulance ride to the x-ray building.

The whir of the x-ray machine is the last thing I remember.

When I opened my eyes, I was lying in a little room I had never seen before. For a while I lay there, trying to recall where I was. All of a sudden I sat bolt upright. The train! I'd miss the train to Richmond!

Now I know that what I am about to describe will sound incredible. I do not understand it any more than I ask you to; all that I can do is relate the events of that night as they occurred. I sprang out of bed and looked around the room for my uniform. Not on the bedrail. I stopped, staring. Someone was lying in the bed I had just left.

I stepped closer in the dim light, then drew back. He was dead. The slack jaw, the gray skin were awful. Then I saw the ring, the Phi Gamma Delta fraternity ring I had worn for two years.

I ran into the hall, eager to escape the mystery of that room.

"Look out!" I shouted to an orderly bearing down on me. He seemed not to hear, and a second later he had passed the very spot where I stood as though I had not been there.

It was too strange to think about. I reached the door, went through and found myself in the darkness outside, speeding toward Richmond. Running? Flying? I only know that the dark earth was slipping past, while other thoughts occupied my mind, terrifying and unaccountable ones. The orderly had not seen me. What if the people at medical school could not see me either?

Suddenly, one thing became clear to me: in some unimaginable way, I had lost my firmness of flesh.

I was beginning to know, too, that the body on that bed was mine, unaccountably separated from me, and that I *must* get back and rejoin it as fast as I could.

Finding the base and the hospital was no problem. I seemed to be back there almost as soon as I thought of it. But where was the little

A Northwestern University student once told about a mysterious note he'd scribbled at the age of four. His mother saved it— the writing resembled shorthand—and gave it to a handwriting expert. Indeed, it was shorthand, a message from the boy's father regarding the location of a safe-deposit box. It was a communiqué from a man who had died two weeks earlier! As Dr. J. B. Rhine stated in Guideposts (1963), "It has been firmly proved that the human mind can transcend both space and time."

room I had left? So began what must have been one of the strangest searches ever to take place: the search for myself. I ran from one ward to the next, past room after room of sleeping soldiers, all about my age. Several times I stopped by a sleeping figure that was exactly as I imagined myself. But the fraternity ring, the Phi Gam ring, was lacking, and I would speed on.

At last I entered a little room with a single dim light. A sheet had been drawn over the figure on the bed, but the arms lay outside. On the left hand was the ring.

I tried to draw back the sheet, but I could not seize it. I thought suddenly, "This is death." It was the first time I had connected death with what had happened to me.

In that most despairing moment, the little room began to fill with light. I say "light," but there is no word in our language to describe brilliance that intense. I must try to find words, however, because incomprehensible as the experience was to my intellect, it has affected every moment of my life.

The light that entered that room was Christ: I knew because a thought was put deep within me, "You are in the presence of the Son of God." I have called Him "light," for that room was flooded, pierced, illuminated, by the most total compassion I have ever felt. It was a presence so comforting, so joyous and all-satisfying, that I wanted to lose myself forever in its wonder.

With the presence of Christ (simulta-

neously, though I must tell it one by one) also had entered every single episode of my entire life. There was no first or last, each one was contemporary, each one asked a single question, "What did you do with your time on earth?"

I looked anxiously among the scenes before me: school, home, scouting and the cross-country track team—a fairly typical boyhood; yet in the light of that presence it seemed a trivial existence.

"Did you tell anyone about Me?" came the question.

"I didn't have time," I answered. "I was planning to, then this happened. I'm too young to die!"

"No one," the thought was inexpressibly gentle, "is too young."

A new wave of light spread through the room and suddenly we were in another world. Or rather, I perceived, a very different world occupying the same space. I followed Christ through ordinary streets and countrysides thronged with people. People with the unhappiest faces I have ever seen. I saw businessmen walking the corridors of the places where they had worked, trying vainly to get someone to listen to them. I saw a mother following a 60-year-old man, her son I guessed, cautioning him, instructing him. He did not seem to be listening.

Suddenly, I was remembering myself that very night, caring about nothing but getting to Richmond. Was it the same for these people; had their hearts and minds been all concerned

His Mysterious Ways: Ellen Daveys' mother had warned her never to ride with a stranger, but one frigid day, she disobeyed (Guideposts 1981). When the driver pulled into an alley, his intentions were clear. He pushed Ellen out of the truck and drew a knife. "No noise," he ordered. Ellen prayed desperately to God for help, and suddenly down the alley came running steps—a woman with a policeman. The woman picked Ellen up, saying, "Thank God I heard your screams." But Ellen had not even whispered.

with earthly things, and now, having lost earth, were they still fixed hopelessly here? I wondered if this was hell. To care most when you are most powerless; this would be hell indeed.

I was permitted to look at two more worlds that night—I cannot say "spirit worlds" for they were too real, too solid. Both were introduced the same way; a new quality of light, a new openness of vision, and suddenly it was apparent what had been there all along. The second world, like the first, occupied this very surface of the earth, but it was a vastly different realm. Here was no absorption with earthly things, but—for want of a better word to sum it up—with truth.

I saw sculptors and philosophers here, composers and inventors. There were universities, libraries, and laboratories that surpass the wildest inventions of science fiction.

Of the final world, I had only a glimpse. Now we no longer seemed to be on earth, but immensely far away, out of all relation to it. And there, still at a great distance, I saw a city—but a city, if such a thing is conceivable, constructed of light. At that time I had not read the Book of Revelation, nor, incidentally, anything on the subject of life after death. But here was was a city in which the walls, houses, streets, seemed to give off light, while moving among them were beings as blindingly bright as the One who stood beside me. This was only a moment's vision, for the next instant the walls of the little room closed

around me, the dazzling light faded, and a strange sleep stole over me...

I woke up in the hospital bed, in the familiar world where I'd spent all my life. It was not a homecoming. The cry in my heart that moment has been the cry of my life ever since: Christ, show me Yourself again.

It was weeks before I was well enough to leave the hospital and all that time one thought obsessed me: to get a look at my chart. At last the room was left unattended: there it was, in terse medical shorthand, "Pvt. George Ritchie, died December 20, 1943, double lobar pneumonia."

Later, I talked to the doctor who had signed the report. He told me there was no doubt in his mind that I had been dead when he examined me, but that nine minutes later the soldier who had been assigned to prepare me for the morgue had come running to him to ask him to give me shot of adrenalin. The doctor gave me a hypo of adrenalin directly into the heart muscle. My return to life, he told me, without brain damage or other lasting effect, was the most baffling circumstance of his career.

Today, over 19 years later, I feel that I know why I had the chance to return to this life. It was to become a physician so that I could learn about man and then serve God. And every time I have been able to serve our God by helping some injured child or counseling some teenager, then deep within I have felt that He was there beside me again.

Virginia Lively (on right)
with Catherine Marshall, 1966

AUGUST 1966

Three Months in His Presence *by Virginia Lively, housewife*

When friends ask how I first discovered that my hands have been given a ministry of healing, I'm sure they don't expect to hear the kind of story that I am about to set down. Apparently, the fact that I am a suburban housewife who saves grocery stamps and has to watch her weight seems a poor beginning to a story of divine intervention.

It started the year my father entered the tuberculosis sanitarium in Tampa. We had long since given up hope. He was too old for an operation and we had seen the x-rays. The last thing on earth that would have occurred to any of us—Mother or my sister or me—was to ask God to step in and change medical facts.

And yet, my husband Ed and I were active church members. As a banker, Ed was head of fund-raising, our two children went to Sunday school and I belonged to all the groups. We were, in short, typical, civic-minded churchgoers. Which is why the tears, when they began, caused Ed and me so much embarrassment.

It was in October, driving home from a PTA meeting, that I suddenly began to cry. I was in charge of the Halloween Carnival that year, and at the meeting there'd been some criticism of the plans. When I was still crying at bedtime, Ed put his arms around me and said:

"Honey, all the carnivals in the world aren't that important."

But it wasn't the carnival. Even as I cried I knew that these tears were for something far

bigger. I cried myself to sleep and in the morning as soon as I opened my eyes the tears started again. I choked them back while I fixed breakfast. But as soon as Ed and the children left, the tears burst out again.

This incredible state of affairs lasted four days. I took to wearing dark glasses even in the house so that the family would not guess how constantly I was crying. I was sure I was having a nervous breakdown.

It was on the morning of the fourth day, after Ed and the children had left, that a curious change took place. I saw nothing. I heard nothing. Yet, all at once there was power in the air around me. The atmosphere itself seemed to hum and crackle as though I stood in the center of a vast electric storm. As I try to put it into words it sounds fantastic; but at the time, there was no sense that something beyond the possible was taking place.

I had sunk into the high-backed chair in the living room when suddenly through the window I saw the eastern horizon. Trees and houses stood between me and it, but I seemed to see right beyond, to the place where earth and sky came together. And there, where they met, was a ball of light.

This light was moving, traveling toward me with incredible speed. It appeared white, yet from it poured all the colors I had ever seen.

And then it was beside me. Although it seemed impossible that anything with such

Marveling at her sister Virginia's faith, Doris Lively thought her own faith was weak by comparison (Guideposts 1978). Her prayers seemed empty… until she gave herself completely to God. The next morning, Doris noticed something extraordinary about her hands. Like Christ in the Garden Gethsemane (Luke 22:44), she was sweating blood. It was an unexplainable experience of His Presence, a confirmation of her deeper faith.

energy could hold still, it took a position at my right shoulder and there it stayed. And as I stared, I started to smile. I smiled because He was smiling at me. For I now saw that it was not light, but a face.

How can I put into words the most beautiful countenance I have ever seen? "He is perfect" was the first thought that came. His forehead was high, His eyes exceptionally large. But I could never fix the color of His eyes any more than I could the color of the sea.

More, much more, than individual features was the overwhelming impression of life— unhampered life, life so brimming over with power and freedom that all living things I had seen till that moment seemed lumps of clay by comparison.

Not for a moment did I hesitate to call this Life at my side Jesus. And two things about Him struck me most. The first was His humor. I was astonished to see Him often break into outright laughter. And the second was His utter lack of condemnation. That He knew me down to my very marrow—knew all the stupid, cruel, silly things I had ever done—I realized at once. But I also saw that none of these things, or anything I would ever do, could alter the absolute caring, the unconditional love that I saw in those eyes.

I could not grasp it. It was too immense a fact. I felt that if I gazed at Him for a thousand years I could not realize it all.

I did not have a thousand years; I had three months. For as long as that, the face of Jesus stayed before me, never fading, never with-

drawing. Many times, I tried to tell someone else what I saw but the words would never come. Meanwhile, I carried on with my tasks— meals and shopping and the PTA carnival— but effortlessly, scarcely knowing I was doing them, so fixed were my thoughts on Him.

At the same time, I had never seemed so aware of other people. How this was possible when my mind was full of Him alone I don't know, but it was true. My husband, especially. Far from feeling that a third person had entered our marriage, I felt that Christ *was* the marriage, as though all along He had been the force drawing us together.

And the Bible! All at once I couldn't read enough of it. It was like tearing open a letter from someone who had known this Presence as a flesh-and-blood person, full of just the kind of specific details I longed to hear. Certain passages in particular had a strange effect on me: when the Bible described Jesus healing someone, the actual print on the page seemed to burn. The hand that touched it would tingle as if I had touched an electric current.

And then one afternoon before the children got home, I was sitting, looking at Him, when all of a sudden in a patch of sunlight on the wall appeared the x-ray of my father's chest. It was all scar tissue and cavities. Then, as I watched, a white mist moved up the wall. When it passed the diseased tissue, there appeared on my wall a picture of a healthy lung.

"Then Dad's well!" I said aloud, and at that the Person at my side burst into peal after peal of joyous laughter, which said that wholeness was always God's way.

Doris Lively, 1978

I thought my heart would burst as I waited for next Wednesday's x-ray. I enjoyed the scene in my mind again and again, imagining the ring of the telephone and Mother's voice stammering with excitement, "Darling—the most amazing—the most glorious—"

But when Mother called, her voice was flat. "The most annoying thing, Virginia. They got the slides mixed up! Poor Dad's got to go back for x-rays tomorrow. Why, they sent down pictures of someone who never even had TB...!"

But, of course, the x-rays next day showed no sign of disease either; Dad was healed and lived out his long life in thanksgiving to God.

And it was Dad's healing that convinced me I must try to describe the indescribable that had happened to me. I went to an elderly pastor whom I had known a long time. To my astonishment, he understood me at once. He gave me some books that described fairly similar things.

Then he said the words I have wished unsaid so many, many times.

"Don't be surprised, Virginia, if the vision fades after a time. They usually do, you know."

"Fade!" I thought, as I drove home with that joyous Presence beside me. Oh, it can't be, it mustn't! For the first time in the whole incredible experience, my attention veered from Him to myself. And in that instant, the vision was diminished, actually disappeared for a second or two, though right away the radiant face was beside me again.

But the damage was done. The seed of self-concern was sown. The bright Presence would sometimes be missing for an hour or more.

The more worried I got, the more self-centered I grew. What have I done? What will I do without Him? When He did return there would be no accusation in His eyes, just a tremendous compassion, as though he realized how difficult it had become for me to see Him at all.

At last, all that was left of this experience was the strange tingling in my hands as I read the Bible stories of healing. One day I was visiting a friend in the hospital. She was hemorrhaging and in pain. On an impulse, I reached out and touched her. My hand began to burn just as it did during the Bible reading. My friend gave a little sigh of comfort and fell asleep. When the doctor examined her, he found that the hemorrhaging had stopped.

Over the next eight years there were dozens, scores of experiences of this kind, all as inexplicable as the first. And yet for me, they were still years of emptiness and waiting. "I will always be with you," He had told me when I last saw Him.

"But how will I know if I can't see You?" I called to Him, for He had seemed so far away.

"You will see Me," He said, and then He was gone.

But the years went by and the vision had not come back. And then one day, while speaking to a church group, I saw those love-lit eyes smiling once again into mine. I looked again. The eyes belonged to a lady in the second row. Suddenly the room was full of Him; He was in the eyes of everyone in the room. "You will see Me...."

His Mysterious Ways: Katy Brown and her husband had long wanted to adopt a child (Guideposts 1982). One July morning, Katy was startled awake by a vivid dream of a baby. Months went by. At last, in December, the adoption agency called to say a baby girl had been chosen for the Browns. Katy took down the baby's date of birth—July 20th. It made Katy wonder. She looked at her journal ... and indeed she'd dreamed of the baby on the very day *God had chosen for its birth.*

I used to wonder what would have happened if the old pastor had never spoken of the vision fading. Might I have had it forever? I think not. I think that the days when Jesus was real to my eyes were the days of the "childhood" of my faith, the joyous, effortless time of discovery. But I do not think He lets it stay that way for long.

He didn't for His first disciples, He doesn't for us today. He gives us a glimpse only. Perhaps He let me look so long because I am slow to learn. But, finally, He takes away all sensory clues. He is bigger than our eyes and ears can make Him, so He gives us instead the eyes of faith, and all mankind in which to discover His face.

NOVEMBER 1983

His Mysterious Ways *by Hazel Houston*

One day a dog appeared at our farm. Somehow, we understood that he had come to stay. We fed him table scraps, but he did not beg for food as some dogs do, nor did he wag his tail with happiness when fed.

He did not have a distinctive coloring. His hair was brown mixed with black, his tail stubby. We did not even give him a name, perhaps because he never had to be called. He was always there.

This dog seemed to think his mission in life was to accompany me as I went about the outdoor duties of a farmwife. When I fed the chickens or gathered vegetables, he was by my side. Sometimes, not only did he escort me, but he also carried one of my hands gently in his mouth.

One day a stranger came. Oddly, he parked his car midway between the house and barn. When I stepped out on the porch, he asked a question about the previous owner of our farm. Then he appeared not to hear my answer. He walked toward me and asked the question again. This time I walked out in the yard a short way before I answered him. Again he seemed not to understand and continued to walk toward me. Now I sensed that he could hear me perfectly well.

Suddenly, the man came to an abrupt stop. "Will that dog bite?" he asked.

I had not realized the dog was beside me, so quietly had he come. This time he did not take my hand in his mouth. His upper lip was pulled back revealing sharp teeth.

"He certainly will," I answered firmly.

The man understood my words perfectly. He hurried to his car and drove away.

Soon after, the dog left. He may have gone to hunt rabbits and just never come back.

Somehow, I do not think so.

Chloe Wardrop, 1977

SEPTEMBER 1977

The Cloud *by Chloe Wardrop, housewife*

Twice in my life I have seen and felt a phenomenon so strange to me, so irrational, that it takes an act of faith to believe it. Twice, each time during a period of grave trouble, a thing that looked like a cloud, a misty white cloud, has come to me. Once it helped save my life. Bizarre? Of course. The only thing I have ever been able to liken it to are the clouds mentioned in the Bible, especially that helpful cloud described in the Book of Exodus and in the letters of Saint Paul.

My first encounter with this cloud was many years ago in Detroit. I was seven months pregnant when a doctor told me that I had diabetes. This was shattering news, not just because of the coming baby, but because my father had suffered from the same disease and I knew all about the needles, diet and strain.

On the way home that day, I saw an announcement for an evangelist then conducting healing services at the Detroit Fair Grounds. Ordinarily this would have meant nothing to me. I was not a very spiritually oriented person. Growing up, I'd passed through a variety of Sunday schools, but I was not a churchgoer; I believed in a Supreme Being, and from time to time I prayed—that was about the sum of my religion. Nevertheless, one evening I went alone, secretly, and stood in the back of the evangelist's tent. I prayed earnestly. Nothing, apparently, happened. Still, I went on praying for several days. And that's what I was doing as I stood at the kitchen stove preparing dinner

late one afternoon when I looked up and there, hovering above me, was the cloud. At first I thought it was some peculiar accumulation of steam from the stove, but it didn't dissolve; it held its shape, a cottony mass about two feet long. I could have reached up and touched it.

Then it moved. Slowly it began to roll, to swirl. To my astonishment, this swirling mist descended on me and disappeared into my body. I could feel it vibrating within me.

I was too startled, too mystified, to tell anybody about it. In fact, I mentioned it to no one until a few days later when a woman appeared at my door in response to a card I must have filled out at the tent. Soon I found myself describing the cloud to her. She nodded. "It was the healing virtue," she said.

I did not know what that meant, and so my visitor explained about the ailing woman who touched Christ's garment and was healed. Together we read the passage from Mark: "The fountain of her blood was dried up; and she felt in her body that she was healed of that plague. And Jesus, immediately knowing in Himself that virtue had gone out of Him..." (Mark 5:29,30)

For a while, I was hopeful that this astonishing experience meant that I had been healed, but that was not so. The diabetes has remained with me from that day to this, though it has always puzzled doctors that my condition has never deteriorated. Since I was not cured, however, I pushed the experience with the

*His Mysterious Ways: Plowing his field, Iowa farmer Robert Barr
unearthed a rock with the outline of a cross on it (Guideposts 1982).
Heeding Deuteronomy 11:18–20, the Barrs kept the rock by their
door as a sign of faith. Later, during a 1979 tornado watch, Bob saw
a twister bearing down on his house. The Barrs hid in the cellar,
fearing their home's destruction. It survived. Neighbors described
what had happened: Twice the twister went up to the Barr's door—
right to the rock of the cross—and twice it backed away!*

white cloud into a recess of my memory, and the years passed.

On November 17, 1974, my husband and I were cruising along in our custom-built motor home heading west on Highway I-10, hugging the Texas side of the Rio Grande. Scotty had recently retired as an executive of the Ford Motor Company in Dearborn, Michigan, and now we were on our way to our winter home in Arizona.

Near sundown, we pulled into a large, paved roadside park. It was surrounded on three sides by desert, nothing but dry scrubby chaparral in sight. There were several cars in the parking area when we arrived. Gradually these left until only one remained, a yellow and black sports car.

I set the table for dinner while Scotty walked our schnauzer, Fritz. When they returned and I opened the door for them, what I saw made me gasp. Coming up behind Scotty was a young man with a pistol in his hand.

"What's wrong?" Scotty said to me, and then the gun touched his back.

"Get in!" the young man ordered. With a rough shove, he pushed Scotty inside. The gunman was about 20 years old, short hair, cleanshaven, neatly dressed in brown slacks and a brown turtleneck sweater. His face was grim, his voice expressionless.

"All right, get your cash." Scotty reached for his wallet, took out the money in it. The gunman stuffed it in his pocket. "Now you."

My purse was on the bed, yet I was so afraid I couldn't move. He snapped. "Move, lady!" I got my purse, and removed three bills.

"Okay, now, a buddy of mine is out there in the bushes. He's got something he wants to talk over with you." He waved the pistol toward the door, but we hesitated. If we stalled for time, somebody might drive in.

"I've made some wonderful chili," I said, grabbing at straws. "Have some with us." He put the gun to my head.

"Get moving."

At that moment, I figured he was going to steal our motor home, and if he did he might take Fritz along with it. "May I please take my little dog?" I asked.

"I won't hurt him, lady," was all he said as he forced us out into the desert. With the sun down now, it was cold. We came to a barbed-wire fence. There were five strands of wire, each spaced a foot apart. The gunman held the bottom wire while I crawled under. This unexpected act of courtesy on his part inspired me to try another tack with him.

"You must have been awfully abused as a little boy to come to this..."

"Shut up. Don't get smart," he snapped at me, but I could see now that he, too, was trembling. A new fear came into my mind: He might shoot us accidentally.

"Help me, Jesus," I cried under my breath. "Help me, Lord," I prayed.

A hundred, two hundred yards we walked. "That's far enough. Turn around. My buddy's behind that bush."

As I turned, I saw no one behind the creosote bush he pointed toward. "Take off your clothes."

"Please," Scotty pleaded. "Don't do any..."

Robert and Lavonne Barr with their "rock of the cross"

"Strip," he said, "both of you."

As we stripped down to our underwear, he made us place our clothing into two piles. "Lay facedown on your clothes," came the command.

I thought he was going to tie us up until I looked over and saw Scotty staring up at the gun. "My God!" Scotty shouted, horrified. "You're not going to…"

Then he began firing, first at Scotty, then at me.

Something rose up and out from within me. A cloud. The misty white cloud I had seen all those years before, hovered over me once more like one of those comic strip balloons.

I found myself floating in the air in spirit form. I could look down and see my own body on the ground below, beside Scotty's. I felt at peace. Comfortable. No pain. But this only lasted briefly.

The next thing I remember I was standing up, staggering somewhere. I did not know where, in my bare feet. Blood flowed over my eyes. I bumped into something. A creosote bush. Swaying, I held on to one of its prickly offshoots. "Help me, Jesus, help me. Lord God, help me," I prayed.

The cloud appeared again, larger this time. I accepted its being there without amazement. "Move to the left," a voice said. I moved to the left. The cloud moved, wrapped itself about my body, buoyed my arms, supported me. "See the lights?" asked the voice. I squinted my eyes open. Yes. Now I remembered, the lights of the roadside park. With the cloud holding me, I groped forward, then stopped. "See the post?" There was the post of the barbed-wire fence. I went to it and clung to it. The cloud went away.

I stood there weakly holding on, trying to focus my mind. If only I could make it to the parking area, I could lie there until somebody drove in. If I collapsed here, I'd die unnoticed.

The very next thing I knew, I was on the other side of the fence.

I could not comprehend how I had got there. Nor did I try, for it was my feet that troubled me now. They were a mass of thorns and sandburrs. Walking on them was torture. I summoned up my energy. I propelled myself, half walking, half crawling, to the pavement of the parking area. The motor home was gone. I stumbled down at last, my head on the cold surface of a picnic table. In spite of the horror, in spite of the pain, I was calm. "Thank You, Lord, thank You," I kept saying out loud with every gasp of breath.

"Chloe, Chloe," came my name, called in a faint voice. Scotty's voice. I looked up and there was Scotty, standing in the middle of the pavement, coughing now as though the words he had spoken were strangling him.

I spoke to him matter-of-factly. "I'm over here, Scotty." He came and slumped down beside me. We were too dazed from the bullets to do anything but silently recognize each other's existence.

I raised my head. A car was coming. Now it was coming into the park area.

"Help, help," we both said, more moaning than shouting. We got to our feet, our arms flailing above us as the lights of the car spot-

*Maude Blanford was dying of cancer. Just when doctors had lost
hope for her, she found herself praying, "God, I don't know Who you
are...Just have Your own way with me." (Guideposts 1972.) Whole
passages from the Bible came to her, Scripture she had never read.
Without benefit of teacher, minister or church, He healed her. As
Christ said to his disciples (John 10:16), "Ye have not chosen me, but
I have chosen you..."*

lighted us. But the car swerved and sped out onto the highway again. I collapsed.

The minutes passed. I could hear another car coming. Then more cars, sirens. I heard the sound of running footsteps. I felt the warmth of a blanket. I felt strong arms holding me.

Much later, safely out of cranial surgery and days of intensive care (though both our skulls were battered, neither of us received any brain damage, any paralysis, or even a concussion) Scotty and I learned of our rescue by a young man named Tommy Rodriguez, who had just driven away from having coffee with the Sheriff at a nearby diner. Spotting us, and not wanting the Sheriff to get away, Tommy had made a fast turnaround—only apparently deserting us—and sped away.

Once the police arrived, I passed out intermittently, but Scotty remained coherent enough to tell his name, age, the make of our motor home, its license number! His years as an automotive executive did not fail him as he told the police about the "two-toned yellow-and-black Dodge Charger with Utah plates on it," enough information for a radio call that enabled the police 15 miles away to pick up the sports car, the motor home (with our little Fritz, safe and sound in it), the young man who shot us, as well as his accomplice. Eventually, these two were tried and sent to prison.

After 17 days in the Eastwood Hospital in El Paso, we were taken back to the roadside park. I wanted to see the scene again, to check a point in my own mind.

It was all there as I remembered it: the spot

where I'd looked down upon our two bodies, the creosote bush I had held on to, the post I had clung to, the stains on it still visible. And there was the barbed-wire fence. To me, that was the real key to the reality of my cloud. It simply wasn't possible that, in my blinded, stumbling condition, I could have crawled through those five close-spaced strands of barbed wire unassisted—without being scratched. Yet, among all my wounds, there were no scratches on my body, or on Scotty's. Now I was certain. Something had helped me through—or over—the barbed wire.

Twice, since that terrible experience, I have read the Living Bible through from beginning to end, and many times I have returned to the same passage in much the same way one seeks out an old and dear friend: "For we must never forget, dear brothers, what happened to our people in the wilderness long ago. God guided them by sending a cloud that moved along ahead of them; and He brought them all safely through the waters of the Red Sea. This might be called their 'baptism'—baptized both in sea and cloud!" (I Corinthians 10:1,2)

Looking back today, I know that that night of terror was not without its blessings. Never again will death frighten me. If it was so that I was dead and my spirit rose above my body, I found the sensation sweet and placid and natural. On the other hand, never will life frighten me either. I savor it. I believe that the cloud that came to me twice dwells within me today. It stirs; I feel loved and wanted. It heals. It comforts. Call it what you will, I believe it is the Holy Spirit of Jesus.

Diane Bringgold, 1978

FEBRUARY 1978

A Promise Made, A Promise Kept *by Diane Bringgold, housewife*

Far up in Northern California, in the awesomely lovely wilderness of glacial lakes and towering granite pinnacles beneath Mount Shasta, there is a rocky height that is called Black Butte. Its slopes are steep and covered with boulders and loose gray shale. A few trees struggle to survive on its surface. To me, Black Butte is the ugliest place in the world and the most beautiful; for it is a place of terrible death, and vibrant life. On a December evening in 1975, I lay on its slope and asked to die, but I was given life instead, and faith to sustain it. It was a faith I didn't know I lacked.

The day after Thanksgiving that year, Bruce and I and our three children flew up into the Shasta region from our home in Southern California. We had an invitation for the weekend from our across-the-street friends in Ventura, Bill and Edy LeFevre, who had a family compound of rustic cabins and huge Victorian house near Dunsmuir. It was an easy trip for us to make, for we were a flying family. Both Bruce and I were licensed pilots and our kids were accustomed to being in the air.

On this Friday, our own plane was down for its 100-hour checkup, but we managed to rent an identical aircraft, which could accommodate the five of us as well as a couple we'd asked along, Jim and Virginia Dixon. Jim, like Bruce, was a successful attorney in Ventura.

The flight north was quick and easy, just like the weekend, which passed much too speedily. The mountain air was tingling cold,

and the kids ran about and played at high speed. Proper Southern Californians, they were excited by the ice on the swimming pool, and when it snowed on Saturday, they flapped around in it like happy penguins.

On Sunday it snowed again, off and on. From time to time, Bruce would put on his jacket and wander outside. He was like that wherever we went; his pilot's instinct kept him sniffing at the weather. We planned to fly home that afternoon, but the ceiling stayed too low.

On Sunday morning, I went to a little Episcopal mission church in Dunsmuir where the priest, Father Torgerson, delivered a Thanksgiving sermon. Had it entered my mind, that quiet Thanksgiving weekend would have been a good time for me to have taken spiritual stock of myself, but when you have a multitude of blessings, you often fail to notice them.

My life was rich. I had Bruce, whom I loved, and our marriage of 14 years was good by any standard. Bruce had a fine law practice and was a leader in civic affairs. Our children were delights to us. They were all exactly two years and nine months apart in age, starting with Scott, who was 11, then Mary, who copied Scott in everything, and then our little Laura.

As for me, I was busy at home and in the community, and in our church especially. Shortly before my marriage to Bruce, I'd made a commitment to Christ; and yet, in spite of all my conscious efforts to lead a Christian life, in spite of all my sincere work in

the three Bringgold children: Mary, Scott and Laura in 1975

church activities, my prayer life was not an active one. I had never really faced the fact that my faith was important to me, but not central to my life. There was always a hidden doubt, something left over from the intellectual probings of college days. I think, that stopped me from turning over my life to Him completely.

On Monday morning, our hosts left for Ventura in their motor home while we waited, our eyes on the sky. Finally, in the afternoon, Bruce made another call to the weather station. "It's breaking to the north," he told me. "I think we can go."

A caretaker drove us out to the Dunsmuir airstrip. Bruce looked up at the sky. "The ceiling looks high enough for safety," he said. But still he hesitated. "Just to make sure, let's see what it's really like up north." We got in the car again and drove to Shasta, about half an hour away. True enough, it was clearing. "We'll fly north," he told me. "We'll take advantage of the wide valley up there. There'll be plenty of room to climb in."

The takeoff was simple. I felt relieved that it had all been so easy, and was just beginning to relax when the weather closed in around us. The clouds pushed lower and lower. We flew lower and lower to keep beneath them. Then they began breaking up into fog. Straining to follow the points on the ground, I tried to help Bruce navigate.

"I can't see, Bruce," I said, alarmed. My always calm husband now seemed to be getting nervous, too. "We've got to turn around," I shouted, and even as the words came out I knew that it would be more dangerous to do that than to go ahead. And then, in the most terrifying moment of my life, I saw the ground. "Bruce, the trees!" I screamed. Bruce saw them, too, and turned the plane to the left, but there wasn't time.

We hit. The plane slid, then jarred sharply. I was knocked unconscious.

We had come to Black Butte.

I don't know how long I was unconscious. A minute or two, I think. The next thing I remember, I felt the weight of Bruce's body against me. He was dead. I looked back. The Dixons were gone—the doors on either side had popped open—and the kids, the kids weren't moving. In the same flashing second that I knew they, too, were gone, orange fire burst out of the instrument panel. I threw my hands over my eyes and screamed as the flames seared my face. I squirmed, struggling to get free of the seatbelt that held me. The belt flipped open. I pulled myself out from under Bruce and through the door. There was no drop, for the plane was level with the ground as I crawled out the uphill side. Flames shot out from the engine to the gas tanks on the wings and everything exploded. The plane somersaulted into the air and came crashing down to lie on its back.

I lay on the slope of Black Butte in the darkness. I couldn't look at the plane. *Bruce*, my mind kept repeating. *Scott...Mary... Laura...* I lay there knowing that I was severely burned, one side of my face in shreds, my right hand causing me agony. *Dead, all my loved ones are dead...* I kept thinking.

His Mysterious Ways: Tom Coverdale was wounded in Vietnam while manning a listening post 500 meters from camp (Guideposts 1983). Later, his platoon sergeant asked how he'd been able to summon help. "My radio, sir," Tom answered, puzzled. "Not with this one," replied the sergeant, holding up a twisted, blackened box. In taking the brunt of the grenade blast, and probably saving his life in the process, Tom's radio had been totally destroyed.

"Diane! Diane!" My name. Called in the mist. Virginia's voice. "Are you there, Diane?"

I did not answer. I did not want to answer.

"Diane. Answer me if you can. Please."

I dragged myself over to some rocks where a tree had fallen. I tried to hide myself behind them. I did not want to live without Bruce and our children. I did not want to face the physical pain of my burned body, or its ugliness. "I can't handle it," I said to myself.

And at that moment, five feet away, a figure appeared in the fog, a figure robed in white. I cannot tell you the color of hair or eyes, but this obviously was a man, a large man, larger than most, and He stood suffused in light, not like the light of a flashbulb, not a beam, but a soft luminescence.

I knew without any doubt or surprise that this was Jesus Christ. He was too far away for me to touch, but close enough for me to hear Him perfectly. He stood majestically in front of me, yet His Presence was not overpowering. I had no sense of awe; a sense of amazement perhaps, but I didn't feel that He was some omnipotent being to whom I couldn't relate.

"It's not for you to decide whether to live or die, Diane," He said. "That's My decision to make."

I still did not want to live, and I replied, "It's easy for You to say, Lord, but I can't handle being widowed, and childless, and being badly burned as well. Maybe two, but not all three." It sounded like a flip statement; I didn't mean it to be. "If You want me to live, I will give You my life. You will have to handle the grief, the pain and the loneliness; I can't."

Suddenly, He was gone. It wasn't as though He walked away. One moment He was there, the next He wasn't. But when He left, I knew that I could conquer the grief and pain and loneliness; I could handle whatever lay ahead, because He was going to be there. For me, that is the meaning of the gift of faith that I received on cold, mist-bound Black Butte. All doubt was abolished. What the Bible said about asking and receiving was true. Jesus was real.

For two years now, Jesus has been with me. Have I suffered? Yes. But He has made it bearable, for He was there when I found the will to call out to Jim and Virginia down the mountainside; they were seriously injured, too, but not critically. Jesus was there when the young hikers who saw the flash of fire arrived, and when the girl held my head in her lap while I kept telling her how brave she was to hold me, looking the way I did, and she kept saying, "No, *you're* the one who's brave." He was there in the emergency ward down in Shasta when my vital signs were so unstable that the doctors thought I'd not survive; but I knew I would, and that I'd recover fully. He was there on the three-hour ambulance drive in the fog to the hospital in Chico where a mass of people in green hats and masks rushed me into surgery. He has been there during all the months of these past two years, and He has kept His promise to handle the hurts that once caused me to prefer death to life.

How has He helped me?

For the first week or so in the hospital, it took all my resources, physical, emotional and

*His Mysterious Ways: Only seconds after Mary D. Wilson mounted
her new black mare, the horse went berserk (Guideposts 1984).
The possessed animal threw Mary and began trying to stomp her
to death. Mary screamed, but there was no one to hear. Nearby,
Mary's gentle six-year-old palomino, Amber, was in her stall,
a restraining chain across its entrance. A second barrier, the stable
door was locked with a metal bolt. Yet Amber charged on to the
scene and held off the black mare. Who set Amber free?*

otherwise, just to begin the healing process. I didn't have any energy left to grieve. Bruce and the children were always in the back of my mind, but by the time I was well enough to face life without them, the sharpest pain of loss had been blunted. Jesus did that for me.

That is not to say that there were not times in the middle of the night when I'd start to ask the "Why me?" questions, but those depressions would only last a little while, because I'd pray and He would help me cope.

"Lord, why did You take them?" I said out loud one night, but the words were no sooner out than I felt ashamed. *How selfish I am,* I thought. And I was. Knowing that Christ was real, knowing that I myself had seen Him, how could I begrudge my loved ones the life they now had with Him? To this day I miss them, and sometimes I ache to have them back, but I rejoice for them, and I'm always grateful that they didn't suffer or be crippled or live in pain.

As for my own pain, He has taken care of that, too. For anyone like me, who once dreaded the tiny sting of a hot iron, who was a sissy about needles, I've felt astonishingly little pain. There were a few bad times, early on in the hospital during the four times a day when we changed dressings, but I've gone back to Chico five times for additional surgery in the last two years, and except for one pain pill, I remember no postoperative suffering.

Loneliness? Yes, from time to time I feel it. But the surprising thing is that when I tend to get depressed it isn't when I'm at home. I continue to live in the same house we lived in before the crash. There are pictures of Bruce and the children around me, just as before. But this house is full of good memories. I don't feel alone here. No, if ever I'm inclined to get sad, it's in the hospital, or as an outpatient in a motel room. At times like that I've learned to say, "Hey, Lord, I really need somebody to be here," and then the phone will ring and some friend will be calling. If it's late at night, too late for anyone to be phoning, I'll start to pray hard, and He will come to me. I don't see Him, not the way I did on the mountainside; but I can feel Him, and it's just as if someone were there holding me, saying, "It's okay, you're all right."

Often when I tell people about meeting the Living Christ on Black Butte, I can see by their expression that they think I dreamed the whole thing up out of my own need. I can understand this. I also know that a lot of people have been watching me, waiting for the full realization of loss to hit me, waiting for me to fall apart. But the longer it goes on, the longer I show my strength—the strength He has given me—the more these people themselves are going to start believing that the Lord is alive and working in the world, their world. I know that He presented Himself to me because He wanted me to have the faith I lacked, the faith I want everybody to know about, the faith that says you can go through fire and come out strong, and beautiful.

the late Dr. and Mrs. S. Ralph Harlow

DECEMBER 1963

The Host of Heaven *by Dr. S. Ralph Harlow, college professor*

It was not Christmas, it was not even wintertime, when the event occurred that for me threw sudden new light on the ancient angel tale. It was a glorious spring morning and we were walking, my wife and I, through the newly budded birches and maples near Ballardvale, Massachusetts.

Now I realize that this, like any account of personal experience, is only as valid as the good sense and honesty of the person relating it. What can I say about myself? That I am a scholar who shuns guesswork and admires scientific investigation? That I have an A.B. from Harvard, an M.A. from Columbia, a Ph.D. from Hartford Theological Seminary? That I have never been subject to hallucinations? That attorneys have solicited my testimony, and I have testified in the courts—regarded by judge and jury as a faithful, reliable witness? All this is true, and yet I doubt that any amount of such credentials can influence the belief or disbelief of another.

In the long run, each of us must sift what comes to us from others through his own life experience, his view of the universe, his understanding. And so, I will simply tell my story.

The little path on which Marion and I walked that morning was spongy to our steps, and we held hands with the sheer delight of life as we strolled near a lovely brook. It was May, and because it was the examination reading period for students at Smith College where I was a professor, we were able to get away for a few days to visit Marion's parents.

We frequently took walks in the country, and we especially loved the spring after a hard New England winter; for it is then that the fields and the woods are radiant and calm, yet show new life bursting from the earth. This day, we were especially happy and peaceful; we chatted sporadically, with great gaps of satisfying silence between our sentences.

Then from behind us, we heard the murmur of muted voices in the distance, and I said to Marion, "We have company in the woods this morning."

Marion nodded and turned to look. We saw nothing, but the voices were coming nearer—at a faster pace than we were walking, and we knew that the strangers would soon overtake us. Then we perceived that the sounds were not only behind us but above us, and we looked up.

How can I describe what we felt? Is it possible to tell of the surge of exaltation that ran through us? Is it possible to record this phenomenon in objective accuracy and yet be credible?

For about ten feet above us, and slightly to our left, was a floating group of glorious, beautiful creatures that glowed with spiritual beauty. We stopped and stared as they passed above us.

There were six of them, young beautiful women dressed in flowing white garments and engaged in earnest conversation. If they were

aware of our existence they gave no indication of it. Their faces were perfectly clear to us, and one woman, slightly older than the rest, was especially beautiful. Her dark hair was pulled back in what today we would call a ponytail, and although I cannot say it was bound at the back of her head, it appeared to be. She was talking intently to a younger spirit whose back was toward us and who looked up into the face of the woman who was talking.

Neither Marion nor I could understand their words, although their voices were clearly heard. The sound was somewhat like hearing—but being unable to understand—a group of people talking outside a house with all the windows and doors shut.

They seemed to float past us, and their graceful motion seemed natural—as gentle and peaceful as the morning itself. As they passed, their conversation grew fainter and fainter until it faded out entirely, and we stood transfixed on the spot, still holding hands and with the vision still before our eyes.

It would be an understatement to say that we were astounded. Then we looked at each other, each wondering if the other also had seen.

There was a fallen birch tree just there beside the path. We sat down on it and I said, "Marion, what did you see? Tell me exactly, in precise detail. And tell me what you heard."

She knew my intent—to test my own eyes and ears; to see if I had been the victim of hallucination or imagination. And her reply was identical in every respect to what my own senses had reported to me.

I have related this story with the same faithfulness and respect for truth and accuracy as I would tell it on the witness stand. But even as I record it, I know how incredible it sounds.

Perhaps I can claim no more for it than that it has had a deep effect on our own lives. For this experience of almost 30 years ago greatly altered our thinking. Once, both Marion and I were somewhat skeptical about the absolute accuracy of the details at the birth of Christ. The story, as recorded by St. Luke, tells of an angel appearing to *shepherds abiding in the field* and after the shepherds had been told of the Birth, *suddenly there was with the angel a multitude of the heavenly host praising God, and saying, Glory to God in the highest.* (Luke 2:8–14)

As a child, I accepted the multitude seen by the shepherds as literal heavenly personages. Then I went through a period when I felt that they were merely symbols injected into a fantasy or legend. Today, after the experience at Ballardvale, Marion and I are no longer skeptical. We believe that in back of that story recorded by St. Luke, lies a genuine objective experience told in wonder by those who had the experience.

Once, too, we puzzled greatly over the Christian insistence that we have "bodies" other than our normal flesh and blood ones. We were like the doubter of whom St. Paul wrote:

But some man will say, How are the dead raised up? and with what body do they come? (I Corinthians 15:35)

Prayer For Tomorrow by Carlene A. Wallace

Beyond today will be tomorrow,
But what it will bring of joy or sorrow
I cannot know. I only pray
Your guidance, Lord, each hour, each day
Your strength to bear whatever may be
Your loving wisdom has for me.
So sweet or bitter, sad or gay,
Be with me, Lord, beyond today.

In the 30 years since that bright May morning, his answer has rung for us with joyous conviction.

There are also celestial bodies, and bodies terrestrial: but the glory of the celestial is one, and the glory of the terrestrial is another....So also is the resurrection of the dead....It is sown a natural body; it is raised a spiritual body. There is a natural body, and there is a spiritual body....And as we have borne the image of the earthy, we shall also bear the image of the heavenly....For this corruptible must put on incorruption, and this mortal must put on immortality. (I Corinthians 15:40–53)

All of us, I think, hear the angels for a little while at Christmastime. We let the heavenly host come close once in the year. But we reject the very possibility that what the shepherds saw 2,000 years ago was part of the reality that presses close every day of our lives.

And yet there is no reason for us to shrink from this knowledge. Since Marion and I began to be aware of the host of heaven all about us, our lives have been filled with a wonderful hope. Phillips Brooks, the great Episcopal bishop, expressed the cause of this hope more beautifully than I can do:

"This is what you are to hold fast to yourself—*the sympathy and companionship of the unseen worlds.* No doubt it is best for us now, that they should be unseen. It cultivates in us that higher perception that we call 'faith.' But who can say that the time will not come when, even to those who live here upon earth, the unseen worlds shall no longer be unseen?"

The experience at Ballardvale, added to the convictions of my Christian faith, gives me not only a feeling of assurance about the future, but a sense of adventure toward it too.

For Us at Guideposts

Norman Vincent Peale has often said that God has His hand firmly on Guideposts. We, the editors, and all the men and women who have worked at the magazine over the years have good reason to agree with him. Not just because of the publication's phenomenal growth and acceptance, but because in so many ways Guideposts' success has been so unlikely.

The magazine began with a simple idea: "to disseminate the gospel" by letting people who have felt the power of God in their lives tell other people. That one idea was its one great asset, for the people who first put the magazine together were essentially publishing amateurs, and they had precious little money—sometimes no money—at their disposal. No scientific studies were made beforehand to see if anybody out there wanted an interfaith, inspirational publication. No fancy promotion kits were sent forth to herald its birth. Its fund-raising was done in kitchens and living rooms on wobbly card tables and borrowed typewriters. But one day in March 1945, a four-page leaflet called Guideposts was mailed from the Pawling, New York, post office to a thousand unsuspecting recipients.

Little by little, the leaflets grew into a magazine and a regular, day-to-day staff began assembling in a progression of offices in upstate New York, first in Pawling, then in nearby Carmel. That early staff was an unusual mixture. They were people like Len LeSourd, a young pilot just out of the Army Air Corps, who had been wandering about trying to figure out what to do with his life. Len cast in his lot with the little magazine for $25 a week. There was Starr West Jones, an ex-actor, Army officer who had taken up farming as a career. Mostly, the young staff learned to edit a magazine by doing it.

By the time Guideposts was strong enough to open a tiny editorial office in New York City, a few bona fide professionals drifted in, attracted by the peculiar appeal that Guideposts had for them. Gradually the spirit born in Guideposts touched everyone who worked there. We became a magazine of friends who worked and prayed and played together. Our lives became interwoven, and as personal crises came—sickness, death, heartache, money and emotional problems—we Guideposters found that there was little difference from the events we ourselves were living through and the stories we were publishing. And the answer to all of these problems was the same: faith in our Almighty God.

—the editors of Guideposts

Dr. Peale at age five

AUGUST 1963

Something Infinitely Precious *by Norman Vincent Peale, editor-in-chief*

In my apartment in New York, I keep a little time machine. It's an old-fashioned door-bell, the kind with a key that you twirl to make it ring. It came from the front door of my grandparents' home in Lynchburg, Ohio, (population 1,000) where my brother Bob and I spent our summers as children.

A lot of water has flowed under the bridge since then. But whenever I want to go back to that little town, all I have to do is turn the key gently, and the roar of the Manhattan traffic grows dim, and I'm eight years old again; and all around me is Lynchburg, drowsing in the first decade of this century.

I can see it all so plainly: the three churches (Methodist, Baptist, Carmelite); the white frame houses, each with its broad front porch, big maples overhead, and usually a barn or sta-ble out back; the little railroad station where the B. & O. came through; the livery stables along the main street.

The people are just as real to me, too. See that somewhat stern-looking gentleman over there with the gold watch-chain and the bowler hat? That's my Uncle Herschel—Herschel Henderson—coming home for midday dinner. Uncle Herschel is a bank, an insurance company, a building-and-loan asso-ciation—a leading citizen. First man in Lynchburg to own an automobile. He doesn't drive it much, and won't let anyone else drive it; he just likes to own it.

Uncle Herschel's a strict disciplinarian; he's always leading his two sons—my cousins Philip and Howard—out to the woodshed for sessions with a razor strop. Doesn't seem to cause any neuroses, though. I doubt if anyone in Lynchburg ever heard of one.

Uncle Herschel's a rock-ribbed Republi-can, so rock-ribbed that when William Jen-nings Bryan came through town on the train and made a speech from the observation car's platform, Uncle Herschel wouldn't even come out of his office to hear him. Probably heard him anyway, though; Bryan's voice carried for about half a mile. I was spellbound.

That quiet-looking fellow over there, that's my Uncle George DeLaney. You wouldn't know it to look at him, but he's the greatest cornet player in Ohio, maybe in the whole coun-try. Saturday nights when they have a concert at the bandstand, everyone turns out to hear Uncle George's amazing trills and runs. Sometimes he goes off with the circus and plays in their band for a few weeks. Then he comes back and shows up at Sunday dinner the same as ever.

There, on the edge of town, you can see the distillery. That's run by Uncle Otto, who mar-ried into the family. Nobody's very comfortable about Uncle Otto's occupation. He tries his best to disassociate himself from the Demon Rum. "I make it," he says; "the fools drink it!"

See that corner over there? That's where my father first saw my mother. He was standing in Peale Brothers' Store (general merchandise)

Norman Vincent Peale has a genius for discerning the power in a good idea. In the autumn of 1944, Raymond Thornburg—a friend from Ohio Wesleyan days and a neighbor in Pawling, New York— came to him with the concept of an inspirational newsletter for businessmen. Dr. Peale sensed immediately that there was an important need asking to be answered. By the spring of 1945, the concept had evolved into Guideposts magazine.

and he looked out and saw a new girl in town passing by. He gave a long, low whistle and asked, "Who's that?" "Anna DeLaney," somebody told him. "I'm going to marry that girl," my father said. And he did.

Peale Brothers' Store was not exactly a roaring success, and one reason was the checker games that used to go on in the little back room, presided over by my Uncle Wilson—we called him Uncle Wilse. "Shush!" he'd whisper if an exasperated customer was heard banging on the counter in the unattended store. "Maybe if we keep quiet she'll go away." The result was that finally there were no customers, but Uncle Wilse's reputation as a checker player spread far and wide.

I have one vivid and melancholy memory of another uncle, William Peale. It was a Sunday, and everyone was coming to dinner at my grandparents' house. In those days there was a dreadful custom of calling on children to perform before the assembled guests—play a piece on the piano, or recite something. I had a premonition and hid in the woodshed. But Uncle Will found me and dragged me to the parlor where I stumbled through that lachrymose epic, "The boy stood on the burning deck...."

Those Sunday dinners were the high point of Sunday, though, just as Sunday was the high point of the week. Oh, summer weekdays were fine for small boys. You could go swimming in the creek, clothes hung on bushes, all girls excluded. You could go down to the station at four o'clock to watch the train come through. If somehow you had acquired a nickel, you could go to the picture show at the Bijou on Saturday afternoon. But Sundays had a different tempo, a stately quality. Sundays were where life got its meaning and purpose.

Those Sundays really began on Saturday night. First there were chores to be done: Sunday-school lessons studied, coil-oil lamps trimmed and cleaned, food prepared in advance for dinner the next day—Grandma wouldn't cook on Sunday. Baths for grubby small boys in the kitchen or the wash shed, water from the pump heated on the wood stove and poured into two tin tubs, one soapy, one for rinsing. Then upstairs to the big old double bed where Grandma, half-moon glasses sliding down her nose, would read us a story from *Youth's Companion* or *The Christian Advocate*. She'd hear our prayers and pray over us herself. Then, without fail, she'd peer cautiously under the bed. Once, I asked Grandma what she'd do if she found a burglar hiding there. She said serenely that the Lord would tell her what to do. I was sure He would.

Then she'd kiss us good night and go away down the hall, the yellow light of the lamp receding as she went downstairs until we were in total darkness—and glad of each other's company.

Next morning, when the sun rose, it looked down on a town where virtually every activity that was not church-related had stopped. The basic idea of Sunday was simple, really: It was a time to turn away from mundane or commercial things and give yourself to your church, your family, your relatives and your neighbors.

Lowell Thomas, famed writer-broadcaster-adventurer, went to live in Pawling in 1926. That was the start of the Guideposts-Pawling connection: For later, Lowell's sister Pherbia and her husband Raymond Thornburg moved there; and then their friends, the Peales. Lowell was a vigorous Guideposts supporter—never more so than when on his radio show he told how a fire had destroyed the Guideposts subscriber list. Result: 40,000 listeners became subscribers!

Casual diversions were put aside. Everyone went to Sunday school. And this was followed by church, also for all ages.

The church was always packed. In those days many churches had Scripture passages cut into the beams or painted on the walls: *Remember now thy Creator...Peace be within thy walls...Come unto Me...Holiness unto the Lord...* Our church also had an all-seeing eye painted on the wall behind the pulpit. It was not a stern or baleful eye, but it did effectively remind small boys that no unworthy activity could escape God's gaze.

Families sat together; the father at one end of the pew, children next, and mother at the other end. Little boys sat scrubbed and solemn in their Sunday suits and squeaky shoes; little girls in hair ribbons and white dresses. All the ladies wore gloves; I can still remember the kid-glove smell that emanated from Grandma's end of the pew where she sat erect and attentive in her dark dress with a cameo pinned to her bosom.

And the grand old hymns, which everyone knew by heart. And the sermons, which could be long. Sometimes an impatient listener might surreptitiously consult a gold watch with a protective case. If he snapped the case shut, the sound might echo all over the church and the minister, glaring down furiously, would remind his audience that this was *his* pulpit and *his* sermon and he would make it as long or as short as he pleased.

After church, everyone went home for Sunday dinner. Uncles and aunts came two by two (followed by cousins), like the animals in the ark, each aunt bearing a dish that was her contribution to the meal. All the women put on aprons and went into the kitchen. The men smoked and talked. Small boys fought for the honor of cranking the ice-cream freezer, the ice chipped from a great burlap-wrapped cake in the cellar and sprinkled with rock salt. The reward was the privilege of licking the dasher when it was removed from the churn.

The meal at the big extended dining-room table began with Bible reading and a prayer. And what a meal! Platters heaped with crisp fried chicken and roasted meat. Mounds of snowy mashed potatoes streaming with golden butter. Gravy boats, where you could see little yellow flecks of hard-boiled eggs making the rich sauce even richer. Hot biscuits and vegetables of every kind. Iced tea or lemonade to drink. The only thing I don't remember was salad; nobody seemed to serve salad. Nobody ever mentioned diets or calories, either. The food was God's gift, a sign of His goodness. People were supposed to eat it. They ate it.

After dinner came the part of Sunday I liked best. The men carried the rockers from the porch out onto the lawn and arranged them in a circle under the great maple trees. We youngsters could sit on the grass inside the circle, if we liked, and listen while they talked. And marvelous talk it was! They discussed the sermon of the morning, thoughtfully, not critically. And the fortunes of the Cincinnati Reds. And crops. And sometimes politics—but not too much after a heavy meal. And finally, when

Lowell Thomas (right) broadcasting with son Lowell Jr., 1948

all the standard topics were dealt with, they would begin to tell stories.

Uncle Herschel might tell of his first trip down the Ohio on a flatboat. Uncle George would spin tales of circus life. The Civil War always came up because some of these men had actually been in it. "Come on, Sam," someone would say to Grandpa. "Tell us how your company stopped that Rebel charge at Chickamauga." And Grandpa would tell them. In those Civil War stories there was never any bitterness, never any disparagement of the vanquished foe. They were considered brave men, honorable adversaries who happened to be fighting for the wrong cause, that was all.

Through all the talk came a quiet pride in the nation and complete confidence in its future. We had won the Spanish-American War, hadn't we? We were building the Panama Canal, weren't we? The French had failed at it, but we wouldn't, you could count on that. Yes, there were still problems to be overcome and challenges to be met, but Christianity was on the march, man with all his faults was still a perfectible creature, the country was strong, the future was bright.

Finally, when everyone was talked out, Grandpa might take us for a ride in his surrey. Out we'd go along Grady Road, the tasseled whip (never used) swaying in its socket on the dashboard, out past the distillery, past the cemetery, along the dusty road so narrow that if you met another buggy or wagon you had to pull off to the side. Five miles per hour, at the most ten, through the long, lazy Sunday after-

noon. The horse knew the way; if he stopped to snatch a mouthful of sweet grass, nobody cared. Then home at last, to a supper of cold meat and cold chicken, and afterward a few hymns, perhaps, with Aunt Mae playing the wheezy old melodeon. Or maybe just sitting in the porch swing watching the stars come out, and the fireflies beginning to sparkle in the lilac bushes, and the oil lamps being lit in the houses along the quiet street.

Was it all as idyllic as I'm making it sound? No, not all of it. In those days children still died of diphtheria or were crippled by polio. Alcoholism was widespread, despite the thunders from the pulpit, and there was no Alcoholics Anonymous to help. Privies were cold and uncomfortable; in most houses indoor plumbing was still a dream. No electricity meant no appliances; housewives worked long hard hours cooking and cleaning and washing.

But the basics of life were rock-solid. Marriage was forever; divorce was almost unheard of. Honesty in business was taken for granted. A man was supposed to work hard, keep his word, and pay his debts; if he didn't, he was regarded not as evil so much as weak. Evidently crime didn't pay; there was little of it. Drugs were just a form of medicine. Pornography was beneath contempt. Politics were concerned mainly with state and local issues; Washington seemed dim and far away. People didn't travel much. Why should they, when the rich soil needed tending and children needed raising, and right at home was the tight-woven supportive network of family and neighbors,

Len LeSourd was the editor of Guideposts for 27 years, beginning in 1946. These were the formative years when the magazine's character and thrust were determined. Len and Guideposts were young together, and as Guideposts grew, so did he—in faith. An intuitive editor, gentle and unflappable, Len put his own lasting stamp on the magazine with his knack for bringing together disparate people of talent. What was the one quality that bound them all together? They were people who cared.

and the church to point to the eternal verities, and the flag bright against the sky?

They were not spectacular people, perhaps, but I wonder sometimes if we haven't short-changed them a bit in our history books. When we're asked who built America, we're conditioned to think of Pilgrims and frontiersmen and covered wagons and pioneers. And they did indeed conquer the wilderness. But these quiet, solid people two or three generations ahead of us gave us values. They gave us pride and patriotism, and honor and uprightness. They gave us neighborliness, and loyalty to God, and love of family. They gave us morality, and in so doing they gave us strength. And when you look back at them you can't help wondering whether modern America hasn't lost something—something infinitely precious—and doesn't know it.

In my grandmother's backyard, I remember, was a tree loaded with marvelous fruit—damson plums I believe there were called. Every summer we waited impatiently for the plums to ripen, and when they did—no fruit ever tasted sweeter.

Through the years, I've searched in many places for such plums. But I've never found one, and I never will, because the sweetness was not just in the plums. It was the taste of childhood. And when that goes, it goes forever.

But the memories remain, and when I twirl my doorbell key they all come flooding back. I can see the farms where a bell summoned the workers from the fields for dinner, and the washbasins on the back porch, and the combs hanging from chains, and the mirrors that always seemed to be crooked. I can hear the owner of the land saying grace—not a hurried blessing but a real prayer—the sunburned faces bowed, the work-roughened hands folded.

I remember the country churches where the great green ocean of corn seemed to lap at the threshold, and the wagons and buggies hitched under the trees where the horses snorted and stamped. I can see my father preaching in his swallowtail coat, fishing a handkerchief from a pocket in the tails to mop his perspiring forehead, telling the people what Jesus had done for him and what Jesus would do for them if they would just accept Him in their hearts. I can see my mother listening, full of pride, and through the open windows I can hear the sleepy whistle of quail and the sigh of the wind in the trees....

Sunday. American Sunday. When I was a small boy. Long, long ago.

Leonard LeSourd in the Air Corps during World War II

That Saturday Night at Ramapo *by Leonard LeSourd, editor*

He peered at me quizzically from behind his coffee cup, then posed the question that was to start a revolution in my life.

"Would you like to join a group of us on a weekend retreat next month?"

I was suddenly wary—and a bit confused. "What do you mean, 'retreat'? I don't 'retreat' from anything."

It was a pompous statement, typical of me in the year 1948. A former Air Corps pilot, I was 28, single, arrogant. The main reason I had come to this big Fifth Avenue church was because of the Thursday-night dances where I heard you could find an attractive date. Harold Brinig, an older businessman and the leader of this Young Adult Fellowship, along with his wife, Mary, had for some reason taken an interest in me. A look of amusement crossed his face at my statement.

"Let's not call it a retreat then," he said, "but an *advance*. The purpose of this weekend is to have fellowship together away from the world."

The music had started again. I pushed my coffee cup back and got up from the refreshment table. "Let me think about it." Then I turned my attention to a chic young Wall Street secretary who'd just been dancing with me.

Things religious were anathema to me then. To be sure, I had been reared in a Christian home, been taught Christian values, but the religion I'd seen was lifeless. I sought excitement, adventure. Sports, flying, writing were my interests.

Right after the war, I'd stashed everything I owned in the trunk of my Studebaker—golf clubs, typewriter, flying togs, Air Corps uniforms and some new civilian clothes—and traveled up, down and across the country for a year, searching out old Air Corps buddies, trying ineffectually to write a novel about postwar American life.

It seemed almost ironic that when nothing worked out for me that year, I had ended up in New York City going to Thursday-night social events in the basement of historic Marble Collegiate Church. And working as a reporter for a small inspirational magazine called Guideposts. What was happening to me?

The irony was intensified when Harold Brinig reported the theme of this particular weekend—*commitment to Jesus Christ.* That smacked of old-time emotional religion.

"I don't think I can make it, Harold. Something has come up."

Harold smiled at me. "I understand, Len. You don't want to be committed to anything at this stage in your life."

"It's not that," I lied. "I have an…er, interview I must do that weekend."

"Too bad. While everyone else is out having fun on Memorial Day weekend, you have to work."

Harold was pinning me against the wall and we both knew it. I began to wriggle off. "I'll see

One unusual thing about Guideposts is that husbands and wives of employees have often seemed like a part of the staff, too. Certainly that was more than true in the case of Catherine Marshall. Len interviewed the famous author of A Man Called Peter *in January 1959. When they were married in November of that year, with Len's Methodist minister father and Catherine's Presbyterian minister father officiating, Catherine became part of us—for always.*

if I can change the interview to another time," I said lamely. Harold had been more on-target than he realized. I had just broken my engagement to Debby, a lovely and gifted woman, because I didn't want to commit myself to marriage.

At that point, I think I was typical of many males in America. I wanted inner toughness... to be strong...cool. The *macho* philosophy. I hated to lose my composure. I'd never forgotten my embarrassment when, at the age of 13, I'd been out with my friends and I'd cried copious tears while watching a sad movie. Tears, I decided, were a sign of weakness. I gave myself an order: *I will not cry again— ever.*

To obey this order had been costly. A hardening process began, climaxed by three years in World War II. I became a selfish, self-centered, egotistical, spiritually dead person. Frozen on the inside. My arrogance was a front for a starved spirit and a parched soul.

Yet I didn't want to change. To appease that part of me so repelled by the weekend theme of commitment, I said to myself: "It's no big deal. Didn't I make a kind of commitment at age 12 when I joined the Church?"

If Harold Brinig had heard this, he would have chuckled at the self-deception. He and Mary had encountered many recalcitrant individuals like me who had first come to Marble Collegiate Church to further their social life, certainly not wanting a religion that made demands on them.

The truth was that this particular church, located in mid-Manhattan at a crossroads of busy life, had a special mission for its young people's work—to salvage mixed-up lives.

The strategy was to attract them first to evenings of fun and dancing, then encourage them to attend Sunday nights for some spiritual substance. Soon they would be coming to church Sunday mornings—if they could find a seat—to draw inspiration from Dr. Norman Vincent Peale.

This was my pattern over a period of weeks. What gradually began to penetrate my thick outer shell was the caring attitude of so many of the young people. I had never felt this kind of *agape* love inside or outside a church.

One clerk-typist with large eyeglasses told me one day she was praying for me.

Startled, I asked, "Why?"

"So you will find fulfillment in your work," she answered with a smile.

I thanked her. It was strangely unsettling, even frightening, but also touching.

So, little by little, I began to change my mind. I decided that I'd go to the "retreat" after all.

Twenty-six of us crowded into cars that Friday afternoon for the two-hour drive from mid-Manhattan across the Hudson River to Ramapo, New York, not far from the New Jersey line. Included were young executives of both sexes, secretaries, typists, an auto mechanic, a tugboat operator, a Wall Street broker, a dress designer, an accountant, an editor plus assorted students.

On Friday night, we forgathered in a spacious lounge at the retreat center for our first meeting. Right away I knew I was in trouble. A young man told of an experience he'd had

Catherine Marshall (1914–1983)
and Leonard LeSourd at their wedding

upon arrival at the retreat center that afternoon. He had gone into the small chapel, knelt at the altar and prayed that the Lord would melt any cold hearts among the weekend group.

He didn't know it, but he was talking about *my* cold heart. I quickly calculated what would happen if I slipped out of the meeting, grabbed my suitcase and drove back to New York alone. Then I sighed. If I did that, the people who came with me in my car wouldn't have rides back to the city. Grimly, I hunkered down for a miserable weekend.

By dinnertime Saturday night, I had relaxed a bit. There was some fun and sports recreation mixed in with the meetings. To my surprise, Harold Brinig played a strong third base in a softball game. And he was approaching 50!

As we left the field, Harold put a sweaty hand on my shoulder and with that disarming smile said, "Len, we all love you."

A knot of hardness dissolved inside me. I began giving more of myself to people at mealtimes and between meetings.

After dinner that night, an episode occurred that shook me. A few of us were discussing personal honesty in workaday situations. I agreed that taking company property was wrong, but scoffed at the idea that employees should be honest dealing with superiors or co-workers.

"To get ahead you say what the boss wants to hear," I told them.

Merle Wick, an accountant, sharply dissented. "A Christian who lies in situations like that violates his commitment to Christ."

In the discussion that followed, I was in a minority. By the time the Saturday-evening meeting began, two opposing forces inside me were in mortal combat.

One side said, *You don't belong here, Len. You don't share the beliefs of these fanatics.*

The other side said, *Your life's a mess, Len. When are you going to do something about it?*

It was the carefully crafted but emotionally frozen person versus an emerging individual who called for a revolution in his nature. During the meeting, one person after another described how a life run by Jesus freed them from past bonds. Mary Brinig summed it up by reading this statement of Jesus to His disciples: " 'Ye have not chosen Me, but I have chosen you…that ye should go and bring forth fruit.' " (John 15:16)

"How exciting to think that Christ is choosing each one of us to be a disciple for Him in New York City," she concluded.

The meeting then ended and I escaped out into the night, unaware that people immediately began praying for me. I walked about aimlessly under a starry May sky, my emotions churning, knowing somehow that my feet would take me to the chapel. Finally I opened its door and stepped inside.

It was a simple, crudely furnished room with folding chairs for about 20. Up front was an altar; behind that, a picture of Jesus with outstretched arms.

But the chapel wasn't empty! A young woman sat on one of the chairs praying. Embarrassed to be there, I turned to leave, but

John Sherrill joined Guideposts in 1951, shortly after our editorial department moved to tiny quarters in the Beekman Tower Hotel in New York City. He soon discovered that he had a reporter's nose for sniffing out unusual true-life stories. The "adventure" piece became his forte, and a permanent staple in the magazine. Eventually, John's inquiring mind led him deeper into his Christian faith, a personal adventure that resulted in such seminal books as The Cross and The Switchblade *and* They Speak With Other Tongues.

my feet wouldn't move. Instead, they took me slowly down the center aisle to the altar.

Inside me a dam was ready to break and I fought to prevent it. *Cool it, Len. Strong men don't cry. Get out of this place and tomorrow you'll be yourself again.*

The other voice said, *Jesus wept. And He is the strongest of all.*

Then the first voice took another track. *Don't kneel! That's a surrender of your manhood.*

For a long moment I stood there, frozen in time, aware of the shallowness of my self-centered life, hating it, wanting forgiveness for it, seeing a vision of something so much more worthwhile—if I took this next step.

My knees bent. As I knelt, I looked up into the face of Jesus and the dam inside me broke. Tears flowed. In a stumbling prayer, I gave myself to Him.

When the group met the next day after breakfast, I knew what I had to do. These people who had loved me and prayed for me wanted a report. When I gave it, I wept once again. To my surprise, no one was embar-

rassed. Instead, my tears washed away more barriers between me and those who were becoming closer to me than any friends I had made in the course of my whole life.

The fascinating twist to my story is this—in the years that followed, a Christ-centered life brought me adventure, challenges and fulfillment beyond my wildest dreams. During those 36 years there were, of course, painful defeats and low points as well. But when they came and my faith grew shaky, I had one unfailing remedy. I would go back in time to that Saturday night at Ramapo, New York. Once again, I felt the love of a church fellowship thawing my hardened heart. Again I knelt before an altar, accepting the forgiveness of Jesus Christ as I recommitted myself to Him.

That compact I made with Jesus back in 1948 is unchangeable and irrevocable, my rock-solid foundation in the shifting sands of life. And with it goes the promise of a marvelous and infinite future.

And to think I could have missed it!

John Sherrill, 1951

JANUARY 1958

Why Men Pray *by John Sherrill, editor*

Dear Dr. Peale:
   I would like to tell you what happened after I was given the prayer assignment.

Friday morning (it was September the 20th) started off as such an ordinary day. After breakfast, we held four-year-old Donnie and one-year-old Elizabeth up to the window to wave good-bye to our seven-year-old boy, Scotty, headed off to school. Scotty had just disappeared from sight when Tibby remembered about the ice cream.

"I meant to tell him I'd be at the ice cream counter today," she said. Mothers here in Mount Kisco take turns selling ice cream at the school cafeteria. It's just as well Tibby did not tell Scotty; because she never got to the cafeteria.

A few moments later, I was upstairs at my typewriter. Spread out on my desk, were the notes I had collected during seven years as a Guideposts reporter. People who had found their strength in prayer. Why? It was a fascinating question.

The phone rang. It was my doctor.

"I need to see you," he said.

"Well, of course, doctor. When?"

"Right now."

I hung up the phone, mystified. I hadn't been to the doctor's in months, except for a brief session two days earlier, when he had removed a small mole from my ear.

"It's nearly noon," I called to Tibby. "Do you want to come along?"

The first inkling we had that something was seriously wrong was when the doctor held my chair for me. He didn't hold Tibby's chair; he held mine.

"I don't know how to tell you this," the doctor said. "How can I tell a young husband and father that in all probability he's going to die?"

Shock is an amazing defense, Dr. Peale. It allows us to function with perfect calm just after hearing bad news. We sat there and listened to the doctor explain that I had a malignant melanoma. We heard him say, "It's a particularly vicious kind of cancer, especially if it gets in the blood stream. Without an operation, the statistics say you have one chance in nine of being alive at the end of the year. With an operation, you have one chance in three."

We said nothing at all. After a moment, he went on.

"I don't want you to take my word for this. Get at least two other opinions—from Presbyterian and from Memorial Hospitals."

Tib drove home to start the endless succession of phone calls and I walked over to the Mt. Kisco Hospital to have x-rays taken. I walked through the brightly colored trees of our early fall, whistling and humming. I wasn't being heroic. I really felt that way. My body's defenses had set up a wall that the news had not yet breached. With the x-rays under my arm, I walked home. I stopped and chatted idly with some workmen repairing the road. We

Tessie Durlach was a brilliant Jewish woman who, early on, helped Guideposts financially. But her greatest contribution came when she replaced money with a philosophy. "You're all thinking lack," *she accused the Guideposts staff—then moaning over a mountain of unpaid bills. "Take command of your thoughts. Visualize success." And so, "As we think, so do we become" became a cornerstone of positive thinking and a guide to Guideposts' future.*

laughed together over something; I don't remember, now, what it was. But we laughed.

That afternoon, Tibby and I drove into New York City. We took my slide and x-rays to the huge Presbyterian Hospital. But the second report came down: Malignant melanoma. Immediate surgery.

By the time we got to Memorial, its pathology labs were closed until Monday morning. We left the slide and x-rays and drove back out to the country.

As soon as we got home, we went upstairs to my office and closed the door, and turned on the air conditioner, because the machine made a buzzing noise that drowned out the house noises below. And then, without warning and without embarrassment, we both suddenly began to cry. It was the moment that we first let reality peek through.

Fear. Fear is such a devastating emotion, Dr. Peale. Once it had broken our defenses, it harried us night and day. I woke up in the night and knew that I was afraid. I answered the children's questions automatically; my mind was elsewhere. I spent hours with Tibby going over insurance, wills, finances. Then I tried to force my mind to more healthy matters, but I could not: I was afraid.

And then, Dr. Peale, something remarkable happened.

On my desk sat the unfinished manuscript on prayer. Why Do Men Pray? I had come to the conclusion that men always pray in response to a specific need, great or small. As

our friends began to hear the news of the cancer, they needed to feel they were helping and their immediate response was to pray.

The first prayer that we learned about, I think, was the prayer that you said for us from your pulpit that Sunday. After that, prayer rose about us like a flood. There was prayer at Guideposts, both in the New York office and the Carmel office. Did you know, Dr. Peale, that your friend, Tessie Durlach, asked her synagogue to pray for us? Our assistant art director, Sal Lazzarotti, told me he almost drove off the road saying the rosary on his way home Friday after he heard the news.

Prayer was in the air we breathed. We were surrounded by it, submerged in it. Prayer from trained groups and from people who had never tried it before. Prayer from people we knew well and from people we had never met.

We had known the man who handles our health insurance only as a fun-loving, poker-playing businessman. In a letter explaining our insurance coverage, he told us, "Don't forget to pray. Remember that with faith all things are possible." A night-club singer told us she was praying for us after work each night, and a Catholic friend who had left her church when she married, admitted that she'd slipped into a chapel and lit candles for us.

On Tuesday, we got the report from Memorial. It confirmed the previous reports, and I was admited to the hospital on Thursday, for an operation on Friday morning.

And to my amazement, the atmosphere at the hospital was one of prayer, too. No sooner

Back in 1948, John Beach's five-year-old son, Brooks, was killed in a tragic accident. One day, as John and his wife Marilee grieved, a magazine called Guideposts arrived in the mail. Sent by their Aunt Mamie, it was filled with true stories that gave them great solace. The Beaches started sending the magazine to friends, and when they were flooded with extravagantly grateful letters, John sent the letters to Guideposts. And that's how we became aware of John Beach, asking him to be our first circulation director. He's never left.

had I settled down in my bed in room 609, than I heard a weird and haunting note, almost a cry, permeate the corridor. In the room next to mine, an Orthodox Jewish patient was celebrating Rosh Hashanah (the Jewish New Year). The nurse told me I had heard the cry of the ram's horn, which for centuries has been used to call men to prayer.

During all these days, what about my own prayers? They were vibrantly real. But I do not intend to discuss them here, except to say that they were not for myself, they were for others.

I must emphasize, Dr. Peale, that I am trying simply to report facts. I prayed for others, not from any deliberate sense of selflessness, but because I genuinely did not feel the need to pray for myself. This struck me as a little strange until I realized the reason. *Suddenly, on the night before the operation, I was aware that I was free of fear!*

Was this the tangible result of all the prayers? I think it was. On the night before the operation, I felt such a surge of health that it was hard to realize I was in a hospital.

At six o'clock the next morning, a nurse roused me and gave me a needle. "This will make you sleepy," she said.

I laughed. "You wake me up to give me something to make me sleepy?"

They came and wheeled me into the operating room. It was as if I and the white-masked nurses and the doctors were in the center of a force that dispelled fear. The closest I can come to describing it, is to say that I felt as if I were deeply and personally loved.

And that, of course, must be a perfect condition for healing....

The operation was over.

There was a week of tortuous waiting. Then the doctor brought in his report. He did not tell me the result of the operation right away. He shined a light into my eyes, probed and thumped, and then, in a matter-of-fact voice, he said: "Your report is the best one I could possibly have for you. There is no evidence of residual melanoma."

Does this mean that there has been a cure?

I am not a doctor, and I do not pretend to understand the vagaries of cancer. Has it all been removed? Will it come back? No one really knows. But I do know about another kind of cure, one that may be more important.

Before the operation, I lived as I think most of us do, in a kind of twilight fear of cancer. Then, when I learned that I did have cancer, this vague fear blossomed into a monster. The fear had the power to destroy just as surely as did the melanoma.

But after the experience in the hospital, I feel there has been another cure.

With as much honesty as I can possibly muster, I must say that I personally have experienced the power of prayer to heal the most devastating disease of all—the power of prayer to heal fear.

Van Varner and John Sherrill were grammar-schoolmates in Louisville, Kentucky, where they spent their playtime hours together laboriously copying favorite books by hand, their own idea of "no-cost" book printing. John hailed Van into Guideposts in 1954, and later they actually saw their early publishing dream come true when they became two of the four founders of Chosen Books. PS: Van was appointed editor of Guideposts in 1982. PPS: Van and John Sherrill are still close friends.

APRIL 1958

When to Pray *by Van Varner, editor*

It was a day of anguish. For months my mother had been ill, for weeks she had been suffering agony from the cancer that was killing her, and today was the day when she was returning to the hospital. I was preparing to leave the office to take her there when my executive editor called me for a conference.

"I'd like to do an article on the subject of *'When to Pray'*" he said to me. "Why don't you consider Paul's exhortation to *Pray without ceasing*? (I Thessalonians 5:17.) Try to delve into that idea in your own life. You might even try to pray without ceasing for a day and see what it means to you."

It was difficult to think of exploring an article while deeply concerned with something else, but this assignment was obviously fitting to the circumstances. If anything, it was too fitting; the events of this day could not be interpreted as proper examples of routine living. Still, the idea was challenging. What did it mean? How could one make all of life a prayer?

As I arranged last-minute details in my office, a fellow editor dropped in, and very casually and skillfully (I realized later) told me something quite funny. I laughed. And when it came to me that I was laughing, I said my first prayer—a prayer of gratitude for good humor, which can keep us all in balance, and for this friend who had come purposely to cheer.

Down on the street, I saw a father bawling out his son who, in turn, was responding with squealing argument. I said a prayer for them that each should find understanding and respect. A newspaper headline yelled out at me about a teenage killer. I prayed for him, and for the two families. My taxicab driver complained limply about the blistering summer heat before lustily indicting another cabbie for his driving tactics. I prayed for him, too.

There was a tense quietness in my mother's apartment. The nurse moved about the rooms silently, now laying out a dress, now gathering together the few essentials for the hospital suitcase. Briefly, as I watched her, my appreciation for her care and vigilance was translated into prayer, and then my thoughts returned to Mother. It was not easy to present myself as calm and assured, to act as though this journey to the hospital were a good thing, that there, soon, the terrible pain would be softened. In my own mind, I was not sure.

It had been two weeks since the specialist in charge of her case had gone on vacation; his substitute had not telephoned or visited since then. A faithful general practitioner had come daily, but still I worried for fear Mother was not receiving sufficient attention. She was unable to take any sedative stronger than aspirin and her pain was constant and excruciating. Finally, I had taken it upon myself to call the substituting specialist and suggest hospitalization simply as a "psychological move." The doctor felt the idea had merit and said that he would telephone the general practitioner about it, and would come to see Mother. A day

Van Varner, 1954

later he had done neither, and so I made arrangements without him.

Father, guide me. Help me to have acted wisely.
Father, give my mother the strength for this short but difficult trip.

She had the strength and, in fact, seemed to benefit from the sun and air and change of locale. While the hospital made its inaugural tests and Mother was wheeled away for x-rays, I went downstairs to brood over a cup of coffee. There, I found myself in conversation with a woman who was obviously under great strain.

"My son," she said to me, "was operated on two days ago. He's fine they say, but I worry so much and I stay here all day. He's only 21, too young to have a hernia."

I thought of my mother who seemed young to me, at 60—at any age—to be riddled with cancer, and I became annoyed by this woman's monologue. Then I remembered my pledge to pray unceasingly, and I addressed God again, this time for a young man's return to robust activity, and for the easing of his mother's deep distress.

By the time I had left the coffee shop, I actually recognized a kind of tranquility within myself, and thereby made a vital discovery about prayer. The idea was so basic, so obvious, that it hardly needed discovering—but then, what is "discovering" if it is not the finding of something that is already there? In this case, my sudden peace of mind was, I believe, directly related to being absorbed in the problems of another. "Dwell on your own peril and you may be reduced to gibbering panic," Fulton Oursler once wrote in an article about finding presence of mind. "Think of others and you may well find yourself doing the precisely correct thing." This is what prayer offers as well.

For the remainder of the afternoon, Mother and I talked cheerfully together—and then, as the emergency painkiller she had taken at home lost its potency, the agony returned, vengefully. It was hours before she was quiet again. By then I had been called into the dark, barren hall by a new surgeon and his assistant who had been summoned. The x-rays had revealed a desperate condition. The doctors told me that my mother could not live more than 24 hours without an operation and there was little chance of her surviving that.

I do not know whether they were asking permission to operate or not. I simply looked at them. What other course of action could there be?

In the warmth and murkiness of the night, I sat beside my mother and held her left hand as she drowsed. Her other hand was strapped to a board while liquid strength flowed into her veins. I wondered why, in the absolute stillness of the room, I could not hear the steady dripping. My eyes watched her face steadfastly and I tried to regulate my thinking, to crystallize a lifetime while there was still the opportunity. I must pray, I told myself.

But I could not. Pray without ceasing? I couldn't pray at all. It was simple to pray for cab drivers and ladies with vigorous sons, but pray for my mother's life? I could not ask that much of Him.

The men and women who've always worked at Guideposts? A real hodgepodge. Catholic, Protestant, Jew. Editors like Protestant country-living Starr West Jones. Writers like Sidney Fields, a city-bred, Jewish newspaper reporter who first wrote for us in 1948. His newspaper column, first seen in the New York Mirror *and later in the* Daily News *was called "Only Human." With it, he proved that whether he was reporting for Guideposts or a huge, metropolitan daily, his beat was always the same: the human heartbeat.*

The minutes melded into a quarter hour, then a half, and my mind seemed empty. Slowly, without rationalizing, without focusing my thoughts at all, I began to repeat the same inaudible words to her:

"Love and contentment...love and contentment..."

I don't know where the words came from, but they were there to the exclusion of everything else. It was as though I wanted literally to swathe my mother in love, to bring her utter comfort, and that by keeping her hand in mine I could transfuse the power of those silent words.

The night passed and the next morning, surgery was performed. Mother underwent it successfully, as I knew somehow that she would.

That afternoon as I returned home to sleep, my prayers diminished in gratitude as a feeling of anger took their place—anger against the doctor who might have come and who might have foreseen the critical situation. I was in a white fury when I telephoned him. I castigated him for what I considered was his dereliction of duty, and when he replied with what I thought were lame excuses, I swore at him.

What had happened to my praying without ceasing? The past 24 hours had been challenging ones and I had failed to pass muster. I could pray in situations that did not touch me near, but I was not prepared for those that struck the raw nerve of emotion.

In retrospect, I recognized the value and importance of formal periods of prayer, be they in church, upon rising or going to bed, in specific quiet moments. I believe, now, however, that just as a man should not be a Sunday Christian only, neither should he restrict himself only to a prayer schedule. When Paul said *Pray without ceasing* he was, of course, saying that God should be foremost in man's mind at all times, but more, he was offering man a practical instrument—prayer—for accomplishing this end. He was prescribing a conduct of life that would include all eventualities.

"It is," Alexis Carrel said, "when prayer becomes a habit that it operates on the character." Prayer and God are not sometime things.

"Love and contentment" was a prayer from deep within me. It came unconsciously when I thought myself empty. The oaths I flung at the doctor, however, represented a collapse of the prayer fabric because I did not care. Had I been prepared by a life of praying, had I learned the value of silence in which prayer is most effective, I believe I would not have sworn at that physician. I most certainly would have taken him to task as I saw the facts, but if I had had the resources from which to form prayers, both for him and for my own equanimity, I would not have allowed my argument with him to be dissipated in frenzy.

On a Sunday morning, after two weeks of numb struggle, Mother died. By then, for me, as I am sure it was already for her, the continuity of life had been affirmed. And one of the insights into living that her death had given me was that we come closest to God, Who is with us always, in times of prayer. When we pray without ceasing, difficult as it is to achieve, we are with *Him* always.

Sidney Fields, 1948

JUNE 1983

From Our "Sincerely" Page *by Sidney Fields, editor*

The month of June always makes me think of Helen Keller. She was born in June and died in June, at the age of 87 in 1968. Blind and deaf from infancy, living her life in a world of darkness and silence, Helen Keller was the most extraordinary person that I interviewed in 40 years as a newspaper columnist.

The first time we met was in her home in Connecticut. Her round face was smiling and alert; she made me feel good at once. As we talked, her optimism seemed boundless, but it was her curiosity that impressed me the most. I was the interviewer, but she was asking *me* the questions. She wanted to know everything. Her hands were in constant motion, reaching out to my lips and hands (it was the way she "saw" and "spoke"). Albert Einstein called her eagerness to know everything "a holy curiosity." Later I learned the derivation of the word "curiosity"—from the Latin, "cura" meaning "care."

I met Helen Keller on three occasions, and after each encounter I'd come away exalted. She was a living lesson for me in what the human spirit can achieve no matter how badly the body is shackled. And she was a lesson for others, millions of others, as she traveled over the world, always sharpening awareness and spurring help for the blind, the deaf, the lame, the disabled.

One time, I saw her just after she'd come home from a nine-week trip assessing the needs of the blind all over South America. "Life is an exciting business when it's lived for others," she told me. Another time I asked her to do an article for Guideposts; she was immediately eager. She called it *My Luminous Universe.*

"Blind or seeing," she wrote, "one is not happy unless one's heart is filled with the sun that never dissolves into gloom. God is that sun, and if one's faith in Him is only strong, He will somehow reveal one's power and brighten the darkest days with His divine beams."

I went to see her when the article was finished. I put her finger on my lips so she could feel me thank her. "You have been so good to Guideposts, Miss Keller," I said, "now what can Guideposts do for you?"

Her reply came quickly: "Does Guideposts have a Braille edition?"

In the June 1956 issue of Guideposts, *My Luminous Universe* by Helen Keller appeared, with the announcement of a new Braille edition for the blind. Today, almost 220,000 visually impaired readers receive Guideposts in Braille or large-print editions, on records or cassettes. All because of Helen Keller.

Yes, June always makes me think of Helen Keller. It's a joyous month, a month of hope and summer's promise.

Arthur Gordon, 1949

JUNE 1966

A Sharing of Wonder *by Arthur Gordon, editor*

Many summers ago, a small boy lived in a tall house by the sea. The house had a tremendous peaked roof made of weathered shingles that towered above all the surrounding cottages. In this roof, near the top, was a trapdoor that could be reached only by a ladder propped up on the attic floor. Children used to play in the attic sometimes, but no one ever climbed up to the trapdoor. It was too high and forbidding.

One sunny day, however, when the boy's father was storing some boxes in the attic, he glanced up at the underside of the great roof. "Must be quite a view from up there," he said to his son. "Why don't we take a look?"

The boy felt his heart lurch with excitement and a touch of fear, but his father was already testing the shaky ladder. "Up you go," he said. "I'll be right behind you."

Up they went through the mysterious darkness, each step a terror and a delight. Up through the tiny sunbeams lancing through the cracks, up until the boy could smell the ancient heat-soaked shingles, up until the trapdoor, sealed with cobwebs, touched the top of his head. His father unhooked a latch, slid the trapdoor back...and a whole new universe burst upon his dazzled eyes.

There lay the sea—but what a sea! Gigantic, limitless, blazing with splintered sunlight, it curved away to infinity, dwarfing the land, rivaling the sky. Below him, queerly inverted, were the tops of trees and—even more un-

imaginable—the backs of gulls in flight. The familiar path through the dunes was a mere thread where heat waves shimmered; far away, a shrunken river with toy boats coiled into the sea. All this he saw at a glance from the protective circle of his father's arm, and the impact of such newness, of such violently expanded horizons, was so great that from that moment the world of his childhood was somehow altered. It was stretched, it was different, it was never quite the same again.

Decades have passed since then; most of the minor trials and triumphs of childhood have faded from my mind. But I remember that moment on the roof as if it had happened yesterday. And I think of it sometimes when the day set aside as Father's Day comes round, because it seems to me that the real Father's Day is not this sentimentalized, over-commercialized occasion at all. The real Father's Day is the day that exists only in memory, in the mind of some happy child or nostalgic adult, the magical day when—just for a moment or perhaps simply by accident— a chord was struck, a spark jumped the gap between generations, a relationship was suddenly achieved so warm, so intense, that it was caught and held in the meshes of the mind, impervious to time.

My father has been dead for many years now, but he left so many Father's Days behind him that he doesn't seem to have gone very far.

Arthur Gordon had been a Guideposts roving editor for two decades when he was persuaded to become Executive Director and Editor in 1975. Arthur was only filling in temporarily—he thought—but he led us for seven expansive, quality-filled years. The Savannah-born Rhodes Scholar, former Editor of Cosmopolitan *and author of hundreds of magazine pieces, is much admired for such books as* A Touch of Wonder. *Indeed, "a touch of wonder" was the very quality he brought to countless Guideposts stories.*

Whenever I want to feel close to him, all I have to do is choose one from the assortment in my mind labeled "the time we…" Some are little-boy memories like the day on the roof, some are teenage recollections, some no doubt would seem trivial to anyone else, but all have the same quality: a sense of exploration, a discovery of newness, a sharing of wonder.

There was the time we went to see a captured German U-boat that our Navy had brought into the harbor. We climbed down into the maze of machinery smelling coldly of oil and war and claustrophobia and death. Another visitor asked my father bitterly if he did not consider the German soldiers murderers who struck without warning from the depths of the sea. I remember how he shook his head, saying that they, too, were brave men caught like their adversaries in the iron trap of war. The answer did not please his questioner, but somehow brought relief and pride to me, as if a sudden test had been met and mastered.

Or the time we explored a cave, and at one point—far underground—snapped off our flashlights and sat there in darkness and silence so profound that it was like being in the void before the beginning of time. After a while, Father said, in a whisper, "Listen! You can hear the mountain breathing!" And such is the power of suggestion that I did seem to hear, in the ringing silence, a tremendous rhythm that haunts me to this day.

Did my father deliberately set out to manufacture Father's Days for his children? I doubt it. In the episodes I remember so vividly, I don't think he was primarily seeking to instruct or inspire or enlighten us. He was satisfying his own curiosity—and letting us in on his discoveries. He was indulging his own sense of wonder—and letting us share it.

This is the stuff of which *real* Father's Days—and Mother's Days also—are made. Sometimes, when the formula works, the parents may not even know it. But sometimes you do know, and when this happens there is no satisfaction in the world quite like it.

Not long ago, our family visited one of those marine establishments where trained porpoises—and in this case a small whale—put on a marvelous show. I was so fascinated by the whale that I lingered after the performance to ask the trainer how it was captured, what it was fed, and so on. He was an obliging fellow who not only answered the questions but summoned the whale herself to the side of the pool. We patted her back, smooth and hard and gleaming like wet black rubber. This evidently pleased her, for suddenly she raised her great barrel of a head out of the water, rested it on the coping and gazed with friendly, reddish eyes at our eight-year-old daughter, who was nearest.

"Apparently," I said, "she wants to rub noses with you."

Our daughter looked both interested and aghast.

"Go ahead," the trainer said good-naturedly. "She won't mind."

There was an electric pause, then the briefest of damp contacts, then both participants hastily withdrew. And that seemed to be the

If you ever want to know anything about Guideposts, just ask Dina Donohue. She was our computer before there was such a thing. Quick and tireless, with a catchall mind, Dina started with us part-time when her children reached school age in the early '50s. "Part-time" didn't last long. Neither did her "retirement" in 1978, for true to the dictum that nobody ever really leaves Guideposts, at least twice a year this writer, editor and deeply feeling friend swoops back from California to "organize" us—again.

end of it, until bedtime that night. Then, staring pensively at the ceiling, my daughter said, "Do you think any other third-grader in the whole world ever rubbed noses with a whale?"

"No," I said, "I'm pretty sure you're the only one."

She gave a deep, contented sigh, went to sleep, and hasn't mentioned it since. But 30 years from now, when her nose tingles, or when she touches wet black rubber, or sometimes for no reason at all, maybe...just maybe ...she will remember.

JANUARY 1983

His Mysterious Ways *by Dina Donohue, editor*

India Albery was, perhaps, the most unusual person ever to work at Guideposts. Lady Albery—for that was her title—seldom spoke about herself. We knew only that she had come from England, that her early life had been privileged, but that when she first came to Guideposts, she was old and alone and impoverished, living in a shabby room with a few cherished keepsakes.

She met adversity bravely, but with a stern and haughty demeanor. I myself tried hard, but I could not break through her British reserve. I used to pray that I'd find some way to reach her, but she was too proud to let any emotion show.

One lunch hour in December, I was browsing in an antique shop, a favorite pastime. I seldom purchased anything, but this day was different. I spied an enamel pencil in a silver case. It had a large "A" in its elaborate mono-

gram and I felt an urging—almost a physical nudge—to buy it for Lady Albery.

"What's this?" she asked brusquely when I handed her the tiny package.

"Just a little Christmas something," I said apprehensively.

When Lady Albery opened the package and saw the silver case, her body tensed, and her eyes filled with tears. "Dina," she said—never before had she used my first name— "Dina, how did you know?"

"Know what?" I asked.

"This once belonged to me," she said. "I had to sell it years ago, when I was hungry and desperate. It was given to me by someone I loved. And now your kindness has brought it back."

A circle of love, I thought, *I've been part of a circle of love.*

And Lady Albery never forgot it.

Dina Donohue, 1958

OCTOBER 1957

Thy Neighbor's Husband *by Dina Donohue, editor*

When this article was first published, Dina Donohue used a pseudonym. Since that time, many of those mentioned have died, but Dina still feels more comfortable in retaining the fictitious names in her true story.

This is a story of what can happen when one of God's commandments is broken. It isn't a pleasant story, but disobeying the admonition, *Thou shalt not covet thy neighbor's goods nor thy neighbor's wife...* can be an unpleasant matter.

It started years ago when a secretary "coveted" my father. The fact that he was handsome and well-to-do evidently meant more to the secretary, Julia, than the reality that he was 17 years older. Not to mention that he was a married man with three children: ages 15, seven and four. I was the four-year-old.

In time, Julia's affections were returned and there followed a period of great unrest, indecision and unhappiness. Finally, my father asked for and received a divorce. He and Julia were married. The custody of the children was divided; my sister and I stayed with Mother, and my brother Bill went to live with Dad and his new wife.

Julia's disregard of the Tenth Commandment hurt five lives. My father, first of all, was never the same again.

When my sister got into trouble at school, the principal told my father: "It's quite usual for children from broken homes to become behavior problems." Dad was disturbed by this and subsequently never got over the feeling that he had wronged my mother and his children. Once, after I was grown, he told me, "If I had been a poor man, there probably would have been no divorce; there simply would not have been enough money to support two households."

For the remainder of his life, he gave the major portion of his income to us and spent every Sunday and one night a week trying to be a father to us. Julia, who had "coveted her neighbor's husband," had to be content with only a share in his life.

We came to know Julia after a while, and to realize she wasn't the "Jezebel" or "fallen woman" my mother had told us about. She had simply been lonely and had put her wants first, but her resultant married life was a frustrated one. It was years before she was accepted by Dad's family and friends. Even my brother Bill, who had gone to live with them, rejected her.

At 16, one can be so idealistic and moral that there is nothing but right and wrong, black and white. To Bill, Julia was wrong. Although she cooked and cleaned and took care of his needs, he refused to speak to his stepmother. When a baby girl was born of this second marriage, my brother would not acknowledge her presence, even when the child tried to climb onto his lap or tugged at his hand.

"It nearly broke my heart," Julia once told

She came looking for work, but didn't want to be paid for it. She was young, beautiful—and famous. When June Lockhart started her days at Guideposts in 1951, she'd already made movies and had been a dazzling star on Broadway, but "it was all unreal and flat," she told us. In seeking spiritual perspective, she saw that "to find myself I have to give myself." And for five months she gave the little magazine herself, her shine and some much-needed office help. Then on she went to marriage, motherhood and a memorable TV career.

me, "when the baby would point at Bill, then look at me and say 'who that?' and Bill wouldn't bother to answer." As soon as Bill was 21, he left home. We seldom saw him after that.

Losing her husband to another woman meant years of heartbreak and loneliness for my mother. It was demonstrated in little things. For example, she had been quite active in a fraternal organization whose special charity was a home for the crippled. When we were very young, my sister and I often were given miniature cotton stockings to fill with pennies. "For the crippled children," mother told us.

After the divorce, there suddenly were no more stockings to be filled. Divorcees, who 30 years ago were subject to more social ostracism than today, could not be members of the club. There were many such heartaches for my mother; however, never once did she openly criticize or blame Dad as an individual. Yet there was one word she used that explained it all, "Men!"

My mother could say just this one word, and it would be a curse on the whole species. I think perhaps it was that word, more than anything else, that disturbed the early years of my sister and myself.

As soon as we were old enough, we were sent away to girls' boarding schools and camps. Until I was 17, I hardly ever talked to a man or boy. Both my sister and I were painfully shy; we behaved as though we were afraid of men, and of love, because of my mother's unhappiness.

My sister carried this early fear into later life and never married. For a while, I wasn't sure I wanted to either, but fortunately for me, a very understanding man helped change my mind.

"Because your parents' marriage was a failure is no reason for your life to be empty," Carl told me before we became engaged.

At this time, Carl was working for a comparatively small salary. He thought he should have a larger income before marrying. But I remembered Dad's statement that he might not have obtained a divorce if he'd been less well-off. It made me decide that money would not have first importance in our lives.

So Carl and I married despite his very modest salary. Then, just before our daughter was born, Carl was promoted to assistant manager of his company. When our son was born two years later, there was another promotion. We hadn't put money first in our lives, yet it came when needed.

But more than anything else, I wanted the children to have something I had missed as a child—a feeling of being wanted, of security, of roots. When I was young, we moved often, and before I graduated, I had attended high schools in four different states. My own children have lived in the same house since they were born. Although the neighborhood could be more attractive, the neighbors couldn't be finer.

I believe our children have also developed a sense of belonging. Carl and I and the children have done things together—as a family. Then something happened several years ago

June Lockhart in motion picture "Son of Lassie," 1945

that brought me in touch with the Tenth Commandment again. It involved our son.

When David was nine, he was offered a scholarship at a private school, many of whose students came from wealthy homes. Would he be envious of them? Carl and I spent hours trying to decide whether or not we should accept the scholarship.

After much praying and careful thought, we accepted the scholarship; and soon David was firmly established at the school.

One weekend, David went to visit the sumptuous country home of a classmate, Jimmy, who was the son of a leading actress and a wealthy businessman.

Several days later, we listened carefully to David's excited account of the visit.

"I couldn't count the rooms, the house was so big..." he told us. "The maid can't speak much English, just French...We had fun in the swimming pool...Jimmy's mother wasn't there, though...She's away making a picture and he hasn't seen her in over two months... Jimmy feels terrible about it...."

David expressed no envy of Jimmy's very obvious material advantages; just sorrow for the boy's unhappiness.

As I listened to David's excited chatter, a burden was being lifted from my heart. Subconsciously, I had been afraid that my own unhappy childhood would color the lives of my family. Instead, here was my son's demonstration of the positive side of the Tenth Commandment, *Thou Shalt Not Covet.*

Sal Lazzarotti, 1964

JUNE 1964

Why Should I Get Involved? *by Sal Lazzarotti, art director*

One way to avoid involvement in other people's problems is to play the monkey game—hear no evil, speak no evil, see no evil. It's a simple matter of withdrawing yourself from a situation where you might be asked to give something like time or money or talent.

Most of us are 50 percenters, I suppose. That's about the category in which I fall. Sometimes I act when I see a need, other times I just "pass by on the other side."

Not too long ago, I stood face-to-face with a tough decision. The choice I made taught me a lesson I won't soon forget.

It was such a refreshing, bright spring day— the day that I tried to cover my eyes, ears and mouth—that I lingered at the top of the subway steps to catch a couple of extra breaths of air. But finally, the sound of an approaching train sent me scurrying into the cavern below. Aboard the train, I took a seat beside the door and began reading the morning paper, a regular ritual for the 45-minute ride to our Guideposts office in New York City.

As an artist, I like to study people. That day, a graying grandmother-type sat across from me sleeping. Her head sagged to the left in a 45-degree list. A lanky, dark-haired boy of about 18 stood holding the center post, a brown paper sack under his arm. Directly across from me, an attractive young lady— brunette, maybe 25—was a portrait of poise as she sat erectly reading a paperback book.

As we pulled into the 57th Street stop, "Grandma" rubbed her eyes, ran her fingers through her hair, jumped to her feet and bounded out the door.

Next was the 50th Street stop near Rockefeller Center. People were standing, but it was nowhere near the usual morning jam. The brunette placed her bookmark and closed the paperback.

As the train lurched to a stop, she rose and walked to the door, passing the dark-haired boy. Suddenly, the young lady whirled and screamed:

"You fresh punk! Don't look so innocent! I know you touched me!" Her pretty face was now contorted in anger.

Then the girl began flailing the astonished boy, who in defense, threw his arms up and tried to push her away. In doing so, he must have hit her in the face because suddenly her mouth was all bloody.

At last the boy broke free and made a dash down the platform. The girl pursued—her high heels clicking as she ran.

"Police, police!" she shrieked.

With the sound of her voice and the noise of her shoes still echoing through the station, the doors of the train closed and we continued on our way. I sat staring at the door not sure that I wasn't dreaming. When it came shut, it was something like the curtain closing on the first act of a play.

By 1955, we still had no full-time art director. Norm Mullendore, head of a huge ad agency's art department, "moonlighted" for us. Then in January, he hired an assistant, Sal Lazzarotti—fresh from the Korean War, it was his first job out of art school. Sal was to become the typical Guideposter. His marriage to June, their three children, June's losing battle to cancer, his happy marriage to Sheryl, all the events of his life not only became our concern, but they seemed to reflect the very things our readers were living through.

Inside the car, passengers smiled, amused, and then almost in unison, they shrugged their shoulders and returned to papers and books. I smiled rather smugly myself until the full impact of the incident hit me.

I had seen that boy standing, and had detected no move to touch the girl. I wondered what would happen to the boy if he were caught. The girl's story would carry more weight, I told myself.

He might be taken to a police station and be charged with molesting her. Was it fair for me—a witness—to remain silent?

"It's not your battle…don't stick your nose in someone else's business…he probably ran away and nothing will come of it." These thoughts turned cartwheels in my mind as I left the subway and headed for the office.

Still, I felt a compulsion to help the boy—if he needed help. At the office, I got some coffee, made a couple of phone calls and worked on a rough sketch, but I could not forget the sound of that girl's voice and those high heels echoing through the subway, "Police…clickety click, clickety click…police!"

What was the right thing to do? As I thought about it, I remembered Christ's parable of the Good Samaritan who helped a man he didn't know. I knew I should do the same.

It took four calls to locate the right police precinct. The desk sergeant listened to my story. "You saw it all, huh? Well, the boy has been sent to Juvenile Court, downtown."

I called Juvenile Court and obtained the boy's name, Steven Larsen, and his parent's address. By the time I got in touch with Mrs. Larsen, she knew the details. There was a quiver in her voice and I could tell she was fighting back tears.

"We don't have any money to help Steve, Mr. Lazzarotti," she lamented.

Through a girl in our office, I learned of a lawyer named George Fleary. He was contacted and agreed to represent the boy without charge. Later, he called back and asked me to meet him in court the following Monday. I was to testify.

When I arrived Monday at the courtroom, Mr. Fleary took me aside and briefed me on what he had learned: Steve had been in trouble once before when he was 15. Police picked him up on suspicion of stealing a car with some other boys, but he had not been charged. Then Mr. Fleary outlined the accusations that would be brought by the girl's attorney.

"If Steve's found guilty of these charges, he could receive a sentence from six months to a year," he said.

Steve's mother arrived, her face was painted with worry. Steve now entered the courtroom, accompanied by an officer, and was seated at a table with Mr. Fleary.

"Is Steve still in school?" I asked Mrs. Larsen.

"No, he quit when he was a junior," she answered. "He works in the mail room of an advertising agency. He wants to be a copywriter some day. My husband is a longshore-

*When Jack Haring's name went on the masthead in 1975,
Guideposts had become a mature organization with a two-
million-plus circulation. He was just the kind of experienced
professional that the magazine was then attracting. Jack came to
us via newspapers (Washington Star) and magazines (Saturday
Evening Post, Ladies Home Journal, Boy's Life). At ease in the big
city, he's never lost touch with his Boyertown, Pennsylvania roots.*

man. He wanted to come today, but he couldn't afford to take the day off."

The judge came into the room and proceedings began. Counsel for the girl presented charges that seemed a mile long to me. Then the judge began questioning the girl. Without inhibition, she described what Steve supposedly had done. I shook my head in disbelief. Nothing she said possibly could have happened. Steve flushed with embarrassment and squirmed in his seat.

At one point the judge interrupted, asking her to be more specific:

"There is a witness to the incident present, so be sure of what you say."

The girl's eyes searched the room and then came to rest on me. She looked at me incredulously. Then a strange reaction came over her. She started fumbling with words, qualifying previous statements and contradicting herself. Within five minutes, the judge called the two lawyers forward. They huddled, whis-

pered, nodded. Then Mr. Fleary came back to where we were sitting and said:

"The case has been dismissed. The judge feels the girl needs psychiatric help."

Steve grabbed my hand firmly to show his gratitude, but he was too choked up to speak. Through tears of joy, his mother thanked us over and over.

After Steve and his mother left, I talked with Mr. Fleary and told him how much I admired him for giving his time to the case.

"Our job is made easy when witnesses will come forward and testify," he said. "Too many people say 'It's none of my business.'"

On my way home that night, I thought how close I had come to saying, "It's none of my business." How close I had come to playing the monkey game.

"Thank You, God," I said. "Thank You for giving me the courage to act. Help me be more sensitive to others in need. Open my eyes and ears and mouth—and heart."

Jack Haring during World War II

DECEMBER 1977

Out of the Night *by Jack Haring, editor*

*Christmas Day
1944*

Dear Mom:
This is a very different Christmas Day than I have ever spent in my life. Right now I'm living in the hayloft of a farmer's barn, and I'm very glad to be here rather than out in a foxhole somewhere...

The Battle of the Bulge. The final desperate attempt of the Germans to break through Allied lines in Belgium and dash to Antwerp and the sea. For six days our 84th Infantry Division had been diverted from the Ninth Army in the north to the beleaguered First Army area in the Ardennes forest. The fiercest fighting of the war, and I, a 19-year-old private, was in the middle of it.

My letter home to Pennsylvania was written on a Christmas morning that was sunny and quiet—deceptively quiet. "The barn I slept in last night," I wrote, "made me think of the place where Jesus came into the world." Then I began reminiscing to Mom about the good Christmases we'd had as I was growing up—always starting with the traditional dawn service at St. John's Lutheran in Boyertown. Church had always been an important part of my life. I'd started college thinking I might go into the ministry.

The letter home was upbeat all the way. I didn't mention anything about the things that had been troubling me. How I had become disillusioned with organized religion because I saw so few Christians either at home or in the combat zone—certainly not Christians trying to live the way Jesus had taught. Or how the weather had been so miserable and the fighting so blazing that I feared I'd never live to see Pennsylvania again.

The last straw was being sent to these snow-covered hills and woods where we might be attacked at any moment from out there, somewhere. I was beginning to think that God had forsaken me.

Still, even though we'd spent the last five days floundering around trying to stop the Germans, even though our supply trucks had been captured, at least we'd had a barn for shelter on Christmas Eve, and our cooks were promising us a hot meal for Christmas Day.

"Let's go, men," Sergeant Presto, our squad leader, shouted. "Collect your gear and fall out. We're going on a mission."

I groaned. We all groaned. There went our first hot meal in a week!

We drove for about ten miles and then the trucks dropped us and sped away. It was dusk. Troops were strung out all along a dirt road that circled through some hills. When Presto came back from a meeting with the platoon leader, he gathered the ten of us—we were one man short in the squad—around him.

"Okay, men, here's what we're going to do. This won't take long and we're going to travel light. Leave your packs and entrenching tools here." He made it sound so simple. Intel-

Even though Guideposts couldn't afford to pay topflight wages, a number of topflight writers were attracted by the little magazine's spirit and intent. Glenn Kittler's by-line was already well known when he started coming to those marathon Monday-night idea sessions. Soon this wry fellow found himself our Roman Catholic "expert," and one of the first of many roving editors. Glenn even roamed as far as Africa for a remarkable interview with Albert Schweitzer at his Lambaréné outpost.

ligence had said that some German infantry were dug into a nearby hill and were causing havoc by shooting down on the roads in the area. Our battalion's job was to go up and flush them out.

Single file on each side of the winding road, we moved up the hill. We moved quietly, warily. At the top, we were surprised to find, not Germans, but an abandoned chateau in the middle of a clearing. Our squad went into the building. We found a billiard table and the tension broke as we played an imaginary game of pool using our rifles as cues.

Then Presto came stalking in. The Germans, he said, were in the woods beyond the clearing. Our orders were to chase them out into the waiting arms of another battalion positioned at the other end of the woods.

"There'll be three companies in this deal," Presto said. "Two of us will stretch out along the edge of the forest while the other hangs back in reserve. Now, as soon as we push into the woods, everybody fires, got it?"

We spread out, walked through the darkness to the forest's edge, then, at a signal, we burst in, opening up with everything we had. We kept up a brisk pace, keeping contact with our buddies along the moving line, walking and firing for about a mile. But the forest was empty. There was no movement...

The trees in front of us exploded. Suddenly, the night went bright with every kind of firing I'd ever seen or heard of—rifles, rifle-launched grenades, mortars, machine guns, tracers over our heads, bullets at our thighs.

But worst of all, Tiger tanks. At least six of them, opening up point-blank with 88-millimeter cannons. Their projectiles whined and crashed all up and down our line.

Our intelligence was wrong, I thought angrily, as I flung myself down on my stomach. *They told us there were no tanks up here. Now we're really in for it.*

Within seconds, men were screaming in pain all around me. I saw a tree with a big trunk and made a sudden lunge to get behind it, but I wasn't quick enough. Something tore into my thigh. There was hot, searing pain.

We were completely pinned down. The Tiger tanks kept scanning their turrets and firing on every yard of our line. The German ground troops sent their small-arms fire into anything that moved.

The minutes went by. Five. Ten. Fifteen. Then came a lull in the barrage. I called over to my best buddy, Kane. We called him "Killer." He was the gentlest guy in our platoon, but we'd nicknamed him after the popular comic-strip character, "Killer Kane."

"Are you hurt, Killer?"

"Naw. But I think everybody else over here is. Presto's hit bad."

I called to Cruz on my right. He was our squad's B.A.R. man. There was no answer. Then I barely heard him whispering, "I'm hurt. Real bad. Floyd's dead. Corporal John's hit bad."

Well, I thought, *if Presto's out and the Corporal, too, we don't have a leader.*

The pounding started again, this time with flares so they could spot us better. We did

Glenn Kittler, 1949

some firing back and then the action subsided into another lull.

Down along the rear of our line came a figure, crawling. It was our platoon runner. "Captain says we're getting nowhere," he whispered to Killer and me. "We're pulling back in five minutes. Move out when you hear our covering fire."

I crawled over to Killer. "We've got to get our guys out of here," I said. "You go up your side and I'll go down mine, and we'll drag as many as possible to that big tree back there."

"How're we going to get them out of here, though?"

"I don't know," I said. "But we can't leave them lying here."

We were trapped. I lay there on the cold ground feeling helpless, that forsaken feeling again. Where was the God that I had prayed to during all those years of church and Sunday school back home in Pennsylvania? "And whatsoever ye shall ask in My name, that will I do," the Bible had said to me clearly. Was it necessary, when I needed help so badly, to ask?

"Oh, Lord," I mumbled, "help us. We're trying to get our wounded buddies out of here. Show us the way."

I had no sooner started dragging Corporal John toward our meeting tree when the firing started up in the center of our line. *There's the signal for pulling back,* I thought frantically, *but we can't do it. The Germans will sweep in on us; they'll mop us up before we can pull back.*

Just as I got to the tree, I saw that Killer had

brought back three wounded squad members. So we had six in all to get back. I closed my eyes and in desperation said: "In Your name, Lord, help us."

I opened my eyes. In the black of night, moving mysteriously among the shattered trees, a giant hulk came toward us. *The Germans,* my heart thumped, *they've broken out of the brush. They're bearing down on us.* No, it was something else, something unbelievable. It now came into full view and stopped beside our tree.

A horse.

A big, docile, shaggy chestnut, standing there without a harness, as though awaiting our bidding.

Killer and I looked at each other in disbelief. We didn't question then where the horse came from, or how, or why; we just got to work. Moving swiftly, we draped Cruz and the Corporal on the chestnut's broad back, then Mike and Presto. Then, with Killer carrying one of our buddies and me carrying the other, we led the horse out of the woods. At the clearing the horse trotted on ahead of us, straight to the chateau, and by the time Killer and I got there, our wounded were already on medical stretchers. The two men we carried in were cared for; the medics gave a quick look at my shrapnel wound; and then, as fast as we could, Killer and I went to find the horse. We wanted to pat him, give him some sugar, anything to make him sense our gratitude.

But he wasn't there. We looked everywhere, asked everyone we saw, but no one could tell us anything about him. He had simply van-

She's the daughter of a minister and the wife of one. She has a listing in Who's Who *that runs as long as her husband's. She's been a teacher, a writer-editor-publisher, a public speaker, a world traveler, a recipient of awards, medals, honorary degrees—all recognizing her contributions to innumerable boards and missions. Born in a little town in Iowa, she'd fit in easily if she went to live there today, for Ruth Stafford Peale's values have changed little over the years. She believes in God and hard work and that first and foremost she is a mother and a wife.*

ished—gone from us as mysteriously as he had come.

The next morning at the aid station the shrapnel was removed from my leg, and at noon Killer and I lined up for our much belated Christmas dinner. The day before, 190 men in our company would have answered the chow call; today there were only 35 of us. All the wounded men in our squad had survived, however, though some were never to see action again.

Killer and I looked at the turkey and sweet potatoes in our mess kits. Hot and savory and long-awaited as this food was, we had no appetite. We were still too full of our emotions: the sorrow for lost buddies; the shock of our own survival; the strange, deeply affecting arrival and departure of the horse. We could not get the horse out of our minds then, nor have I since, for that noble creature did more than just save our lives; he reaffirmed my faith. I have always believed that on that Christmas night 33 years ago, God sent that horse to reassure a doubting soldier of His presence, even as He had sent His Son for that purpose on a Christmas night twenty centuries ago.

APRIL 1983

This Thing Called Prayer *by Richard Schneider, editor*

"Pray for me, will you?"

How many times have people facing some crisis asked you that question? And how many times have you replied, "Yes, of course I will" —and then didn't? Naturally you meant to, but somehow it just slipped your mind.

Well, it used to slip my mind too, until one day while talking on the phone to my friend John Sherrill, I mentioned something that was troubling me. "Let's take this to God right now," John said. Then and there, on the phone, he asked God's help for me. By the time we hung up, I was already feeling better.

The next day, another friend told me of a dilemma he was having with his job. I started to assure him he'd be in my prayers—then stopped. "Bill, let's pray about this now," I said. When we parted, Bill was talking optimistically about his situation.

Nowadays, I don't wait. I pray *now*—on the bus, over lunch, walking on the street. If someone needs a prayer, the sooner the better!

Mrs. Peale and Dr. Rosen, 1977

JUNE 1977

The Remarkable Doctor Rosen *by Ruth Stafford Peale, editor-in-chief*

The first time I realized I had a hearing problem was when I tried to listen to my watch tick and found I couldn't. With my left ear I could still hear it, but not with my right. When I consulted a doctor, he confirmed that I had a serious hearing loss. At that point, he wasn't sure why.

Months of tests and examinations followed. Fortunately, the hearing in my "good" ear remained normal. But if a person sat on my "deaf" side, I had to twist my head awkwardly to hear. It was troublesome and a bit frightening at times.

It was during this time that I learned to have a feeling of compassion for people with hearing problems, which has never left me. A blind person or any disabled person arouses sympathy immediately. But many people are insensitive about deafness or partial deafness in others. They can't "see" the affliction, and so they tend to be impatient with it. This causes a lot of unhappiness, because there are 14.5 million people in the United States alone who are hard-of-hearing or deaf.

My doctors finally came to the conclusion that my problem was otosclerosis, an overgrowth on a tiny bone called the stapes inside my right ear. This bone is the smallest in the human body; ten of them would just about cover the small fingernail. It's shaped like a stirrup, and is the closest bone to the auditory nerve. Sound makes the stapes vibrate. This stimulates the nerve, which in turn sends the sound-message to the brain where its meaning is deciphered. But in my case the stapes had become rigid, unable to vibrate or react to sound.

Time went by. More treatments and one operation didn't seem to help. Then one day by chance (or was it chance?) I happened to mention to Dr. Louis Bishop, our personal physician, that I had this problem. Louis' wife Kitty, who had a similar problem with both ears, had just been greatly helped by an operation performed by a Dr. Samuel Rosen. A new technique, they told me. A real breakthrough. They urged me to go and see Doctor Rosen in New York. I did, and met a most remarkable physician.

Doctor Rosen was in his 70s, gentle, reassuring—fatherly was the word that described him best. I told him about my problem and asked if he could help me. He smiled. "If God is willing," he said.

He used the same phrase from time to time during subsequent visits when I came in for testing. One day, I ventured to ask him why. "When my parents prayed," he said, "whether it was a prayer of supplication or of thanks, they always ended it with, 'If God is willing.' That's a cornerstone of my faith and work."

Doctor Rosen told me that his parents were immigrants. His father had peddled some crockery, and his mother had suffered from severe asthma. He recalled that one morning,

Our Prayer At Guideposts

*Lord of all things, whose wondrous gifts to man include the shining
symbols known as words, grant that we may use their mighty power
only for good. Help us to pass on small fragments of Your wisdom,
truth, and love. Teach us to touch the unseen, lonely heart with
laughter, or the quick release of tears.*

when he was six years old and preparing to go
off to school, his mother had such a severe
attack that she could not catch her breath.

"To a child that meant that she would suffo-
cate," Doctor Rosen said. "A doctor came and
gave her some medicine, which relieved her,
but I would not go to school. I sat by her
bedside all day. When I told her that one day I
would be a doctor and cure her, she took my
hand in hers and said only, 'If God is willing.'"

Doctor Rosen's mother died when she was
quite young. His older brothers pooled their
labor, their savings and love to send him
through medical school. For over 40 years,
Doctor Rosen has been an ear surgeon at Mt.
Sinai Hospital in New York City and has
taught ear surgery in its medical school. In his
early days, he was baffled by otosclerosis, as
were all ear specialists. They knew what it is,
but not what causes it. The standard surgery,
called fenestration, took over four hours, and
required the removal of the second of three
bones in the middle ear. Sometimes it helped;
mostly, it didn't. It usually left the patient dizzy
for weeks, even months, and often totally deaf.

Like so many dramatic discoveries in medicine, Doctor Rosen's was an accident. Or was it?

One day, in 1952, while operating on a
woman who had had a hearing loss for
over 20 years, he was startled to find that her
stapes was not entirely rigid, even though
otosclerosis had been diagnosed.

"I wondered how many times fenestration
was performed on patients like her," Doctor
Rosen told me. "I decided that from then on, I
would first try to test the stapes with a long, thin
needle to see if it was rigid before I operated."

In the next five operations the stapes were
rigid. So was the sixth, in the case of a 42-
year-old engineer, who had been almost deaf
for 15 years. But when Doctor Rosen inserted
the long needle to make the test, the engineer
suddenly shouted, "Doctor, I can hear you!"

"I knew something remarkable had happened," he recalled. "But what?"

He did not remove the bone from the ear;
the engineer recovered his hearing. Afterward, Doctor Rosen tried desperately to recall
every detail of what he had done. His nights
became sleepless, as he tried to find the answer to the question: "How can I do deliberately what I did accidentally?"

For the next 18 months, after his day's work
was done, he performed autopsies, studying
the tiny stapes. What was its structure? How
much pressure could it take? How could he get
through the complex labyrinth of the ear to try
to move the stapes without damaging it or the
other fragile bones?

He designed and made at least three-dozen
special instruments. None worked. When he finally made one that promised to work, it broke
the arms of the stapes. The search seemed
endless, the frustration was deep. I asked him
what had kept him going.

"Only the Lord knows how the human mind
works," Doctor Rosen said. "But there was
something that filled me with hope. How do
you reinforce hope? You pray. I did, every day."

One night, he twisted the delicate sides of
one instrument in the hope that it would grasp

Let us portray the courage that exists defiant in the face of pain or death; the kindness and the gentleness of those who fight against the anger of the world; the beauty hidden in the smallest things, the mystery, the wonder of it all…Unstop our ears, unblind our eyes, unlock our hearts. Speak through us, Lord, if it be Your will. Amen.

the neck of the stapes, its strongest part, without damaging it. He wiggled the instrument, and gasped when it moved the base of the stapes—without breaking it. He tried it again and again, and finally murmured, "God *is* willing!" He labeled the instrument "The Mobilizer," and used it 400 times before he ventured to try it on a living patient.

"Until then, I don't think I really understood what my parents meant when they ended their prayers with 'If God is willing,'" he said. "I do now. It could not have happened without His help."

After a series of successful operations, (each takes 30 minutes and requires only a local anesthetic), Doctor Rosen published his findings in medical journals. He was invited to demonstrate and teach the procedure all over the United States and the world. He has done so in 45 countries including Arab and Iron Curtain nations. He always leaves the special set of surgical instruments behind when he departs. He has trained over 1,000 doctors to perform the operation, and they in turn have trained others. Doctor Rosen charges no fees for such teaching. Over 750,000 people have been spared possible deafness in this chain of unquestioning love.

On the morning that I arrived for my operation in 1969, I prayed that God would guide Doctor Rosen's gentle hands, and prayed for the strength to accept the outcome, no matter what it was. Doctor Rosen began his work. There was complete silence. About 25 minutes later, I thought I heard someone speaking. Was it a fantasy? No. The voice was whispering, "I love you." I looked up in amazement. Doctor Rosen was bending over me, smiling, his lips close to the ear that had been deaf. Now the sound was coming through in the form of the three most beautiful words in any language. "Oh, Doctor Rosen," I said, "I love you, too!"

Since then, my hearing has been perfect. My husband Norman wrote a grateful note to the surgeon. "Only God," he wrote, "could create a Doctor Rosen." I agreed with all my heart.

Doctor Rosen continues to be an active and sought-after consultant. At 80, he feels spiritually and physically ready for any challenge.

Doctor Rosen's latest challenge is to find a cure for nerve deafness, a problem that has baffled medical science for generations. When I asked him if he thought one day he might find the answer, he smiled. "If God is willing," he said.

A Note From The Editors

This book was created by the staff that prepares *Guideposts*, a monthly magazine filled with true stories of people's adventures in faith.

If you have found enjoyment in *A Very Present Help*, we think you'll find monthly enjoyment—and inspiration—in the exciting and faith-filling stories that appear in our magazine.

Guideposts is not sold on the newsstand. It's available by subscription only. And subscribing is easy. All you have to do is write Guideposts Associates, Inc.; Carmel, New York 10512. A year's subscription costs only $5.95 in the United States, $7.95 in Canada and overseas. Our Big Print edition, for those with special reading needs, is only $5.95 in the United States, Canada and abroad.

When you subscribe, each month you can count on receiving exciting new evidence of God's presence, His guidance and His limitless love for all of us.